FOREWORD BY MARK CAVENDISH

For fifteen years or so, an age group of British cyclists flooded the professional peloton and made seeing the Union Flag at the top of the results sheet a pretty normal occurrence. If you scroll through that list of riders, you can pretty much guarantee that at some point they'd have been a guest in the Rowe household, bikes ready to roll in the garage and a cup of tea immediately in their hand.

I think a good portion of those names too, myself included, will have been helped to bed over a Rowe shoulder after getting a bit too acquainted with hugging the toilet bowl at some point. But we won't go further on that . . .

The simple point being that when you're with a Rowe you can be sure you're going to be looked after. As every single one of Luke's teammates could testify, this was something that was just as apparent within the environment of a professional cycling team, both on and off the bike.

From the neo-professional who led me out for near on a kilometre to win my final race as UCI world road champion, to an almost predictable presence on the very front of a Tour de France peloton, Luke got the job done. If there was a big race to be won, then you knew who you wanted as your soldier.

Cycling is a special sport. A team sport. But with only one victor. There's a strange logic to it, as the hardest workers often aren't publicly acknowledged. But in the relentless world of professional cycling, you can see very easily who's doing it as just a job and who regards it as something much more than that, who's determined to give their very best in every race, while also being prepared to put that cup of tea down, open the garage door and just enjoy riding a bike with their mates.

And that's why, for many years, Luke was professional cycling's MVP.

ROAD CAPTAIN

ROAD CAPTAIN

My Life at the Heart of the Peloton

LUKE ROWE

bantam

TRANSWORLD PUBLISHERS

UK | USA | Canada | Ireland | Australia
India | New Zealand | South Africa

Transworld is part of the Penguin Random House group of companies
whose addresses can be found at global.penguinrandomhouse.com.

Penguin Random House UK, One Embassy Gardens,
8 Viaduct Gardens, London SW11 7BW

penguin.co.uk

Penguin
Random House
UK

First published in Great Britain in 2025 by Bantam
an imprint of Transworld Publishers

001

Typeset in 12.5/16pt Minion Pro by Jouve (UK), Milton Keynes
Printed and bound in Great Britain by Clays Ltd, Elcograf S.p.A.

The authorized representative in the EEA is Penguin Random House Ireland,
Morrison Chambers, 32 Nassau Street, Dublin D02 YH68.

A CIP catalogue record for this book is available from the British Library

ISBN: 9780857507822

Penguin Random House is committed to a sustainable future
for our business, our readers and our planet. This book is made
from Forest Stewardship Council® certified paper.

I would like to dedicate this book to my mum, Alyson Rowe. She sadly passed away in 2023. The wonderful lady who always put others first, gave the best hugs, was solid as a rock and my number one dance/drinking partner. I wouldn't have achieved the career I had or be the man I am without you. I aim to follow in your footsteps and to become half the person you were. Always take time to smell the flowers x

CONTENTS

PROLOGUE

Winning is everything in professional sport, although my own record does undermine this a tad. I had just two victories in thirteen years as a pro. Cycling, though, is a sport like no other. I wasn't paid to win, but in my role as road captain I was paid to secure victory for others.

What does a road captain do? Essentially, almost anything to ensure that their leader ends up on the top step of the podium. And I mean *anything*.

It's a role very few riders are qualified for and which almost no one outside the professional peloton really understands. In this book, I'm going to take you inside the peloton and into the heart of my career as a road captain. I'm going to start, though, with an insight into what *anything* can mean.

So let's scroll back to 4 March 2017, the day before the start of Paris–Nice, arguably the most prestigious one-week race on the calendar. Known as 'The Race to the Sun', it starts on the outskirts of Paris, where winter is still firmly in charge, and finishes in early spring sunshine on the Côte d'Azur. To win it, you've got to be at the top of your game in every aspect of racing, especially if the weather's shit and the wind's blowing. One mistake and it's game over. Paris–Nice doesn't offer second chances in the way that a three-week race like the Tour de France can, and that's one of the reasons I love it. Another is that it's renowned for full gas racing, especially on the opening two or three days close to Paris when the roads are exposed and that bitter wind comes into play.

Going into the 2017 race, Team Sky had won the previous editions with Richie Porte and Geraint Thomas, and we were looking for a hat-trick with Sergio Henao as our leader for the week. But he'd need to ride the perfect race to beat Spain's three-time Tour de France winner Alberto Contador and Richie, who'd left Sky to become the outright leader at BMC.

You go to Paris–Nice with a squad of two halves – guys who can get the leader through the crosswinds and then guys who can get the leader up the climbs as you approach the coast. Our directeurs sportifs, Nico Portal and Servais Knaven, knew the first two days were going to be windy and the evening before the race started they told me, 'Right, Luke, you've got to look after Sergio. If we can get him through these first two days, we think he can win the race. The only problem is that he hasn't got a clue in the crosswinds. This is a baptism of fire for him.'

I was thinking, 'Fuck, that's a big ask with the team we've got.' We had Sebastián Henao (Sergio's cousin), David López, Mikel Nieve and Philip Deignan for the climbs, which meant everything was on me, Michał Gołaś and Christian Knees for the opening days in the crosswinds. I went to the bus and said to Nico, 'You can't do this to me. You can't put this team together and then say, "Right, it's on you for two days," ' because it was largely on me. We had Gołaś and Knees, who could ride the wind, but the rest couldn't. If any of the three of us had a mechanical or other issue, we'd be skating on thin ice because riding in crosswinds is not the kind of job you can do on your own.

After we'd had dinner in the team hotel that evening, I got Sergio to sit down with me and I explained to him the basics of riding in an echelon, at an angle across the road, using the salt and pepper pots on the table to illustrate what I was saying. 'Sergio, if it splits, we've got to share the work. I can't protect you all the time,' I told him, using the pots to demonstrate how I'd make space for him and how he'd then have to do it for me, protecting our place in the echelon and taking turns to bear the brunt of the wind.

When the first stage got going the next day, we didn't have to wait too long to find out whether Sergio had understood my instructions. With 50K of the 148K gone, the hammer went down and the bunch split. There were fifty-odd riders at the front. We had three in there initially – Sergio, Gołaś and me – which was great because all of our major rivals for the overall title had been left behind. Then, just as we were coming into a roundabout, we had a setback. The group split to go around it, and at precisely that moment we heard on the radio, 'Hey guys, make sure you go the right-hand side of the roundabout. There's oil on the left.' As we heard this, I was on the right, Gołaś was on the left. We looked across at each other and made eye contact. As I looked ahead again, I heard bikes crashing on to the tarmac. The whole left-hand side of the peloton had gone down, Gołaś with them. So it was just me and Sergio with twenty-five other guys.

It wasn't a surprise to see that QuickStep had six riders in there. If there was wind and you were wondering 'Could it split? Could it split?' you'd look around and if there wasn't a QuickStep jersey you'd be saying, 'It can't split because QuickStep aren't here.' They were the team for crosswinds, a team of monsters, like orangutans on bikes. The Belgian outfit was up against another team with six at the front, FDJ, and ultimately it was the French team that clinched victory, their sprinter Arnaud Démare, strong enough to bridge up to a late solo attack by QuickStep's Julian Alaphilippe, outgunning him in the two-up dash for the line. All that mattered to us, though, was that we'd got Sergio through the mayhem and he'd gained time on his two biggest challengers – thirty-eight seconds on Richie, fifty-five on Contador. Job done.

The next stage went 195K in a straight line south. Lotto-Jumbo had totally missed out the day before, completely blown out of the water. So they started day two as if they had a vendetta. It was pissing down, 2 or 3 degrees, and after 5K Jumbo made their move and the bunch started to split in the crosswinds. I was looking after Sergio again. He seemed to be doing OK, but it was hard to tell as he spoke almost no English and I had no Spanish.

After 50 or 60K, I said to him, 'Sergio, did you eat? You have to eat.'

'No, too cold, too cold!'

If he didn't eat, it was game over. So I got this rice cake out of my pocket in the crosswinds, unwrapped it, put my hand out, and he ate it off my hand like a dog. There was rice all over his face. 'Thank you. Thank you,' he kept saying.

Another 20 to 30K further on: 'Have you eaten?' And that became the theme of the day. For 200K I was literally feeding him like a dog out of my hand or squeezing gels into his mouth. It was perhaps above and beyond the job of a road captain literally to hand-feed my team leader, but he was so cold he couldn't get his hands off the bars.

At the finish, I was so cold I couldn't either. I rode back to the bus and the first person I met was Slarky, our driver. He helped me get off the bike and up the stairs on to the bus. My hands were frozen rigid, so he stripped me out of my soaking kit till I was bollock naked and bundled me into a warm shower. Like I said, *anything* . . .

When Paris–Nice finished six days later, dealing with the craziness in the crosswinds paid off. Sergio took the title, winning by just two seconds ahead of Contador, who ultimately paid for missing out on the very first day.

1

What is a road captain?

Hats off to anyone who can remember the two races I won in thirteen years as a professional cyclist with Team Sky and the Ineos Grenadiers. They were a stage of the Tour of Britain in 2012 and another at the Herald Sun Tour in 2017. I had an all-round talent as a bike racer, but didn't stand out in any particular domain. I could climb OK, sprint pretty well, and I was average against the clock as a time triallist. In fact, there was just one area in which I stood out – as a tactician. It was this skill that was the foundation of my long career.

Although I only won once in a blue moon, my ability to 'read' a race led to me becoming Sky's road captain, a role in which I helped some of the greatest riders of my generation capture many of the biggest titles, including five Tours de France, Paris–Roubaix and Milan–San Remo. While the likes of Chris Froome, Geraint Thomas and Egan Bernal had physical and competitive attributes that were well beyond my limits, they depended on me putting them and our teammates in precisely the right position to race for victory and, above all, to win.

In this book, I'm going to take you inside the road captain's role, explaining the tactics and strategy that go into winning. I'll lead you through every aspect of racing, up mountains and down descents, over cobbles and hills, into the heart of the peloton, the sprint lead-out train and the front echelon in a windy race. By lifting the lid on the unparalleled insight that I offered to Froomey, G, Egan and many others, my goal is to provide a better understanding of the complexities of bike racing. Before I get to that, though, let me start by explaining my path into racing and towards the road captain role that would become my niche.

Like all budding bike racers, my dream as a kid was to ride in the Tour de France. No matter what your favourite sport when you're seven or eight, at that age you always look to the pinnacle, unaware and not really caring about the many steps you've got to climb to get there. I was doubly lucky, though. I not only came from a family with quite a long history in the sport, but was fortunate too that the sport was on the verge of an unprecedented boom, largely triggered by National Lottery funding.

Up to the end of the 1990s there'd been no formal structure in place for British cyclists who wanted to test themselves on the Continent. They had to pay for and find their own way into the sport's elite. However, by the time I was at that stage I went from well-organized junior racing to the academy pro-gramme at British Cycling's HQ in Manchester. From there, the next step, in 2012, was to Team Sky, which would win the Tour de France with Bradley Wiggins that year. Three years on from that, my dream became a reality. I was selected for Sky's Tour team, my job to act as road captain to a line-up led by 2013 Tour champion Chris Froome. It's a role very few are familiar with, one that I barely understood before I joined

Sky, but the rider tasked with it is absolutely critical to success for any elite-level bike team.

The term 'captain', when applied to a sports team, will bring certain personalities to mind. It might be David Beckham or Harry Kane if you're talking about the England football team, Sam Warburton or Alun Wyn Jones if it's the Wales rugby team. All four of them have been great leaders and motivators, renowned for setting an example to their teammates on the right way to play. Yet their role was partly symbolic. They were their manager or coach's mouthpiece on the pitch, and it was down to the coach to set or change the team's tactics. Sitting right on the touchline, on the very edge of the action, this is relatively easy to do. In stadium sports like football and rugby, strategy can be tweaked very quickly if the coach sees the need.

Road cycling's the same as those sports to a degree. The directeur sportif (DS), or team director, decides on and sets out the strategy for the race ahead. However, once the flag's dropped and the action gets under way, the DS's ability to dictate what the riders on their team should do is immediately compromised. They're sitting in cars that are 100, 300 or maybe many more hundreds of metres behind the peloton. Not only are they not on a touchline, they're not even in the same stadium as their riders.

As a result, they've frequently got no clue at all about what's happening on the road ahead of them. Their only connections with the sharp end of the race are messages from the riders relayed by radio, occasional updates from the event's officials via Race Radio – who's punctured, who's in the break, the distance covered – and a small TV on their dashboard that tends to be delayed by at least a minute. What they're watching on that screen has already happened. Consequently, they're completely dependent on their riders doing the right thing, and in particular on the team's road captain. Like Beckham or Warburton, that designated rider is responsible for making sure the team's strategy remains on track, but has to act with a degree of tactical independence that's rarely allowed to their peers in other sports.

Towards the end of the 2024 season, my final one as a professional rider after thirteen seasons with Team Sky and Ineos, I got a first-hand insight into how cut off from a race a DS can be when I got my debut in this role at the Czech Tour, working as assistant to my former teammate Ian Stannard. When a DS is planning their team's strategy the night before a race, it's so easy to look at a map, to suss out the route (or the 'parcours' as it's generally known), to think about the various qualities of your riders and make a plan. It's not too hard either to predict what's going to happen in the race, but it never, ever goes exactly how you think it will. There's always a hiccup, always something that goes wrong.

It could be something as minor as a rider missing a feed, or the race hitting a section of road with some potholes that you don't know about and someone puncturing. It could be a much more significant incident, like one of your leaders crashing. When you're in the team car, you react as soon as you become aware of these moments occurring, but it's almost certain that your road captain and his teammates will already have taken action simply because they can't wait for the DS to give them instructions when the race is on. A decision has to be made right then. Even if it doesn't turn out to be the best one, it'll still be better than doing nothing. Generally, it's the road captain who takes that decision.

When you're racing – and this applies to any member of the team including the road captain – you've always got to remember the DS is the boss and has the final call. They put together the plan for the day and, ultimately, you have to go with what they want. But a good directeur sportif doesn't make decisions in isolation. They know that every plan they make will need to be adapted, that tactics will have to evolve, that split-second decisions will have to be taken that will have an impact on the end result, and this is where the road captain's role is fundamental to a team's success.

In some instances, you see something on the road that makes you think a change of tactic is required. Often it's a tweak that's quite simple to agree on – switching the order of riders in the pace-setting train perhaps. I might radio back to the DS with a concern about a teammate, let's say German rider Christian Knees. 'Hey, I know we were supposed to ride with Kneesy. He's carrying a bit of fatigue. Stannard says he's fresher. We can use Kneesy on a climb later. What do you think about starting with Stannard?' That's an easy discussion, a run-of-the-mill conversation that contributes to the overall goal for that specific day, and there are plenty of interchanges like this between DS and road captain, especially when the peloton's rolling along without a great deal of urgency.

However, you really get to find out how good your road captain is when the racing is full gas and they have to react when things go wrong, usually in a pressure cooker situation when they have to make a split-second decision. 'Should I scream for the team to move left, or scream for them to go right? When should we accelerate into a corner?' You might be coming into a sprint finish or into a key moment of your race – perhaps you're approaching the Oude Kwaremont climb in the Tour of Flanders or the key section of cobbled road through the Arenberg Forest in Paris–Roubaix – and you've only got a few moments to decide where you and your teammates need to be.

As I've already said, at critical moments like this the DS in the car behind the race may be watching footage with a lag of anything between a few seconds and a handful of minutes – they're hostage to the reliability and strength of the network coverage, just like anyone else. They likely don't have a clue where you are. When I was DSing at the Czech Tour, I kept getting caught out. I'd be on the radio and essentially guessing where the riders were at times. It underlined to me how dependent the DS is on the road captain in these moments, on them picking the right way to move. And it's in those moments that you spot the difference between a good and a great road captain. It's not my place to say where I sat in this hierarchy, but I know from messages and chats with teammates during my last racing season in 2024 that they really missed having me alongside them after I was sidelined by concussion in March that year.

The fact that directeurs sportifs are often tactically blind during races also blows a hole through the frequently stated argument that they control their riders like puppets on a string. We used to hear this a lot when Team Sky were dominating the biggest races with that 'train' of riders setting the tempo at the front of the bunch in order to protect our general classification (GC) leader, usually Chris Froome, Geraint Thomas or Egan Bernal. We were made out to be robots riding to the numbers that were displayed on the Garmin computers mounted on our bars. Sometimes I felt people assumed it was like playing *Pro Cycling Manager* on your laptop, where you're going, 'OK, move right, go to the front, accelerate, prepare your train, do a sprint.' Whereas, the constant movement within a peloton means that you're always evaluating and re-evaluating.

This process is happening back in the team car as well, and you do pick up things that the riders can't see – who's been dropped or has had a mechanical issue, for instance. Above all, though, you get an overview of what's happening in the race rather than the specifics. So it's down to the riders and particularly the road captain to take care of the details, the spur-of-the-moment decisions that can make the team's task easier when you get them right, or scupper your chances if you don't.

Say you're moving up the peloton and you see a wave of riders moving to the right. That's the ideal moment to say to your teammates: 'Accelerate as it's going to the right.' Space should open up on the left to move towards the front of the bunch. Or, let's say you're trying to move up and you're blocked. You might look at your Garmin and see that in 500 metres the road bends to the right and in that instance you can once again try to get to the left so that you can move up.

Rather than pulling the strings at any and every moment, it's down to the DS to give you the broader picture, to say, 'Guys, in 5K you need to be in the front.' How we get there is pretty much up to us. In Flanders, there'll come a point when the DS tells us, 'In 3K you enter the Kwaremont.' Then it's down to me to gather the troops. I'll say, 'Right, Kim Heiduk, you're first, Connor Swift, you're second. Luke goes third.' We know from the pre-race briefing that the leader, Tom Pidcock in recent editions, will either be in front of me or stay on my wheel and come around me at the last minute.

I'll be waiting, waiting, waiting. Is this the right moment? When I think it is, I'll say, 'Kim, go!' If you accelerate too early, you get exposed, blow your troops away and get swamped by riders coming from behind. If you move too late, you can't get past and you're stuck behind when you need to be at the front. That timing is purely down to the road captain. Experience is crucial in these moments. You've got to have a feel for the race. If you're a first-year pro and you see there's a bend going to the right . . . well, right is the shortest option, but the problem is that everyone's going to go to the right. It's only with the experience of having tried to move up on the right, as I did myself when I was twenty-one that you realize it's not possible to do it at that point.

Often, you do have to accept that tactics have gone a bit awry and not press the issue. Say you enter the Kwaremont and you're behind. You're in thirtieth place when you'd like to be in tenth place or fifth place. You do have to recognize when you've got it wrong and not stress in those situations. This happens a lot in the Classics, in races like Flanders and Paris–Roubaix where you turn on to these roads that are only wide enough for four or maybe five guys at a push riding abreast. Sometimes you are going to be caught behind. It happens to everyone, and when it does you always see guys scrambling at the side of the road, risking a crash. In those instances, you've got to tell yourself, 'I'm caught behind. I'm a long way back. There's nowhere to go. I am where I am. We've slowed down because it's a narrow road, so now I'll use this opportunity to fuel.' I'll have a drink, a gel. I'll say to my teammate next to me, 'Mate, fuel up now and then when you get to a bigger road try not to make the same mistake again.'

It's interesting when I look back at races and understand

how I saw them, as it provides another perspective on the road captain's role. I'm not that good at recalling the race result on a particular day, if we managed to win the stage perhaps or our GC leader ended up battling with a particular rider on the final climb, because at that point I'd be way behind, perhaps riding beside the second team car trying to get an idea of what was going on at the front. But I always remember how things went earlier in the race and what my role was, how I felt that day, particularly if it was a bad one as they stand out more. You don't forget the suffering as easily.

If I think back, for instance, to that Paris–Nice that Sergio Henao won, I could probably list most of the twenty riders who were in the front echelon on that opening stage that was hit by crosswinds. This is because, as road captain, you're always evaluating the situation. When I was in that group of twenty, I'd have been looking at which GC guys were there, which teammates they had who would commit all the way to the finish line, which sprinters were there and whether they had teammates who would commit to keeping the break going. I'd be analysing everybody in that group, constantly.

On the flip side, I'd also have been thinking, 'Who's missed this move? OK, Alberto Contador's missed it. Has he got a strong team? Will they pull? Will they chase?' I'd be trying to work out who was going to be pulling behind. What level of firepower did we have among the riders at the front and how did that match up against the firepower in the group behind? Who would be willing to chase in that group behind?

I'd also be making calculations like this even when there was nothing happening in a race, maybe to a crazy extent. We might be riding along with 150K to go and the breakaway had gone, but I'd still be looking at our rivals, and especially at the main guys. I'd look at everyone I was passing or who was passing me, trying to work out whether they were in good shape. 'Does he look a bit overweight? Does he look really lean?' I'd scrutinize the way they were sitting on the bike. When someone was next to me, I'd look at what they were eating and drinking. I'd definitely be taking note of how much they were taking on, thinking, 'Is this guy under-fuelling?' Because that's what you'd be looking for, hoping they were being a bit lax and spotting that weakness.

I wouldn't just be focusing on the other riders either. I'd be looking at the weather, checking the temperature. Riders have different stats showing on their Garmins. Some do want to be able to see their power output, but I'd always have the temperature showing just to have a gauge of how hot it was. Sometimes it might not feel that hot on the bike, because you're rushing through the air and get cooled by it. But when you looked down, it'd be 29 degrees, so I'd not only make sure that I was drinking more, but I'd also try to tell my team-mates to drink more.

This incessant evaluation and assessment also extended to keeping a close eye on my own teammates on and off the bike, because in cycling you're only as strong as the weakest link within a team. If someone seemed a bit quiet or down, I'd be wondering, 'What's up with him? Is he sick? Is there something going on at home? Or is he pissed off about being here at this race because it's a smaller race and he wasn't selected for something bigger?' The cogs in my head were constantly turning, checking over every detail, storing these titbits away in my mind for when I might need them.

As a road captain, you can't exclude from that recall the

mistakes that you and your teammates have made. The harsh reality of cycling is that there are twenty-two teams on the start line and twenty-one aren't going to win. There'll be twenty-one losers every race, every day. Let's just compare this to football. If you're playing for a team in the Premier League and you're tenth in the table, you're bang average: you'll win a third of your games, lose a third and draw a third. So, you're winning one game in every three. That's a much higher strike rate than for almost every professional cyclist. There are some racers who might sometimes approach that level of success – in 2024, Tadej Pogačar did win more than a third of the races he started. But Pogi's an anomaly, a rider in a class of his own. On the whole, the best cyclists in the world won't have the same strike rate as an average Premier League team. Most of the time you're not going to be winning, even if you're one of the best in the world. And if you're on one of the bottom teams in the top flight of professional cycling, if you're Cofidis or Arkéa, for example, what's your win-to-loss strike rate? One in fifty perhaps?

Let's look at what was Team Sky and is now the Ineos Grenadiers, where I spent the whole of my professional racing career and which I still consider to be one of the better teams in the world. In 2024, we won fourteen races over the course of around 200 race days, so that's a strike rate of 7 per cent. As a racer, you've got to accept that's the nature of the sport, that you are going to lose far more often than not. Which leads to one of the oddities about cycling, and that's the need to lose in the right way.

When you're at a three-week event like the Tour de France, the twenty-two teams in the race are all trying to do the exact same thing each day and only one of them can manage it perfectly. Behind them, there's a sliding scale of success. The other twenty-one teams all fail to a certain extent, some of them insignificantly, but others drastically. As a GC team defending the yellow jersey hopes of a rider like Froomey, G or Egan, you'll probably go into most stages with the goal of simply not losing any time to key rivals for the overall title. The stage win doesn't really matter. But even when you come through a day of racing without losing any ground in the GC battle, it's almost inevitable that mistakes will have been made. Someone will have fucked up in some way, and I've always felt that it's important for the road captain to take a lead in weighing up why errors occurred and trying to ensure they're avoided in future.

Bearing in mind the significance of the road captain's role, it stands to reason that they're likely to fuck up as much and probably more than any of their teammates, because they're making so many vital calls. There's no way to escape the inevitability that you're going to make mistakes and it's important, essential even, to take responsibility for any errors you have made. If I was looking after a leader and had to enter a certain climb in a good position, but ended up delivering them in the wrong position, when I got back to the bus I would always say, 'Sorry, mate, that's on me. I got the timing wrong and I got boxed. That's my bad.' It's all well and good to take the praise when you do a good job, but you also have to hold up your hands and be accountable when you do fuck something up.

One other area in which the road captain can play a significant role within any group of riders is off the bike. Team spirit is one of the pillars of success. I learned this when I was racing for the British Cycling Academy team during the three seasons before I turned pro, and it was cemented when I joined Sky. But that desire to bring people together, to ensure that we all knew we were all committed to each other, has always been important to me. Off the bike and on it, I was the glue in that team.

2

Apprenticeship

Cycling was always likely to play a big part in my life. My grandparents rode quite a bit, and my father was passionate about cycling. My parents met through the Cardiff Byways Cycling Club and dipped in and out of the sport. When my older brother Matt and I were growing up we did every sport, but cycling became a family thing. My parents bought two tandems, and I'd be on the back with Mum and Matt was always with Dad, and together we explored South Wales. When I was seven or maybe eight, our grandparents bought us both purple Peugeots and we never looked back.

We rode at Cardiff's Maindy track and formed a good team of four with the Thomas brothers. Matt is the same age as Geraint and I'm the same age as his younger brother, Alan. From that point on I pretty much followed in G's footsteps, a couple of years behind him, minus a few gold medals. A big early turning point for me was winning the Junior Tour of Ireland in 2006, when I was still actually an under-16. That year I'd upgraded my licence so that I could compete as a junior. I began to think then that I might be able to make a career in the sport, that racing on the road as opposed to closed criterium circuits suited me better. I also won a Peter Buckley Trophy junior series race that season, the Bath Road Race, and those successes made me believe that I had a real shot at being a pro rider. As soon as that got into my head, my schoolwork was pushed to one side. I had little to no interest in education. Even though I was quite smart, I didn't really apply myself.

Looking back, my parents were quite relaxed about this change of focus, although they made it clear that I couldn't just ride my bike every day, that I had to get some kind of qualification or a job. So I did my A/S levels at seventeen, and failed them all. Then I found a college course at Ystrad Mynach to do PT and become a gym instructor. It was pretty basic stuff, and it ended with a two-part exam. The first bit was practical, so I brought my mum in and talked her through a PT course while being observed. I passed that OK. Then there was a written exam, which coincided with the Münsterland Tour, a four-day stage race in Germany for which I was selected by Great Britain – one of my first call-ups for GB. I told my parents that I'd spoken to the college and that they'd said I could do the exam a week later. But it was bullshit. I hadn't spoken to anyone. I just wanted to go to this race, although this ultimately rebounded on me in two ways. Not only were the college upset, I also managed to get disqualified from the race on the final stage.

I went into that stage in second place, three seconds or so behind the winner. There were some intermediate bonus sprints where you could pick up three seconds. At the first one, Mark Christian led me out and suddenly Guillaume Van Keirsbulck, who was being led out by his Belgian teammate Tosh Van der Sande, both future pros too, came flying past me at double the speed. I wondered how that had happened and one of my teammates said that he'd got a Madison handsling, as that speed had come from being flung forward. So I asked Mark to do the same for me at the next sprint, which he did. However, the person who gives the sling always gets thrown backwards, and in doing this Mark caused a massive crash.

It was madness then. There was a massive fight in the race, while their DS was going at our DS, Darren Tudor, trying to run him off the road. It was horrific. In the end, though, I won the race. But as soon as I crossed the line I was surrounded by all the Belgians and their families. Their aunties, their mothers, their grandparents were all fuming. One of the old guys had a newspaper and was trying to hit me with it. Mark was there too and we were trying to fend them all off. It was ridiculous. Then, of course, it was announced that Mark and I had been disqualified. I then had to go home and break the news to my parents that I'd missed the exam and got kicked off the race. I was also told that I should write a letter to the head of the GB team, which was Dave Brailsford at the time, to apologize for my poor decisions. Even so, I was still set on being a pro racer. Nothing was going to get in the way of me doing all I could to achieve that.

When G made the jump into the pro ranks with Barloworld it made being a professional seem even more realistic, especially when we could also see him winning track titles on the GB team that featured the likes of Ed Clancy, Mark Cavendish and Ian Stannard. I was part of the next batch of riders who were emerging behind them, along with Ben Swift, Pete Kennaugh, Jonny Bellis and Mark Christian.

I joined the GB Academy in 2009, and for the next three years my time was split between summers in Italy and winters in Manchester. We had a ball, some of the best times of my life to be honest. What's more, without me being in the slightest bit aware of it, I also began to take the formative steps towards the road captain role for which I became renowned during my thirteen seasons racing with Team Sky and the Ineos Grenadiers. At that time, under-23 racing was a jungle, a dog-eat-dog world. It was a big pool of very talented bike riders, and everyone simply wanted to climb out of it and turn professional. There weren't many teams or many riders organized enough to commit or work for each other. Everyone wanted to get that result that made you turn pro, and as a consequence of that there were very few team tactics.

Italy was the wildest jungle of all, home to many of the biggest and most competitive races, and we were guided through it by former pro Max Sciandri, who lived in the same Tuscan town of Quarrata where the GB Academy had its Italian base. Max was the perfect guy to run that part of the programme. He'd put an arm around you when you needed it, he begged, borrowed and stole equipment and shoes for us, he did everything he could for us. He was old-school Italian when it came to training and racing. As the sport has become increasingly robotic, he's stuck with his traditional approach. He would never write anything down on a computer. His plan was always in the back of his head, or he'd jot something down on a piece of paper with a pencil. We'd do a training session, say a three-hour loop, and finish on a climb. He'd sometimes be riding with us and he'd tell us, 'Make an effort on the climb. Guys, go make a sweat.' What did that mean? We didn't have heart-rate monitors or power meters. So we'd get to the climb and we'd just knock lumps out of each other as we raced to the top. I loved that laid-back approach and, needless to say, Max and I hit it off right from the outset.

When we were preparing to race, Max would keep things equally straightforward. It'd be something like, 'These two guys, they're the leaders. Look after them.' It was really all that was needed, though, because the strongest come to the fore at under-23 level and you soon had your pecking order. You kind of knew where you were.

Even then, without being aware of it, I would say I developed into the road captain. I used to look across the whole team and try and get the most out of everyone, and try and give everyone an opportunity. Obviously, Max would decide the way we raced and who would be the leader and what roles we would all have. But I would also have conversations with Max about how we would race and who we should work for, and I know that wasn't something he did with all of the riders. He would ask me things like, 'How's so-and-so going?' It would always be quite informal, on the bike or in a café. He appreciated that little bit of input into how we raced and it was all part of the learning process for me.

During those early academy years, we were probably the one nation and team at the time that did commit to each other, along with the Australians, and I definitely committed to others more than I should have at times. I know I worked for people who, as it turned out, weren't as good as me, but that's the way my cogs worked. We definitely felt, though, that we were all in it together and were organized and loyal enough actually to commit and sacrifice ourselves for the good of the team. At the back end of that first year, for example, Pete Kennaugh had his pro contract with Sky sorted and I knew I was staying with the academy, while a few other guys were moving on and some others were in limbo, among them Johnny McEvoy.

He was a good rider and a brilliant bloke, but it was touch

and go whether he'd stay in the GB set-up. We went to this race and Max said we were going to ride for Pete, but I spoke to Pete and we decided to flip the system and try to help get Johnny a result. The pair of us worked for him in this race and he had a decent finish, although, unfortunately, it didn't change the decision to release him in the end. Again, though, I was looking at things like a road captain would, thinking it's not just about the leader or the second guy. The most important thing is the group, keeping everybody pulling in the same direction.

Of course, one other thing we all had in common was the desire to turn pro. I shared a room with Pete during my first year in Italy, who'd shared it with Ben Swift the year before. To fill some of their spare time, they'd started to make a mural, cutting out pictures of professional racers from magazines and sticking them on this huge wall on one side of the room. They'd covered a small part of it, and Pete and I continued with it and ended up covering most of the wall. 'We want to be on that wall,' we'd say to each other, and at that moment in Italy it did seem possible. But when we started racing, I thought, 'Fuck, this is never going to be possible.' Honestly, we got absolutely battered.

Those races were harder than a lot of pro events I've done subsequently. The Italian club teams were run almost like professional outfits, and some of the riders on that scene seemed to be copying the bad habits that were quite rife at elite level then. I'd be sitting in the wheels thinking, 'Who's on the front of this peloton because I'm literally staring at this wheel in front of me and hanging on . . .' We got a few results, but for the most part I just got my head kicked in. I was pretty sure that they were up to no good because as soon as we went to a UCI Nations

Cup race and competed against more international fields, the speed and intensity were totally different. I won the ZLM Tour, a huge win. Then I went back to Italy and got battered again. I didn't finish the Baby Giro, the under-23 Tour of Italy. I couldn't finish. Then I went to the Tour de l'Avenir, the biggest international event, and I could hold my own again. To put it simply, I didn't trust some of those fuckers.

At the same time, though, I loved being in Italy, and I was massively disappointed when British Cycling decided to move the academy full-time to Manchester. I love Italy – the culture, the people, the country and, yes, the racing. I also felt that I wasn't yet ready to turn pro. So Max helped arrange for me to speak to Trevigiani-Bottoli, which was one of the two biggest under-23 teams in Italy. I went as far as signing a contract with them, for 12,000 euros a year, which was a big contract at that level. They ordered my kit, ordered my bike.

I was about a week or ten days from going out on the first training camp in November 2010 when Shane Sutton at British Cycling called me. He'd spoken to Dave Brailsford and Fran Millar, who were nearing the end of their first season managing Team Sky. Dave, of course, had come through British Cycling's management set-up and was still combining the position of performance director there with his role at Sky, while Shane also worked across both organizations and Fran had played a very significant part in Team Sky's formation. The three of them kept a close eye on all of the guys coming through the lower ranks at that time and realized that me going to an Italian amateur team in that era could have been a fucking disaster. Shane said to me, 'Don't go there. Stay in the academy for one more year, and we agree now to sign you for 2012. We'll sort it out with the Italians.' Done! I didn't even ask how much money. I just said, 'Contract? Yep.' Getting that contract was all that mattered.

As it turned out, being full-time in Manchester worked a treat. On the bike, I really found my feet. I won the ZLM for a second time and I was competitive all year. At the Worlds that year in Copenhagen, I rode for Andy Fenn, who finished third behind the French duo Arnaud Démare and Adrien Petit. By the time the season ended I felt I was ready to make the jump to the pro ranks. I hadn't been ready before, physically or in terms of maturity, but now I felt like I was the complete package.

Off the bike, life was good too. We lived in Fallowfield, right in the middle of Studentville and with a Wetherspoons pub beneath us. The temptation was always there to indulge, and quite often we did. We were almost like students who rode bikes. British Cycling weren't naive, though. They knew what was going on, but they just thought it was part of growing up, part of learning who we were. It would make or break us. It was inevitable that we'd push it too far, though.

Riders now wouldn't go out, they're so very focused. But we used to go out and not think about it, then get up the next morning and ride our bikes a bit groggy. The best evening out was a Monday because it was student night and it was as cheap as chips – a pound a pint, a pound a shot. One Monday we all went out, apart from Alex Dowsett, and stayed out till three or four in the morning. Every Tuesday we had to get into the velodrome for an eight o'clock track session. That meant waking up at 6 a.m. and leaving at about half six to ride to the velodrome in the dark, cold and, sometimes, snow. We'd get to the track, get the track bikes sorted, and by five to eight we had to be ready to go.

This one Tuesday, only me and Alex got up – the rest of them phoned in saying they'd all got food poisoning, the bastards! We were working with our coach, Darren Tudor, doing standing quarter-laps, half-laps and laps, really intense stuff. I was doing these drills and feeling increasingly rough. That day, Britain's track superstar Chris Hoy was filming with Jaguar cars in the velodrome, and as we were doing our last efforts, you could see the cars starting to come in, and Chris arriving too. I did this standing half-lap, finished it, and was promptly sick all over the inside of the track. I sprinted down to the toilet and spewed again, then came back up, got back on my bike and rolled around to where Alex and Darren were. I was totally taken aback when Darren gave me a massive pat on the back. 'Alex,' he said, pointing at me, 'this is what giving 100 per cent is, this is what it takes.' Alex looked daggers at me, knowing exactly what I'd been up to the night before, his eyes clearly saying 'You little bugger' as he got a bit of a lecture.

In October 2011, I went on my first camp with Team Sky. It was in Milan, and it was all about getting the admin sorted for the season ahead. We did the team photos, the content for the website and the media, the medicals, and we had some meetings with the backroom staff, outlining what we wanted to do racing-wise over the following year. On the last night we went to a nightclub where everyone was buying rounds. I had a problem, though: I didn't get paid till 1 January and couldn't afford a round. Swifty realized my predicament and gave me 200 euros. 'That's just for tonight so you can buy the odd drink,' he told me. Even now, all these years later, I think what a good lad he was for doing that.

Roll on a dozen years, and I did the same for Josh Tarling.

After that same pre-season camp, we were in an Irish pub in Nice with everyone buying rounds, drinking trays of sambuca and doing Guinness races, and I realized Josh hadn't got a round in. He was in the exact same predicament that I'd been in when Swifty bailed me out. So I said to him, 'There's my card. Go and get a round, but don't tell anyone I've paid.' That shows how things go full circle. Hopefully, in ten years' time Josh will be doing that for someone else, helping to bring them into the team fold.

It was at that first camp that I started to realize how big Sky was. From the outside you just see the team racing, but what hit me on the inside was the number of team staff. I was used to going into a race with six riders, plus Max, a mechanic and a soigneur (responsible for the riders' kit, nutrition and massage). Suddenly there was this huge entourage of people. I got given an iPhone to replace my shitty old phone, a MacBook as well. Then there was the kit, which had my name on it and was all custom made.

There were meetings just for the riders too. The elder statesmen, the likes of Bernie Eisel and Mat Hayman, spoke. They weren't actually that old, it just seemed like it to new pros like me. Bernie was the loudest of them. He demanded respect and got it because of who he was and what he'd achieved in the sport. In addition to those two, Mick Rogers, Mike Barry, Danny Pate and Jez Hunt also took on the road captain role at certain junctures. At the time they were some of the best at that job in the peloton. Looking back now, they're still prominent names when you consider the best riders to have had that role. I was lucky to turn pro and instantly be with these people, mentoring me.

I'll confess, though, that I had absolutely no idea what a

road captain was or what they did. I don't think I even knew such a position existed before I turned pro. When we turned up to the first race, someone said who the road captain was – I seem to recall it was Mat Hayman – and I was like, 'What the fuck's a road captain?' But I very quickly realized the significance of the role and its importance to the smooth running of the team, both on and off the bike. You always need one guy who goes, 'Right, boys, we're doing this. Let's get it organized.' I'd already been filling this role to a certain extent within the academy, but I'd never really thought about it as a specific job within a bike team. If there was a group talking about going to play pool, say, I'd often be the guy who booked it. 'Right, we meet at seven o'clock.' I think every group needs that one person, and my character fits the role extremely well. I didn't know quite how well I would adapt to it at that point, though, largely because it was still very much on the periphery of my thoughts.

My focus then was completely on racing. While under-23 racing is chaotic, I quickly realized that pro racing is organized chaos. Determined to do well, I was equally set on doing exactly what I was told. It's always been the case that the hardest contract to get is your second one. Anyone's prepared to take a punt on what you've done as a junior or as an under-23, but after two years as a pro they can see exactly what you're capable of at the very top level of professional bike racing and if it's not good enough, you're gone. Going into those early weeks of the 2012 season, I remember thinking that I'd do whatever they asked me to. I took whatever they said absolutely literally, and very much so in one early instance during my first stage race for the team.

I made my debut in Sky's colours in Majorca, in the series

of one-day races that take place on the island. When I crossed the finish line on the final one, I got to the soigneurs and they told me straight away that Sky's head coach Rod Ellingworth had been on the phone to say that I was needed in Oman because Mike Barry had crashed earlier that day in the Tour of Qatar and broken his collarbone. I flew to Oman the next morning and not long after I landed I was on a pre-race ride with several of the team's biggest names. Mark Cavendish was there as our leader, and he had Bernie Eisel and all these other boys for his sprint train.

During the course of that ride, Cav said to me, 'Do you know what I want from you tomorrow in the sprint?' I, of course, thought I'd be riding on the front early in the stage, doing some donkey work. 'I want you to be the last man for me, the lead-out,' he stated bluntly. I remember saying, 'OK, yeah, brilliant, I'll do it.' But in the back of my mind I was thinking, 'Shit, he's world champion. He's Mark Cavendish.' I was an absolute nobody.

As it turned out, we didn't even contest the following day. When we were coming towards the finish of stage 1, someone got between me and the man in front of me, Mat Hayman. In the meeting afterwards, I admitted I'd lost the wheel, and Hayman said to me, 'When you've got Cav as your last man, you crash before you lose the wheel.' Those exact words. Of course it was meant with a pinch of salt and it's a crazy attitude to take, but that's what it was. I was even more determined to do exactly what I was told after that.

We had Rod Ellingworth driving in front of us during Oman, giving us details about the road ahead, wind direction and so on. On one of the stages later on in the race he called our DS with some instructions about a roundabout with about 3K to go. By then, after stage 1, I'd been moved back in the pecking order so I had a few boys behind me in Cav's lead-out train. We'd been given markers, set points where each of us was expected to take the lead in the train. My stint covered from 4K to go to 2.8K, so I had to lead the team through this roundabout. You can take the roundabout full gas, I was told. Straight over, no need to brake.

As instructed, I took over on the front with 4K to the finish. Going into the roundabout I was thinking, 'This really doesn't look like it's full gas, but I'm not fucking touching my brakes because they told me it's full gas.' I went into it hell for leather. My wheels started to skip out and I ran really wide, but I managed to hold the bike up. I glanced back and realized the rest of the team had braked a bit because it clearly wasn't a bit of road furniture you could negotiate flat out. 'You fucking idiot, it wasn't full gas!' they said to me afterwards. But when the road captain and the person doing the recon ahead of the race gave me an instruction like that, my mentality was to do exactly what they said. I felt like I was damned if I did what I was told and equally damned if I didn't. That Tour of Oman was a baptism of fire, one that ended without Cav or anyone else on the team winning a stage. That didn't really matter, though. It was still early in the season, and Oman was, above all, a chance for the team to come together as a unit, for the new guys to fit in.

I soon began to find my feet and get a much clearer idea about how the internal chain of command worked at Sky. Essential to this was listening to what the road captain was telling me and his other teammates during races. As mentioned, I had some of the best mentors to learn from, although I still wasn't thinking about myself as anything other than a new pro whose primary ambition was to ensure that his career didn't fizzle out after two seasons. Bernie Eisel was the big voice of the team. A pro since 2001, he'd been with Cav through the Columbia and HTC days, when those teams had been the most successful in the peloton.

Bernie was a big personality, great fun and always good to be around. You'd never sit down for a meal with Bernie without there being a bottle of red wine on the table. 'I'll pay for it, put the wine on my bill,' he'd say. I got on really well with him on and off the bike, and he definitely cared about me. When we were racing, he knew when it was the team's responsibility to ride and take control of the peloton. He didn't ever back away from hard work. He was probably one of the last guys from that generation who had the on-bike/off-bike balance dialled in to perfection. He worked hard and played hard, and very much lived by that motto, which I've tried to do as well.

And then we had Mat Hayman, a rangy Aussie who'd turned pro in 2000 and had been with Sky since the team's formation in 2010. Like Bernie, he would put you in your place if you stepped out of line or did something wrong, even if it was an unintentional mistake. A key part of the road captain's job was to make sure we were aware when we messed up and learned from those errors so we would be less likely to make them again. Mat was a little bit more reserved than Bernie, who probably had the bigger reputation, but I would actually say he was a little bit smarter as a road captain, a bit calmer under pressure. In fact, I'd say Hayman was probably the best road captain I ever worked with, and he was certainly the one who gave me the most time. He didn't ever lose his shit or shout. He was also quite nurturing. He'd put his arm around you if you'd had a hard day. He always led by example. If we had to ride on the front and the terrain or conditions were particularly tough, he'd put himself in that position first.

I remember one thing that really stuck with me from Hayman, to do with racing in a crosswind. I've lived by what he said: 'If in doubt, go.' What did he mean by that? Basic-ally, he reckoned the reason most teams fail in the crosswinds is because of hesitation. When it's like this and the peloton's nervous, you can see teams thinking, 'Is there enough wind to go full gas and try to split the race? They told us in the bus it's 18kph but it feels stronger and the road is exposed . . .' Wondering what to do, riders will be having conversations with their team car. Hayman said that in those situations, where there is some doubt, just go, and I've always tried to do that. What's the worst that can happen? That the peloton all comes back together. If it does, you don't really end up using more energy if you're lighting it up in the front group in the crosswinds because you have to work equally hard in those conditions no matter what group you're in.

Bernie and Hayman were both very direct with their instructions when we were racing, which is the way I liked it and the way I am. In the thick of the action you can't sugar-coat things. You have to take command. You might have to pull people into line, or drop the odd F bomb. Instead of saying 'Go right!' you might say 'Get to the fucking right!' and in the moment that's completely acceptable. One other thing that I picked up from Matt in situations when the action's really kicking off is to make time afterwards to explain the calls you made. If he shouted at me to do something, he'd come to me later on the bus or in my room to give his reasons for that call, and there was so much value in his explanations. It also built respect and understanding within the team.

The other road captain I worked with during my debut season was Mike Barry, a Canadian who'd raced with US Postal and HTC-Columbia before joining Sky in 2010. I didn't do quite so many races with him as he was only on the team with me for that one year, but we did the 2012 Tour of Norway together, with Mike in a kind of deputy road captain role to Hayman. What stands out about Mike, though, is what happened in the days before that race. I was still based in the UK at that point and wanted to go on a camp, so I travelled out to the Spanish city of Girona, where he lived. I rented a place for a week but didn't know any of the roads, didn't know anyone, and he took me under his wing, even inviting me for dinner with his wife Dede and their kids. He was super chilled and really went out of his way to accommodate me. Garmins weren't a thing back then and I didn't know where I was going. I had some 'efforts' to do, as we called them – some tough sessions. So he worked out which climbs we'd go to so that I could follow my training plan. That was a prime example of how there's much more to road captaincy than just giving instructions in a race. Spending that couple of weeks with him, first in Girona and then rooming and racing with him in Norway, taught me a lot, particularly about how to behave off the bike.

Despite his tricky past and the fact that he was riding under a cloud that season after the revelations about systematic doping on the US Postal team he'd been a part of, led by Lance Armstrong, Mike's still a good bloke, and I've often followed the example he gave when I went to Girona all those years ago. Truthfully, the news that he was involved in the scandal really broke my heart. When I was living in Monaco later in my career, I'd often look after young riders in a similar way, usually Australian kids who were based in France or in Italy and were managed by Dave Tanner, an ex-pro who's now an agent. Dave would message me asking if a kid could tag along for a ride and I'd always say yes. If I was riding with G, Caleb Ewan, Sam Bennett or Michael Valgren, I'd tell them, 'Boys, this lad's coming along. It's not negotiable. Just give him a bit of time.' I might only ride with them once or twice, but I can still remember how I was when I was their age and how Mike Barry really helped me off the bike.

Reflecting on the riders who influenced me as a road captain, I must also include another rider whose achievements were tainted by the doping affairs involving the US Postal team. George Hincapie was in the final year of his long career when I was in my first season, and was arguably the best there's ever been in the road captain role. There are two parts to this assessment: what I picked up from watching him on TV, and the way people spoke about him, including Cav, Bernie Eisel and others who raced alongside him at HTC and rated him so highly. They regarded him as one of the ultimate professionals, the archetypal team rider. As a kid, I can remember watching him during the Tour de France, where he was usually the road captain. He was a super-domestique in the true sense of the term, the epitome of a rider who worked solely for the benefit of his team. He was always front and foremost, pretty much for the three weeks; whether it went uphill, downhill, left, right, over cobbles or into crosswinds, he was always so impressive. These all-round skills were fundamental to his ability as a road captain.

We didn't actually race together in that one season we overlapped. The only Classic I did that year, Dwars door Vlaanderen, was the one that he missed. But I've spoken to him a few times since, swapped a few texts. He actually messaged me in the Tour one year – I think it was quite early on in my career, in 2015 or 2016 – saying something as simple as 'Love your work, bro', or something like that. I was delighted to have that kind of recognition from someone who was renowned for their road captaincy and for whom I had a lot of respect.

Not all of the mentoring I experienced was as positive as this, though. That first year I rode the Tour de Suisse, where Thomas Löfkvist was our leader and also the road captain. I actually got on well with him most of the time, but he belittled me one evening during the race. Obviously we all knew that we had to look presentable when we were at races and there was a team rule that no flip flops were allowed at dinner. No one wants to see your big toe while eating their steak. Just put some trainers on. Anyway, I had no idea about this rule and walked down to dinner in flip flops. He really looked me up and down, like I was a piece of shit, and said in front of everyone, 'No flip flops at dinner.' I was like, 'Sorry, like I didn't realize. I won't do it again. Tomorrow I'll wear my trainers.' I was the new kid on the team and Tommy was a superstar, and I felt pretty small. He told me straight off the bat, 'No, no, you've got to go and get changed.' I wish I'd just told him to fuck off, which I would have done later, but at the time I didn't want to piss anyone off. So I trudged off upstairs, feeling really embarrassed, and put my shoes on.

Back then, the older guys had that authority and some of them wanted to be tough. 'You've got to learn the ropes, young man!' – that type of thing. There was a reason he had the nickname 'Tommy long week', because a week could be a long time with him. He was a nice bloke most of the time, but that really got my back up. I'd never adopt that attitude as a road captain. If one of the younger riders had done the same,

I wouldn't have made an issue of it in front of the rest of the team. I wouldn't have wanted to embarrass them. I'd have taken them aside at some point and said, 'Mate, a quick head's up. We normally wear trainers at dinner. Just so you know for tomorrow.' I wouldn't go so far as to say it was bullying, but it wasn't the right way to deal with that situation.

Towards the end of my debut season I felt fully at home at Sky, to the extent that I started to offer some of my thoughts going into races. The one race that stands out most clearly from that year was the Tour of Britain. That week in general was pretty unforgettable, because we had a right laugh. I was rooming with Bradley Wiggins, who'd just won the Tour de France and the Olympic time trial title in London. It was Cav's final race in the world champion's jersey. Christian Knees and Bernie had both ridden the Tour with Brad, while Jez Hunt was in the final weeks of his long professional career. It was like a victory lap for all of them. I was leading Cav out. We went around a right-hand corner with just over a kilometre to go and Cav crashed behind me, leaving only a handful of riders to pass through. I was the little whippersnapper along for the ride, and it couldn't have started any better on day one when I had Brad and Kneesy working for me in a much-reduced front group and I won the sprint into Norwich. That was kind of surreal.

Cav was second on stage 2, then won stages 3 and 4. We split the race in the crosswinds coming into Blackpool on that fourth stage. Jez Hunt earmarked a place where it was exposed and said that we should drop the hammer there. We blew the bunch apart and I led out Cav for the win in the sprint. We were cleaning up in the race, but it was equally memorable for the fun we had off the bike.

In those days, after a stage had finished, the soigneurs cooked up a big pot of rice, gave us a can of tuna with it and we'd cover it in sauce or olive oil and salt and pepper. But as the race wasn't a key objective after what those boys had all done at the Tour, we gave up on the rice and tuna. Instead, after the stage we would stop at a service station and each go to a different shop. Cav would come back with, like, six pasties from Greggs, Brad would have packs of rocky road from Marks & Spencer. Someone else would come back with a big bag of Haribos, and we'd get back on the bus and dive in. After one stage, we stopped at a pub and had a traditional dinner – bangers and mash, steak and ale pie, stuff like that.

It was one of the most enjoyable races I've ever done. I still say it now to the guys on the team: 'If we can have fun off the bike, I guarantee we'll be successful on the bike.' I believe it's got a direct correlation with performance. That togetherness, that sense of wanting to ride for each other, and the energy it brings to a team. That kind of thing can't come from the staff, and as a rider you can't simply say, 'Let's make a good group.' It's got to happen authentically and naturally, like it did that week.

There was one significant hiccup, though, on the night of stage 4. I don't know who thought it was a good idea to put Bernie and Jez in the same room bearing in mind they both had a reputation for racing and playing hard. When the rest of us went to bed, they stayed up drinking in the bar. The next morning, Bernie came into the room I was sharing with Brad saying, 'Guys, you've got to help, I can't get Jez out of bed.' We went into their room and tried to get him up. He must have been having a dream because he was mumbling, 'I'm not a shark, I'm not a shark . . .'

We eventually got him on the bus and he spent the pre-race meeting sitting with his head back, a hat on his face, sleeping. When the stage got under way, Jez was riding on the front as we were defending Cav's yellow jersey, and he was actually doing a pretty good job considering he probably didn't even know where he was. Then, out of nowhere, halfway through the stage, Brad went on the front and absolutely dropped the heel for 3 or 4K, just ripped it. The race exploded going up a climb, we completely lost control, and ended up losing the jersey. Kneesy was our only rider in the front group. When Brad got to the top of that climb, he turned round and rode back to the gruppetto where Cav was, breaking the rule about not riding against the direction of the race.

Brad was pissed off with what happened the night before, so he just tore the race to bits. That night, he got into the bed next to me and when I woke up in the morning he and his suitcases were gone. I went to see the doctor, as we all do first thing in the morning, to get weighed and he told me Brad had been really sick overnight. But I'd been with him and he hadn't spewed once as far as I knew. He had every right to leave, though. He'd just won the Tour de France and this was his victory lap after living like a monk on a volcano for six months. He'd just had enough.

The stage after that took place on roads I knew extremely well between Welshpool and Caerphilly. It went up from Brecon to Storey Arms and then across Penderyn Moor before heading into the finish for laps of Caerphilly Mountain. When I was at home, we used to do a ride every Thursday called the Thursday Dogs Ride, which went across Penderyn Moor. Bernie was the road captain and I said to him, 'Every week it's windy on that road across Penderyn Moor. You can be in Cardiff or anywhere else and it'll be calm, but you go up on that road and it's windy, and it's always coming from the right.' I reckoned we could split the race there but Bernie said, 'No, no, no, it's OK. It's too far to the finish, no stress.' Although I was the novice, I was thinking, 'You're wrong, Bernie.' I pushed back a little bit, insisting it was a good place to go, but I got overruled.

As we approached Penderyn Moor, I stuck close to the front, and, sure enough, it did split. There were twenty or so riders up there, including a bunch from the Endura squad with Jonathan Tiernan-Locke, the eventual race winner. I was the only representative from Sky. I think everyone on the team took note of that. Firstly, because it was hard for a young guy to get their point across in a superstar squad like that, but I managed to. And secondly, because I was right. It's easy to say something on the bus, but when you say something on the bus and then it pans out, you do get some kudos for it.

I gained a bit more credit on the last day, which was Cav's final one in the world champ's rainbow bands. He was really keen to win. The finish was in Guildford and we did a lap there first which gave us a good look at the final section, which was uphill on cobbles. After we'd been through it the first time, Cav asked me what I thought. 'You've just got to go early, haven't you?' I told him. 'Once you've reached a certain speed on cobbles, nobody's going to come past you. So just have the confidence and go early.' For me to say that to Cav, as a first-year pro, was really something. He did precisely what I'd suggested and won on his final time in that iconic jersey.

'That was really fucking good, Luke,' he said to me.

That was probably the first time where I actually gave some information and people were listening, serious people.

I didn't become a road captain for a year or so after that, but that was a turning point.

Another came at the end of the following season, when me, G and Swifty sat down with Fran Millar at our December camp in Majorca. Mike Barry had left the team by then, Mat Hayman was on the verge of a move to GreenEdge, and we explained to Fran that we had a bit of an issue about the road captains, that we thought there'd been a bit of a drop-off in quality. We felt all the team were doing was looking at the start list at each race and making the oldest guy the road captain. I remember G saying, 'Luke, for example, he'd do a better job than a lot of the older guys. I've done races with him and he'd make a great road captain.' Fran was always great at cutting away the bullshit and dealing with issues straight on, and I think she appreciated us being direct with her. The approach seemed to work as shortly after that I was appointed one of the team's road captains.

Rod Ellingworth on Luke

The first important thing for a road captain is mindset
and forming a strong working combination with
their team leader and sports director – that's the key
triangle of information within any team. Reflecting
on Luke's heyday with Froomey as team leader and
Nico as his DS, I think the mindset they all had was
very proactive, focused on gaining control and not
waiting for attacks, being the ones on the front foot,
the team that initiated action in the crosswinds and
so forth. When you look back at Froomey's best years,
he gained more time in crosswinds and through other
opportunities in races than he ever did on climbs. If
anything, he lost time on climbs.

The three of them did a lot of planning that was
focused on how a race was going to work, on how
they were going to make things happen at a certain
moment. They were really good at that. That came
from the fact that they rode a lot together and talked
a lot, and then in the last critical moments – the night
before, or on the morning of a stage on the bus –
there'd be lots of communication between them. The
emphasis was always on being proactive, on taking
the race on rather than waiting. They'd take advantage
of all the information that was coming from ahead
of the race, from the recon car. What's the wind like?
How open is it? They wanted specific information, and
they'd get that over the radio, then make the decision
on how to respond on the road.

Two other qualities that always struck me about Luke in the role of road captain were his spatial awareness and his awareness of where everybody was in the group. With regard to the former, he was confident taking people through gaps, knowing how the peloton was going to move and flow. He knew when some potential issue on the road might arise. If, for example, he knew there was going to be a pinch point over on the right, he'd take our riders over to the left, and when doing so he'd create space for the people around him so that they could move into the position he wanted them to be in. I think this was always quite a unique asset, one that not a lot of people have. It's something that owes an awful lot to track racing, and was a quality Luke shared with a lot of the British lads who came through the academy. Luke made the most of it in the road captain's role.

With regard to his awareness of where everybody was in the group, this applied not just to his teammates, but to everybody, to all the other GC riders he was controlling. Luke was effectively controlling the narrative we'd set for the race, always keeping everybody on track. He was the one who'd call the numbers of the breakaway riders early on in a stage. He was the one who'd take responsibility for deciding whether a break was going to work. He was the one who talked to and negotiated with riders from other teams when we needed to close the race down or whatever.

There was one day – I'm pretty sure it was in 2016 because Mikel Landa was racing for us – and AG2R, I think, had nailed it and put everyone in the gutter going into a climb late on in a stage. Luke knew that his job was basically to see the team through this climb. I was in the car with Nico, and Froomey came on the radio saying, 'I've got a problem. I need to have a wheel change.' I think the only guys in the group with him were Wout Poels, Landa and Michał Kwiatkowski, and even Kwiato was a little bit behind because it had all split, while Luke was in the third or fourth group.

Froomey was full on panicking. Nico was asking everybody what group they were in, who they could see, that sort of stuff, and I remember Luke coming on the radio and taking control, telling everyone what they needed to do. I'm not sure whether it was Kwiato or Wout who ended up giving him a wheel, but Luke and Nico talked the guys through it, worked it all out between them. It was bloody impressive. It was game-changing for us that day because it could have been a complete shit show. But Luke settled everybody down, gave direction on the road, and everybody stuck to the plan he laid out.

Another moment I remember was at Paris–Nice. It was the first time they'd introduced gravel sections and it was going to be crosswinds. On the bus that morning, Luke was really clear – 'This is what we're going to do. This is how we're going to take the race on. We're going to attack here whether it's windy or not. We're going to go for it on this section.' It exemplified the way in which he'd rally the troops. He'd have his meeting points and he'd gee the guys up, telling them they had to be there.

One thing that was quite unique with the team at the time was that Luke didn't really have to say too much over the radio. At times, he'd just kind of look at somebody and they'd know what was going off. It was such a tight group in the team's heyday, which was down to the training camps and the times they spent with our performance director Tim Kerrison, to all that work they did in Tenerife.

Luke has always held court and been the glue between everybody to a certain extent. It wasn't all singing and dancing and not everybody got on with each other, but Luke ensured the core held together. I think Swifty does exactly the same no matter what group he's in. The group always seems to be quite functional, and that's what Luke brought to the table as well.

I think what was challenging for him, depending on how deep we'd got into the race, were those moments when the mountains came quite early in a stage. At times, we'd be controlling the pace to keep Luke in the group, so that he'd be able to manage the race for us a bit longer. Sometimes he'd let the break go quite a long way out just in order to be able to stay in the race and ensure that he could do his bit. I know it was always a challenge for us on the management side. We'd be thinking, 'When are you going to go backwards and at what point are the guys going to have to make decisions on their own?' That concern came partly from the fact that Froomey had quite a flamboyant and wild outlook on bike races sometimes and on the extent of his capabilities. He got away with it, but I think if left to his own devices anything could have happened. Luke was his anchor.

3

The peloton

Bike racing's sometimes described as chess on wheels, and riding in the bunch is very much like this. The peloton may look orderly when you're viewing images beamed from the helicopter above the race, but it feels anarchic when you're in the heart of it, amid a press of racers jostling for position and advantage. The first thing to realize is that even on a straight piece of road you're never riding in a straight line. That goes for each individual rider and for the peloton as a whole. There's guys moving left, others moving right, some trying to move up, others to move back. You have to navigate your way through, constantly manoeuvring around people. During an average racing day, you'll travel across every inch of the road, from the left- to the right-hand gutter.

Unless you're at the very front, you're always trying to anticipate what's going to happen, reading the situation ahead to see how you can move up or even simply maintain the position you're already in – and you want to achieve this with as little effort as possible. Luckily for me, being tall meant that I could see the flow of the peloton, making it a touch easier to predict what was likely to happen and ready myself to take advantage. For instance, if I wanted to move up and saw the peloton moving to the right, I would move to the left, where there would be more space.

Having a strong sense of this flow is a fundamental skill for every rider, and one that many struggle to master. Road captains, though, are blessed with innate ability for picking their way around the bunch and ensuring that their team-mates are riding in the right place within the peloton. You're always trying to find the sweet spot, the place where you and, most importantly, your leader are safe and feel comfortable, where it's not nervous, where there's little risk of crashing and you're sheltered from the wind. When you find that spot, you reduce your physical and mental losses. If you picture your resources as a bag of sand, every effort you make pricks a hole in the bag, allowing your reserves to trickle out. When you're in the sweet spot, however, you can limit these losses.

There's no golden rule laying down the location of this sweet spot. Usually it's quite close to the front of the peloton, but not always. At certain times, I would tell my teammates to go to the back and sit there as a unit, perhaps because we were on a three-lane highway where there was plenty of room to move up if you needed to. Mentally, it's easier to relax when you're at the back end of the peloton, behind the hustle and bustle of things near the front. Riding for a few minutes in this position could mean one less pinprick in that bag of sand, creating an energy saving that could be cashed in when the team really needed it.

The flip side of this, of course, is that if you're too far back and something kicks off at the front of the race, it's likely to take more time to react and get back to the heart of the action. You very often see this happening when races are on narrower roads, where the peloton gets stretched like an elastic band. When the riders at the front go round a corner and then accelerate coming out of it, those at the back are still braking going into it, and the band extends, then contracts again when the guys at the back accelerate as they come out of the corner.

The road captain's decision on where to ride within the bunch is influenced by a number of key factors, including the weather, the terrain and the condition of the road. If the surface is in a bad state, increasing the likelihood of punctures or a rider losing their grip on their bars and causing a crash, it's best to move towards the front of the bunch, thereby reducing the chances of getting caught behind if there is some kind of issue. When you're racing Paris–Nice, for example, you need to be sat far forward almost all of the time, because you're often on poor-quality roads that regularly change direction, and it tends to be wet and windy. Generally, in races like this where the tarmac and weather are poor, and the road is twisty or undulating, you need to sit at or towards the front. On the flip side, if you're on roads that are a bit straighter and wider, better surfaced, that aren't raked by the wind, you can afford to sit further back.

The Ardennes and particularly the Flandrian Classics are renowned for their narrow roads and lanes, and many of them are cobbled too. As everyone knows that the peloton will get lined out once it reaches them, there tends to be a fight for position as the bunch is approaching them. The guys right at the front who win that little contest essentially do the same kind of lead-out you'd see at the end of a race in the run-up to a bunch sprint. Once they're on the narrower section, they'll often ease off because they've done such a massive sprint, with the aim of recovering. They'll be thinking, 'I've poked a hole in my bag of sand to be in the front. Now let's block the road.' Most guys will be on the same wavelength in this situation, and they're not necessarily teammates. They're exactly where they wanted to be and can have a breather, knowing that their position is safe because there's no room for those behind to manoeuvre. They're in control of the race.

At Team Sky and the Ineos Grenadiers, we'd call these key locations 'meeting points'. If we were heading on to a small road at kilometre 100, there would be a meeting point just before it at, say, kilometre 105, on a big road where it was easy for us to find each other and there was room to move. Coming into it, the directeur sportif would be on the radio, reminding us, 'Remember, guys, 105 is a meeting point.' I'd say, 'Right, guys, 105, let's get together, meeting point.' Depending on your role on a specific day, you either had to be in position yourself or be ready to help your leader and teammates to get into position. We'd group up and focus on going into that section with 100K to go as a unit.

Once we were all at the meeting point and in the right place to help each other, we'd stick to one side of the road, creating 'the bubble'. This would involve a few guys doing a big acceleration to get our group into the location we wanted within the peloton, then we'd bubble up. The leaders would be towards the front and there'd be a gatekeeper at the back, a rider whose job was to prevent other riders and teams from breaking into our little cohort. It was almost like an NFL set play, one that we created at Sky. When new guys came on to the team, they'd be completely alien to it and it would take a few races for them to understand how it was meant to work. We'd start practising it at our pre-season training camp in

December. It would always be presented by a rider, because they knew better than anyone how to explain how the bubble worked having been in it when races were full on.

It's largely down to the road captain to decide on how to deal with this part of the racing puzzle, bringing the team together as a unit in a designated place and maintaining the bubble. Unless it was really relaxed early on, I always encouraged my teammates to stay close to each other as much as possible, simply because this makes it easier to respond if you suddenly find yourselves in a bad situation – say your leader punctures and needs to be paced back up to the bunch, or there's an attack that you need to bridge up to. You can react more quickly when you've got the manpower on hand, when you can easily communicate with your teammates.

Another factor that comes into play when the road captain is deciding where to gather his troops within the peloton is the level of the race you're competing in. In the elite-level World-Tour races, such as the Tour de France or Paris–Roubaix, the racing has to be hard for any rider to lose the wheel in front because they're the very best in the sport. If there's going to be a split, it'll almost always be as a result of a steep gradient or a strong wind or a succession of difficult climbs. Consequently, when you're racing in the WorldTour, you can count on the fact that the rider in front of you is very reliable. You can say to yourself, 'Even when I'm a bit further back, unless something serious happens, they're going to hold the wheel and we won't lose contact with the rest of the peloton.'

However, when you drop down to the non-WorldTour races, like the Tour of Britain for instance, splits develop a lot more easily. I don't mean any disrespect, but it's simply a fact that the performance level of the riders is lower, so you have to be more cautious about sitting further back in the bunch in these smaller races. There'll be riders there who are part-time to some extent, who've got jobs on the side. Because they're not as consistently strong and dependable, they can lose the wheel more easily, even when the racing isn't that hard, and you can suddenly find yourself in the second group on the road because a split has happened in a place that you wouldn't usually expect. As a consequence, you do want to sit a bit further forward. The level of bike handling can also come into play here. Some of these guys might not spend that much time in big pelotons, where the riders are used to being handlebar to handlebar with other riders.

There's also a kind of pecking order in some races, one where the better teams get the best spot in the peloton, which on certain roads is towards the front. It's one of cycling's unwritten rules that the team that's riding, the one that's controlling the bunch by committing guys to the front, can take up the position they want, and tucked in behind them you'll have whoever's leading the general classification.

In most of these cases, it'll be down to the road captain to make the call on where he and his teammates should be. But what does that involve? The most straightforward strategy would be to say, 'Come on, guys, switch on, focus, all together for the whole stage.' But trying to remain tightly grouped as a unit through a complete day of racing adds an unwanted degree of pressure. The best approach in what's already a nervous situation where the riders are tense is to do what a good directeur sportif will do and calm your teammates down, to avoid flustering them or trying to pump them up too much.

Like the best DSs, the best road captains are usually pretty calm personalities. If the peloton was just rolling along behind a breakaway or early on in a mountain stage, I'd say, 'Boys, you should chill out here, go sit where you want to sit. We don't have to be together.' If we were on good roads, ones where we could move up without too much hassle, I would probably have offered the same advice. Then, at a certain point as you come into the final, I'd tell them, 'Right, boys, 50K to go. Let's find each other. Let's switch on. Let's focus. We've had a relaxed day, but now it's game time.' Positioning in the peloton for the last part of the race obviously depends on what the final part of the route looks like, but further forward is, generally, better – you're in front of crashes, you're limiting that elastic band effect, you're not making accelerations because you're stuck behind splits or crashes, and you can react to any attacks. So, coming into the final, being at the front is key.

Before I talk about how my personal approach to riding in the peloton changed during the early part of my pro career, I want to touch on a couple more aspects of this fundamental part of the sport. Most days when you get back on the bus after a stage, you collapse into your seat. You're physically tired, obviously, but mentally you're fried too from being in a frenzied peloton for most of the day. You need a bit of time to decompress, to zone out, often for the first time since the start flag dropped.

While everyone thinks bunch sprints are the most dangerous point of a race and the stress mostly stems from this frantic action in the finale, every rider is actually concentrating to the max in those moments. Sure there are crashes then, and at other key points during a race – usually the result of lapses of concentration, quite often by the same regular offenders who aren't paying enough attention when they need to be, or don't react as rapidly as they should. There might be a crash in the bunch, due to a touch of wheels or whatever; everyone beyond it brakes only to be taken themselves by someone steamrollering in from behind who's not braking at all. You're left wondering, 'Were you asleep there? Everyone in front of you stopped, therefore you should be able to stop.' But they've switched off or, just as bad, they weren't covering their brakes, fingers poised over the levers ready to pull the anchors on.

I would never be in a position between kilometre zero (the starting point of a race) and the finish line where I wasn't covering my brakes. The crash that I was involved in at the 2024 GP E3 Saxo Classic, which left me with concussion and effectively ended my career, was the result of someone losing their handlebars when they hit a bump. All I can say about that is, 'Knobhead!' You've always got to be prepared for that, especially when you can't see what's ahead of you because you're in the middle of the bunch. You've always got to grip your bars and never hold them loose on the tops. You absolutely have to have your fingers wrapped round them.

I once went two and a half years without crashing, while there are other guys who crash ten times a season, and that's not down to bad luck. Sometimes you'd see guys involved on the floor and you'd be thinking, 'That guy again?' They might have an issue with bike handling or they don't pay enough attention in the bunch, or both of these things. While plenty of crashes are the result of bad luck and can leave the best bike handlers in the world on the deck, there are crash artists who you simply don't want to be near because of the reputation they've got. If you happen to be close to them, you try to get in front of them rather than be in the danger zone behind them.

While there's never a good moment to crash, there's one place where they happen and really never should. Before events get under way, the racers always ride out from the start in formation through a neutralized section of the route to reach the official start point, usually outside a town where the roads aren't cluttered with traffic furniture. Sometimes the neutral zone can feel very nervous, because you might be heading straight up a climb from kilometre zero or into a crosswind. You might have a hundred guys wanting to go in the breakaway, so they're determined to be towards the front. This can make the neutral zone, which is usually quite a relaxed part of a race, very jumpy.

However, when everything is quite chilled, danger can still be lurking. Say it's a sprint stage and you know that guys from smaller teams will want to go in the break, leaving everyone else to have a comparatively straightforward day in the peloton. Everyone knows what's going to happen, and as a consequence some riders won't be as switched on as they should be. They'll be thinking, 'I'm in the neutral zone, the break's going to go, so I'll go and catch up with my mate.' One moment you'll be talking, having a laugh, and the next you'll find yourself crashing over your bars and out of the race.

One other thing that you watch for in neutral zones is who is riding where. There are a good number of riders who take a different approach to being in the peloton. Rather than being right in the midst of the washing-machine churn at the heart of it, they prefer to be at the back, where they'll need to spend a little bit more physically in exchange for being able to switch off a bit more mentally. Steve Cummings was a great example of this. He was a rider who would weigh up his chances of having an impact and perhaps winning a stage from a breakaway. If he didn't think there was any hope of this, he'd often be right at the back end of the peloton. If, on the other hand, he was towards the front in the neutral zone, everyone would be well aware of his intentions.

Thomas De Gendt has been the most noted breakaway artist of this type in recent seasons. Like Cummings, if he was at the front in the neutral zone, I'd already be thinking, 'He's all in today,' and everyone would have an eye out for him. They were there purely as stage hunters, aiming to win from breakaways. If there was nothing to tempt them on a particular day, they would sit at the back of the peloton, sucking up the extra work they'd need to do there because they were making slightly more accelerations out of corners and so on. Mentally, though, they could just switch off a bit and say, 'I'm getting from A to B and that's it.' You can't say that they were having a day off, because racing's always too hard for that, but they were having an easier day from a mental perspective, saving themselves for a day when they raced full gas.

Over the years, my own attitude to riding in the peloton gradually changed. Earlier on in my career, I got a lot of things wrong. There were moments when it came to battling for position when I crossed the line, when I was trying to be too assertive, and it took me two or three seasons to understand how this was affecting my racing and, to a degree, my ability as a team captain.

There are all kinds of characters in the bunch. When you're in a peloton, you know every rider, what they're like and how far you can push them – *every* rider. Some riders are a bit soft and will give their position away in the peloton without a fight. You'll find yourself riding alongside someone and you'll think, 'They're in the soft category, I can just go in there whenever I want.' Then there are riders who might stand their ground a bit, but they'll soon let you in. In the next category are the riders who'll really put up a fight, but you'll still get the edge in the end. And then you'll have riders who'll fight to the bitter end, to the point where they're almost prepared to crash to keep their position.

There was a time when I was in that final category. It was partly the result of the pressure I felt coming into a winning team and being absolutely set on keeping that success going. I think as a unit, Sky wanted to be . . . feared is the wrong word, but respected. But we'd really demand that respect, sometimes when it wasn't warranted. We earned it because of our palmarès (our results), but we'd occasionally push it to the limit, especially at the Tour de France, where we kind of did what we wanted. When we were winning the Tour with Chris Froome, we used to say, 'Fuck 'em all and say sorry in Paris.' That was our motto. Then, as we got towards Paris and Froomey was in the yellow jersey as race leader, we'd be like, 'I'm not saying sorry.' It was a means to an end, and that ruthlessness was part of what made us successful, and we could get away with it because at that time we were the top team.

We won the race year after year, and I'm not being arrogant when I say that we were dominant in the way we did it. It wasn't entertaining, in fact it was shit to watch, boring even, but we dominated because we had the best leader and the best team. We had free rein – to go where we wanted in the peloton, to dictate stage results, to decide whether the break stayed away or not and who went in it – and that's because we had the strongest guys. We didn't really give a fuck about anyone. We were strong and had it all going for us. I think we were within our rights to do that. Although we never went over the limit, I sometimes went close to it and paid the penalty for a long time, ending up with a bad reputation – the easiest thing in the world to gain and the hardest thing to get rid of.

Immaturity also played a significant part in me ending up with this rep, and I do regret this. It's only when I got more experienced that I understood that I didn't need to be that way, that I realized that you just become the class clown, that everyone hates you when you're an idiot. There are moments when you do think, 'Fuck everyone here. I've got to do what I've got to do. I've got to carve my way through this peloton. Sorry, boys!' But there's a time and a place for that. I took it too far, trying to be the tough guy sometimes when I didn't need to be. In trying to establish myself, I got too big for my boots.

If I was next to someone, and it didn't matter who it was, and the two of us were going for the same position or the same wheel, I would do whatever I needed to do to get on that wheel. I'd be thinking, 'I'm fucking having it.' Finding myself in that same situation in later years, I had realized that if you speak to people life can be easier. I might even say to the other guy, 'Are you going to let me have that or do you want it?' And most of the time they'd actually say, 'Ahh, go on.' Good communication can solve a lot of things.

Being in that situation in the peloton is a bit like being in the queue at the supermarket or at passport control, one of those moments when you're not quite sure who was first and the other person turns to you and says, 'Is it you or me?' Most of the time you'll let them go ahead simply because you've communicated and have both ended up thinking, 'He's a good bloke for letting me go first or for asking who was first.' It's simply better to get into that mindset. I might just give them a tap on the back and say, 'You go, mate.' They do remember it, and if someone lets me in, I'll be thinking, 'Good lad, I'll remember that.' Sometimes I'd look around to see who it was who had done me a favour, thinking, 'Thanks. I'll remember and give you one back.'

Behaving in this way is better than fighting someone to the death for the wheel and having them remember you for the wrong reason. I've had young lads taking the piss in the way I once did, and they leave you thinking, 'OK, I'll remember that, and somewhere, somehow, some day, I'll get you back. If you're trying to go in the break, I might just close that gap.' Or, if you were controlling the breakaway with four guys away and it was reaching the tipping point where it might stay away, I'd squeeze a bit harder, thinking, 'Fuck him!' Being that way did work against me for a few years, but I definitely went full circle. By the end of my career I would like to think I was well respected within the peloton and did things the right way.

4

Breakaways

Being the road captain, I spent most of my time in the peloton, often working to control breakaways. But I would occasionally seize an opportunity to go chasing a bit of personal glory by going on the attack if I sensed the moment was right, in terms of the terrain, the situation of the race and, crucially, the other riders who were looking to escape from the bunch. My final chance to do so came on what turned out to be the last day of the very last stage race I competed in, the 2024 edition of Tirreno–Adriatico.

This tends to be a stage that favours sprinters, with a finish right on the Adriatic. Yet, it's not always straightforward for them. This one began by heading inland from the coast, undulating relentlessly for its first half, before ending with four laps next to the sea at San Benedetto del Tronto.

As I said, it wasn't really my job to be in the breaks, certainly not on that terrain, but I had good legs, and the group came together just as the peloton was slowing down after thwarting a previous attempt to escape. I was in the last chance saloon when I started to jump across to them, a little late making my move, and half killed myself doing it. But I got there and joined up with EF's Ben Healy and Georg Stein-hauser, Bahrain's Antonio Tiberi and Damiano Caruso, plus Jayco-AlUla's Alessandro De Marchi, a powerhouse in the Thomas De Gendt mould who always committed fully when he sensed an opportunity.

The six of us thought this break could go the distance because many of the sprinters had dropped out, the likes of Phil Bauhaus, Biniam Girmay, Caleb Ewan and Cav, while another, Tim Merlier, got dropped early on in that rollercoaster start. It was a strong break precisely because it materialized at a really hard moment of the race, as we headed straight up from sea level to an altitude of around 500 metres.

As soon as you're in a break, the riders in it need to show cohesion and honesty, even though you're also trying to flick each other, to pick a moment to attack. But there's a time and a place to try to do that. When I got up there we had almost 150K to go, and the 30 or 40K immediately ahead of us were on rolling, hard roads. I looked around and thought, 'I'm out of my depth in this group. They're all climbers and I'm by far the biggest.' So I said to them that I wasn't going to ride at all for those 30 or 40K, that I wasn't going to do a single turn until we passed the climbs. How stupid would I have looked if I'd agreed to ride and then got dropped and went back to the peloton after 10K? But I told them that as soon as we got over the last climb and we were on the finishing circuits on the flat I would turn myself inside out. I asked them to trust me, and they agreed to.

There's a famous saying among racers, that as soon as you get in a breakaway you should do as much as the person who's doing the least. The other five could have got the hump with me and the unity within the group would have evaporated.

But they clearly realized that I wasn't trying to screw with them. I couldn't have contributed with five riders who were much better climbers than me, so I just sat on the back and did nothing, waiting for the moment when I would commit fully. When we came down off the last climb, we went into team time trial mode and rode to perfection. I committed 100 per cent, all of us did, thinking that if we could make it into the last kilometre as a breakaway group then we could race it out between us. Whoever wins, wins, but we had to give ourselves that opportunity first.

Behind us, the sprint teams were losing riders. On the finish circuits, the gap went down to less than a minute, then it went back over a minute, giving us a bit more motivation and impetus. Sadly, though, we got caught just after the final lap started after we'd spent 130K away. In that case, being in the break didn't require too much thinking. Our approach was almost the opposite of tactical: we just rode flat out. Sometimes things can be overthought. You could have said that there were two EFs, two Bahrains, so De Marchi and I should have done less. But that's bollocks. It didn't matter that two teams had numbers on their side. We rode as a six-man unit, us against the peloton, and unfortunately they caught us. But we did put them under the pump, they were really under pressure. You can end up being too clever in a scenario like that. If I'd tried to do less once we got to the flat land, we'd have just got caught earlier because there wouldn't have been total commitment. Better to die trying than to die wondering.

As was the case on this Tirreno stage, breakaways fail more often than they succeed, and I'll highlight why in a moment. Before that, though, it's worth explaining the thinking behind an attack of this kind. The first thing to say about any day you're planning to infiltrate the break is that you can't really predict who's going to be in there with you, although you do get some early clues, sometimes even before the start flag drops and the action gets under way.

You can start trying to suss out which teams want to go in the break and which want to control the race when you analyse the specific demands of the day. Is it likely to end with a sprint? Is it a punchy final section where riders who can accelerate quickly on a climb will be on ideal terrain? Which teams have got the riders to suit these options? Working this out will quickly give you an idea of who's likely to control the break by allowing those in it some leeway, but not enough for the escapees to go the distance. Next you think, 'Which teams haven't really got anyone that suits the demands of the day?' These are the teams that are likely to want to go in the break, because that's their only way to success. Finally, if you're considering the breakaway as an option, you need to establish whether there's a viable chance of success if you do manage to go clear. If it's a pan-flat day and you haven't got a sprinter, then the break is an option. But if you join it and there's, say, six teams on the start line with good sprinters, it's not realistic to expect the break to survive. In short, when it comes to breakaways, it's not simply a case of saying, 'We haven't got someone who ticks the boxes when it comes to the demands of the day, so we'll aim to get someone in the break.' You have to be realistic about its prospects of success.

The ideal scenario if you're looking to the break as your best shot at victory is one where the demands of the day are likely to ensure that there aren't many teams who have leaders they'll back as likely winners and, therefore, commit to chasing down the break. Consequently, if there are only two teams who want the race to come together in the final kilometres that leaves a lot of teams who don't have a stand-out leader for the day, thereby ensuring that there's going to be a lot of people who want to go in the break, hugely increasing the chances that it will succeed.

If it can go the distance, the next question to weigh up is whether you can win bearing in mind the race's finale. If you've got little or no chance, then who are the most likely candidates for success on your team on that parcours? If, for instance, the last 50K rolls over third- and fourth-category climbs, I might have been able to cope with them, but that's perfect terrain for Pippo Ganna, so we'd try to get Pippo in the break. If you think back to that day Tom Pidcock won up Alpe d'Huez in the 2022 Tour de France, we'd have been asking ourselves a simple question that morning: 'Who have we got who can win on Alpe d'Huez?' Tom was obviously the man. If I'd been in the break, I'd have been useless, unless I was there purely to help Tom.

You have a very similar mentality towards going in the break whether it's a one-dayer or a stage in a multi-day event. The critical difference is that in a one-day race the early break pretty much never makes it to the finish. In a stage race, though, the peloton will sometimes take its foot off the gas – but, you've still got to remember that the peloton always has more horsepower than the break. Always! So on any given stage, it's the peloton's decision whether they catch the breakaway or not. It's not down to the breakaway. They can ride as hard as they want, but the peloton can just put more and more men into the pursuit. Even if there's twenty at the front, there's 180 behind. When the breakaway does make it, it's almost always because the bunch has opted to save its energy for the next day.

The purpose of going in the breaks in a stage race versus a one-day race is also different. In a one-day race, the early breakaway's only purpose is to get a head start and make it as far as possible. Sometimes that can result in you ending up in the group contesting victory, as has been the case occasionally in Paris–Roubaix. Mat Hayman and Johan Vansummeren were both in the break of the day and went on to win that race, but I'd say that 99.9 per cent of the time the break never makes it to the finish.

In a stage race, you know that certain days will suit the breakaway – the day after a big general classification (GC) battle, for instance. In fact, if you're asking yourself the question 'Who's this stage really for?', then it's a breakaway day. When checking through a race's roadbook, you're looking for stages where lots of different types of rider could win, so not one that finishes up a 10K climb on which the GC guys are guaranteed to be battling for victory. You also want it to be hard enough so that the sprinters can't stay in contention.

When doing this research before the race or the evening before a stage earmarked as having good breakaway potential, you'd also look at the point at which you ought to make your move. 'Where can I go into this break? Where, realistically, is the launch pad? Where are the small roads, the narrow roads?' When doing this homework, I'd tend to look for narrow roads and small climbs where the stronger guys could attack off the front of the peloton.

When the race got under way, I'd always be looking at who was moving, who was at the front, even in the neutral zone. Which teams were there with numbers to control? Which teams were there with numbers to go in the break? Which individuals were there? You're constantly assessing – who's super keen, who's over keen, who's maybe sitting back and waiting for a certain point to arrive? Analysing the opposition in this way was always one of my major assets as a rider. Road captains are renowned for being all-seeing. While other riders were chatting before the action really kicked off, I'd always be watching and evaluating.

On these days, you're speaking with your teammates all the time too. It's very rare for the DS to say, 'We want one rider to go in the break, and it's on you.' Getting a rider or riders into a break tends to require a collective effort by the team. A particular rider might be given the task of going in the break, but they depend on the support of others to get there. I used to spend quite a bit of time trying to help my teammates in these situations. For instance, if the designated man had tried an attack, been chased down and then drifted back in the peloton, I might move him back up towards the front so that he was ready for the next attempt to form a breakaway. Or I might be close to the front and realize, 'Shit, there's twelve guys going, we're not in that one, close the gap,' so that it reset the situation, giving our designated guy the opportunity to try for the break again.

Once you get into a potential breakaway group, you go full gas, hoping that the elastic reaching back to the bunch will stretch and then snap. When that happens, the peloton will slow down and the gap will quickly reach two minutes or so. At that point you can speak to the other riders with you, encouraging them to go easy. The gap might well keep increasing, but the peloton will start to react and begin closing it at a pre-decided moment. One or more teams will have been told by their DS to limit the gap to a certain distance and their road captain will remind them of this – 'Keep this break between four and five minutes.' So if the breakaway decides to go faster, the peloton will do the same. You know that if you ride faster at the front the peloton will ride faster behind and match you. As I said before, they've always got the horsepower to do that.

That's not to say, though, that the riders in the break can't outwit and outride the peloton at certain moments. If you've looked closely at the profile, sussed out the wind direction and strength, there are points where the escape group can turn the screw. The most dependable way of doing so is by taking advantage of the delay in relaying time gaps. On TV, you can see those figures thanks to live GPS. The riders, though, have to rely on the figures chalked on a small blackboard brandished by a race official on the back of a motorbike. Or we get our information from the team car, but it can be delayed by up to a minute.

They update the time gap every 5K. The motorbike goes to the break with the time check first, then stops beside the road to wait for the peloton and show them the gap. The bike halting is often the cue for the riders in the break to start going full gas. If, for instance, the front group has a lead of two minutes, it will take five to six minutes for the blackboard bike to repeat the process. After waiting for the peloton, it has to pass the bunch and come back up to the break to take another time check, then come back up again to the break with the new gap. If the break is going flat out, it can gain a lot of time in those few minutes, and can occasionally catch the peloton out.

If you're in the peloton and you have a guy in the break, the road captain or one of his other teammates can still provide that guy at the front with some vital support. If there's, say, 50K to go and a team is pulling on the front of the peloton to position their sprinter or GC guy for a final surge, and that rider stops for a leak or goes back to the car, I'd radio through: 'Right, tell the guys at the front to go now because he's just stopped for a piss.' Some of his teammates who were pulling on the front will have to wait for him to stop for a piss and then lead him back up. During these moments, the rest of his teammates aren't going to be booting it to chase behind the break. You never stop analysing, especially as the road captain. If I'm in the peloton and my guy's in the break, it's not a case of 'See you at the finish, mate'. There's often a way you can turn a situation to your team's advantage.

On the flip side, if you're in the break, you can also be giving information to your teammates in the peloton. Turning a corner, you might notice that there's suddenly a strong crosswind and tell your team car that's behind the break to pass on a message to the guys in the peloton that you could feel the wind coming pretty strongly from a certain direction at a particular point. They'll then tell the car behind the peloton and your teammates will get that message relayed on to them. So even if you're in the breakaway, you're still trying to feed stuff back to the riders behind that might help them.

Enough of the theory, let's look at some instances when I did get into breaks, why I chose those moments and how the race unfolded given my earlier analysis. Let's start by rolling back to Kuurne–Brussels–Kuurne in 2024. We'd done Het Nieuwsblad, the opening race of the Spring Classics season, the day before and that race had split in the crosswinds. Going into Kuurne, a race with a similar profile initially to Nieuwsblad but much flatter in its final quarter, it was clear what was likely to happen looking back to the year before, when, thanks to the direction of the wind, the race had opened up early on the asphalt climbs.

With the wind coming from that same direction, prior to the start I was thinking, 'If I wait till we reach those climbs and Visma-Lease a Bike whack it with a team of Wout van Aert, Tiesj Benoot, Dylan van Baarle, Christophe Laporte and the rest, I'm not passing that climb. I'll get dropped and be out of the race. There'll only be a very small group at the front. If I wait till that moment, I'm just waiting with a gun to my head and they're going to pull the trigger.' I calculated that the only way I could remain in contention into the final part of the race was to get in a breakaway and have some minutes on them. If I could do this, I figured that either the favourites would bridge up to us on those asphalt climbs or we'd maybe survive a little longer. When the race got under way, it was clear that a lot of other riders had come to the very same conclusion and had a similar plan in mind.

I finally got into a break with four other guys – Dries De Bondt, Fran Miholjević from Bahrain, Jasper De Buyst from Lotto and Luca Mozzato. We agreed that we'd ride a solid pace and see how far we could get. As it turned out, we didn't make it very far. We stayed together for maybe 60K. They just kept us on too short a leash for our plan to work. Visma sussed out what we were doing and started riding almost as soon as we established the breakaway, and all too quickly this roaring peloton just soared through our break and stuck us out the back.

We didn't get the chance to start playing any games with each other in that break, to use the kind of moves you see when a small group is coming towards the finish and the

riders start attacking each other. For us, it was a case of
'There's five of us, let's ride a team time trial, let's ride hard'.
We knew we'd be caught before the finish line, that the breakaway had no chance of going the distance. We were there to
try and survive for as long as possible, basically trying to get a
head start on the superstars, because none of us could go toe
to toe with van Aert and his cronies. Consequently, in that
situation there was real cohesion.

I can't talk about breakaways without bringing in Thomas
De Gendt. The Belgian rider was the breakaway king for many
seasons, winning stages in all three Grand Tours and most
of the other WorldTour stage races. His strategy was always
crystal clear for me: he got into the break and went full gas.
He would just try to break everyone with his brute power.
When he was at his best, he was often unbelievably good and
produced some of the most impressive rides I've ever seen.

The one that sticks in my mind was the second stage of
the 2018 edition of the Tour de Romandie. That day, he was
in the break and QuickStep started riding behind. They had
a strong sprint team with Elia Viviani and Fernando Gaviria
both well supported, but they weren't bringing him back.
I recall GreenEdge being one of the teams that decided to
help QuickStep. They were pulling, pulling, pulling, throw-
ing guys to the front of the peloton. The gap would stabilize,
then, instead of starting to come down, it would go out again.
We were sat as the second or third team and I was thinking,
'Thank fuck I'm not the one chasing'.

As well as being an immense powerhouse, De Gendt was
very canny too. He'd mess with the peloton over time gaps,
riding faster at times, then slowing and deliberately letting the bunch close in before it wanted to. He wanted the

teams leading the chase to start second-guessing, and if that happened he'd give it everything to take advantage of that hesitation. He was also very good at sizing up his rivals in the break. Strong on every kind of terrain, he'd work out where he could make the most of that all-round ability, attacking on climbs, descents, anywhere he felt he had an edge. This was a guy, remember, who finished third in the Giro d'Italia in the early part of his career. As I said, he had it all. He was deadly in a sprint from a small group too.

Another rider who always used his nous to the fullest when he was off the front of the bunch was Thomas Voeckler. In 2015, the year Richie Porte won Paris–Nice for us for the second time, the opening road stage was in the area where Tony Gallopin lived. There were rumours of mad cross-winds, that those roads to the western side of Paris were quite open. Our DS Nico Portal did a recon of them and came back saying that it was the most exposed area in the world, built for full-on crosswind warfare. Gallopin, then racing for Lotto-Soudal, said it was always windy there and the conditions had more of an impact because the roads were higher than the surrounding fields. Buckle up, we were all thinking.

However, when we got there for the start, there wasn't a puff of breeze. Nothing. It was one of the most relaxed starts ever, with everyone just rolling along at 30kph chatting. Eventually a commissaire or one of the guys from the organization came back and told us to hurry up, that they'd arranged road closures for specific times and we'd be late for the TV slot, which they'd scheduled on the assumption we'd be racing at 48kph. Nobody was too bothered though. There hadn't even been a breakaway.

Then Voeckler rolled off the front with another French guy,

Anthony Delaplace. Everyone was laughing at them, thinking they were fools going on a break on a flat stage with a long distance still to the finish. It seemed pointless given the number of sprinters in the field. But the pair of them just played the game to perfection. They rode really easy and eventually we started to chase behind, and they came back straight away, but too soon for the bunch to want to reel them in. Then, with around 25K to go, they opened the taps and gave it everything. We caught them just before the kilometre-to-go banner. They'd almost got away with it. And I remember Thomas saying that he knew people were laughing at him when he went in the break, but he explained that he never went away without a good reason or simply to get TV exposure for his team. He reckoned he could do something, win the stage, and he almost did.

As a team, Sky quickly worked out how to play things in the Grand Tours. We never put guys in the break because that was a risky game to play when you've got your sights set on overall victory. Some teams do it, but if you're leading the race it's just a case of strength in numbers, always strength in numbers. We'd all stay around Froomey at all times. Nobody would leave the ship.

When the peloton is chasing the breakaway in those situations, it's because they want to catch it. On mountain stages, it was always expected that we would lead the pursuit and we were very happy controlling the race in that way, while on flat stages the sprint teams would be in the vanguard and we'd sit right in behind them. In both instances, it was critical not to catch the breakaway too soon, for two good reasons. First, because another breakaway could then materialize, or the race could open out again and you'd suddenly find you had to chase a crop of fresh guys. The other danger was bringing the break too close too soon, within a minute or so of the peloton, which would encourage guys to try to jump across to the front group. Then, instead of chasing three guys in the break, you might be chasing six or eight.

If the goal is to bring the break back, the road captain and the DS will have a conversation and decide how much of a gap they will allow the breakaway. First of all you look at who's in there. Say there's four riders away. If, as road captain, I don't know enough about the four, someone in the team car will go online and research them. They'll come back and say something like, 'Guy X is pretty strong.' Or, 'Guy Y hasn't finished a race, it's the first breakaway he's been in.' You work out the strengths of the individuals and break it down from there. That then allows you to work out how quickly you can bring the break back when you need to in the final 50K, when you start to turn the screw.

Over the years we spent a huge amount of time controlling on the front at race after race. As we were winning most of the one-week stage races and the Grand Tours, we gradually worked out that it was best for the break to contain either a very small or a very large number of riders. Initially, our mantra was 'Don't let too many guys off the front, keep it to six or eight'. But, actually, six to eight was the most dangerous number, because that amount of riders would work perfectly together.

However, although it might seem counterintuitive, if there were more than eight riders in the break it would be easier to control it. We even got to the point where we wondered whether it mattered how many riders escaped. Say, for instance, a hundred riders went up the road and the eight of us were in the peloton together with all of the top ten riders on GC – would that be a major problem for us? Rather than allowing a small number to go clear, we wanted thirty, even forty guys to be away, because they would never all work together. Some of them might pull a bit, but everyone wants to sit on in a group that big, it's inevitable. They all know they're going to end up attacking each other, so they don't all commit fully and hold something back.

We realized we could let large breaks go as long as we weren't greedy and tried to chase them with the aim of going for the stage win. In fact, the breakaway riders loved it when we took the yellow jersey. They'd be thinking, 'Right, now we can go for the stages, Sky always let the breakaway go.' As a result, it would often take a while for the break to form, but we always said, 'Invest heavily at the start and it'll repay us.' So whatever it took, we'd make sure that the make-up of the break was right, even if it took 100K, because we'd get the payback over the next 100K.

One day like this that sticks in my mind is the 2016 Tour stage that started in Andorra and finished on the flat in Revel. We were riding on the front and there were incessant attacks and counters from the start. They just kept on coming. If you're defending the lead in that situation, all you're looking for is the top ten on GC. You only respond if one of the riders in the top ten on GC goes. On one occasion, Alejandro Valverde jumped, so we had to close him down.

At one point, guys were attacking, attacking, attacking, and when we looked ahead it seemed like there was a peloton up the road. Nico Portal was on the radio: 'Just to reassure you guys. If you're sure there's no one up there from the GC, we're fine . . .' I was on the front of the bunch and told him that I'd seen every rider who'd attacked. 'There was no one in GC, all good.' He came back: 'Brilliant job, guys, that's amazing. It's a big group, but don't worry. Fantastic job.'

And then the numbers came through on the radio: 'Sixty-seven riders in the break.' Sixty-seven! Nico came back on: 'Amazing job. Amazing.' We could see this massive group going up the road, with sixty-seven guys. But he was so calm under pressure. What DS would say 'You're doing an amazing job, guys' when there were sixty-seven guys away? But that was Nico. He might have been in that car shitting himself, thinking, 'If they've missed someone, if one of the top ten has snuck in there, then they've got to chase a group of sixty-seven.'

In the end, other teams got a bit nervous and brought it back. But that was Nico – cool, calm, collected, never stressed. If sixty-seven guys went up the road, most DSs would be beside themselves, but he was telling us, 'Great job, guys.' It might have looked like we'd lost control, but quite the opposite. In the end, we finished nine minutes behind the break, but didn't lose time to anyone of significance in the GC contest. It was a good day for us and the break.

5

Riding in the wind

It's the best racing to watch. But when you're on the road, it's heaven or hell. There's no in-between. You either love racing in the wind or hate it. I always loved it for the simple reason that it gave me an advantage. On the morning of a one-day race like Gent–Wevelgem, where short, steep climbs are scattered across a route that's very open to the elements, I'd be praying for the wind to get up. I knew all too well that if I went man-to-man against a lot of the other riders, I'd come off second best. So, if I was approaching the Kemmelberg, Gent–Wevelgem's emblematic climb, within a complete peloton, there would probably be fifty guys who could go up it faster than me. Whereas, if I was part of a twenty-strong group that had formed in the wind before the Kemmel, there might only be two or three who could climb it a bit faster than I could. In short, the wind turned the odds in my favour.

Gent–Wevelgem was always my favourite Classic. I never got a result in the race – my highest finish was twelfth in 2020 – but there was a spell in the middle of my career when I was always in the front group. Yet, no matter whether I was working for someone else, as was the case early in my career, or given free rein, I would always want it to be windy because the sound of flags flapping frantically in a gusting breeze instilled me with confidence. I never imagined a situation where I wouldn't be in the front group in the wind. That might sound arrogant, but I simply knew that it was my element. I felt right at home in the wind, which isn't something many riders would say.

On days when it was blowing, you'd hear the same things over and over again on your bus and in the peloton as it gathered before the start. Some guys would be admitting defeat already: 'As soon as there's wind, I'm fucked. I just cannot make the front group.' Others would be seeking last-moment advice: 'How are we going to make it into the first group? How do you get in position?' Meanwhile, I'd be relishing the next few hours of racing because a crosswind was where I felt most at home.

Watching on TV, you could be mistaken for thinking that being in the front group when it's windy and echelons form is down to a mixture of luck and brute strength. Those two factors do come into play, but there's much more to it than that. Until recent seasons, when teams began to gather more information about weather conditions, particularly thanks to the Veloviewer app, you had to be well prepared before you got to the start line. You'd match the wind direction against the direction of travel of the route and work out where the critical points would be, the places where the race was likely to split.

When racing began, you had to be smart and look at the flags at the roadside. Where exactly was the wind coming from? Was it switching? Was it coming from the right? At what angle? Was it cross/head? Cross/tail? If you were heading into a forest, you'd want to know when you came out of the trees again and the road became exposed. You'd be weighing the same details in towns and villages. How built up is it? How high is that hill on the right? When will it get exposed again? During the first half of my pro career, you had to think for yourself and suss out how the conditions might impact the race, which is where I added more value. I could do that, and that ability was vital to me as a racer and especially to my team leaders.

Nowadays, everyone knows everything. Everyone knows exactly where it's open, where it's exposed. They get that information in the bus before the start, then over the radio during the race, much of it relayed from vehicles travelling ahead of the action. Everyone knows, for instance, that at kilometre 57.3 it is open from the right. They know the strength of the wind, the direction, how it will affect the race at the right-hand turn 4.3K further up the road. They're better prepared. However, knowledge isn't always power when it comes to crosswinds.

There's a special dynamic to a windy stage. Everyone knows what they're signing up for. It's going to be messy, there's going to be argy-bargy, there are going to be arguments, more often than not there's going to be a crash or some other incident. You can sense the nerves as soon as you get on that start line. When you're in the neutral zone, everyone's thinking the exact same thing: 'Fuck! Here we go . . .'

The next key to survival when the wind is strong enough to split a race is that you've got to be ready to move when somebody hits the hammer at the front. If you're too far back, you're going to miss the split and end up riding in one of the echelons behind the first one. If that happens, the only way you're going to see the front of the race again is if the front group eases off for some reason. There is – and every bike racer rapidly realizes this the first time they're in a situation where the peloton splits in the wind – absolutely no way of jumping from the echelon you're in to the one in front. Physically, it's impossible.

An echelon forms when the peloton splits and groups fan across the road, each rider using the one in front as a windbreak. When this happens, everyone within each echelon has to rotate in order to survive – they have to be part of the chaingang, as we call it. Essentially, the riders are like links in a bike chain. When the rider at the front has done their stint in the wind, they peel away, riding parallel, but behind the echelon until they can slot in at the bottom end of the line and start working their way up to the front again.

If you don't rotate and become part of that chain, you get caught at the back and popped out – fodder for the next echelon, if you can get into it, or the next, or the next. The only exception to this I've ever known was Adam Blythe. He could survive a crosswind without putting his nose in the wind at all, just sitting at the back and missing turns. You'd be thinking, 'Oh, Blythe's gone. I haven't seen him for ten minutes,' and he'd just be tucked in at the rear, never rotating in the line but holding his place and staying out of the wind by sticking right at the end of it using the last three inches of the road. It required astonishing skill and nerve to do that.

If you are in the right place – and it was one of my jobs to make sure that our leader was in precisely that position – it's always easier if you've got at least one teammate with you. If you do, your chances of staying at the front are much higher because of the mechanics of an echelon. Holding your place might sound simple, but it isn't. There may be riders in that chain who don't want you in there, because they're following team orders or they regard you as a weak link who might jeopardize their own position in the line. However, if you've got a teammate with you, you can help each other get back on to the end of the line.

Before I go into a specific example to illustrate how difficult it can be to find and then hold your place in the front echelon, I should point out that there's a complicating factor. Let's say kilometre 100 is where the race is expected to split in the wind. As early as kilometre 50 and certainly by kilometre 80 there'll be nerves in the peloton, so you might have to hold your position for 50K before the wind comes into play in order to be in the right place at kilometre 100. A lot of riders won't manage this. They'll get bullied out of the way and find themselves too far back. And, like I said, even if you're the strongest guy in the world, you can't jump from one echelon to the one ahead if you're a long way back when the race does split. Consequently, holding a place towards the front of the peloton is crucial during those 50K.

There were a good few years at Paris–Nice when we won the race in the wind, which was pretty cool looking back. But those days brought a special kind of pressure. I've already talked about the 2017 edition that Sergio Henao won, how I had to feed him out of my hands, and I'm going to go into a lot more detail about the opening couple of days of that race, starting with the post-dinner conversation I had with Sergio in our team hotel the night before it started. Like a lot of GC guys, he was well out of his comfort zone in the wind. In fact, he wasn't at all sure about how to hold his place in an echelon, so I gathered up the salt and pepper pots and showed him how it works.

Sky had selected three riders with the specific job of protecting Sergio on the flat stages in the opening days, guys who could hold their own in the wind: Christian Knees, Michał Gołaś and me. I needed to emphasize to Sergio how we needed to collaborate if, say, three of us were in an echelon together. He didn't speak English too well, so I had to explain all this in pretty basic terms. 'This is you, Sergio. This is me. This is someone else.' Doing this, by the way, epitomized the road captain's role off the bike.

The first thing to highlight was how to stay in the rotation and keep together. As I moved the condiments around the table, I explained the physical commitment required when you're getting over the guy on the front as he drops back to rotate to the end of the line. It might look easy to move from second place in the line to being the rider closest to the leading edge of the echelon, but you need a real kick of power to do it, because you're suddenly taking the full force of the wind. The next issue is to avoid being forced out of the echelon by the few stragglers at the bottom end of it who want to get into the rotation because they're exposed to the wind. The riders who are already in the chaingang need to prevent this, primarily because they can end up losing their place if someone else forces their way in. There is only so much width in the road and that limits how many riders can be involved. I told Sergio that to prevent this happening, as you move towards the back of the line as a three, it's the responsibility of the guy at the rear of your trio to block off anyone attempting to break into the line. Once that guy's in position, having shut the back door, he shouts 'In!' and the teammate ahead of him drops into the position in front of him. That guy then shouts 'In!' and the third guy drops in front of him. Then you circle around again.

Of course, when you come around again, the third guy is now the first guy, the one who has to get into the line and block the stragglers. As on the previous rotation, the other two can slide in when that guy makes it. Until he does, they'll be thinking, 'Don't mess up because if you do, we're fucked.'

If, say, three of you are together and a fourth teammate is on the other side of the rotation, it's best to join forces – there's always strength in numbers in bike racing. So, as he's coming up the line, and even if he's halfway up it, he'll shout 'In! In! In!' to allow the three of you to slide in front of him so that you become a four, even if that means that you're soon at the front again and have to do another turn quite quickly.

The first stage of that 2017 Paris–Nice was relatively short. It was pissing down and really cold, and when we looked out of the windows the flags were going crazy. I remember saying to someone, 'This is going to be on!', and I decided to start in shorts. One of the other guys asked me, 'What are you doing in shorts?', trying to give me a bit of shit, thinking I was an idiot. I just repeated what I'd said before: 'This is going to be on, mate!'

Sergio was shitting himself at the start, but to be fair to him he was far from the only one in that state. He was our leader because, like all GC guys, he was a brilliant climber, but he was well out of his comfort zone in a crosswind, and it was proper windy. When we got going, it wasn't too long before it split, and we managed to get into the front echelon. The first thing you've got to do then is make as many friends as you can. So I befriended Ben Swift straight away. He was in his first year with UAE having left Sky, and half of his kit was still Sky's because they were so late getting everything ready – they were a pretty average team back then, begging and borrowing stuff from all over. Anyway, Swifty, Sergio and me formed a little alliance.

Things were OK initially, then, as we got to the back of the rotation and I tried to let Sergio in, I suddenly realized he wasn't there. I looked round and he was yards off the back. When that happens, you're fucked. I dropped back for him, sprinted to get back on, somehow managed it, got in next to Swifty again, glanced back, and Sergio was nowhere to be seen. I was now the only Sky rider in the front group. I screamed at the top of my voice 'FFFUUUCCCKKK!!!', then sat up and went back to him. I was so pissed off that I got my bottle and hurled it on the floor Italian-style – not my style at all. The next group was a good way behind, so I told Sergio, 'Right, eat, drink. It's OK. We'll go back to the second echelon. We'll be all right.' We did that and, fortunately, we were OK as the second echelon regained contact with the first.

There were times during the stage when the race was in complete bits, with groups everywhere. But Sergio, Kneesy and I were always at the front, holding position right next to each other. Sergio was incredibly gritty, never comfortable, but so determined to cling on, with me and Kneesy taking the lead in indicating where he needed to be and when. At the very end of the stage there was a little kicker up to the line, where Sergio scampered away from us to finish in a small group a few seconds behind stage winner Arnaud Démare. Crucially, he gained time on his main rivals, Richie Porte and Alberto Contador, who were both better climbers than him.

On the second day, we started riding west for 5 to 10K, then we turned due south and it was a crosswind from the right. So it was 5 to 10K cross/head, turn left, then a cross/tailwind for 180K. On the bus, I said to the climbers, 'From kilometre zero, you have to get me and Sergio to the 10K point at the front. You have to do that, and then it's for me, Gołaś and Kneesy to take it on,' and they did it. Even that takes commitment. I remember saying to Sebastián Henao, 'Your finish line is at 10K, just fucking commit for 10K, after that you're going to be at the back of the peloton, the race is over, you just survive.' Imagine having a day of 195K and being told that your finish line arrives with 185K to go. He said, 'Yeah, no problem, I'll do that.' That's what it takes to win.

This, I should add, is the stage when I ended up feeding Sergio out of my hand. Once again, the race was blown to bits, with groups all over the place. The ones towards the front came together near the end and there were around seventy guys in it for the sprint, which Sonny Colbrelli won. If you watch that sprint back, it seems to be happening in slow motion. We were all completely spent.

Gołaś, Kneesy and I were all up there with Sergio again. I remember my gears broke on the final circuit with around 10K to go and I was stuck in the 11, but everyone was so cold and the speed so slow that I managed to hold on without changing my bike. When I got to the bus at the finish line, I couldn't feel my hands, couldn't feel anything. I couldn't undo the zip on my overshoes. That was the moment I had to ask Slarky, our bus driver, to undress me.

We made more gains on GC that day. Richie Porte lost more than fourteen minutes, so we put him out of the race completely. It was one of those days when you get to the finish line and it's like you've won if you're in the front group. Days like that were often the closest I could get to that winning feeling. When it's your job to get your leader into the front group in the crosswind and you manage it, you really feel like you've contributed. You get to the finish, gain time on a big opponent, and think, 'That was mega.' It was probably the nearest I could get to having personal success.

One thing I should add is that the team we had at Paris–Nice that year exemplified how you need different horses for different courses. The likes of Sebastián Henao, Mikel Nieve and Phil Deignan weren't there for the flat, windy days. They were there for the back end of the race, when it reached the hills and mountains close to Nice. Phil was nowhere in the crosswinds, but ended up having an excellent race. He was really good on the last stage into Nice when Contador went ballistic on the Col de Peille, where I was already ten minutes down. He saved our bacon there, and that underlines why teams need to be well balanced.

Going into that race, we also knew how much Richie hated the wind – he loathed those conditions. He'd spent four seasons with us, winning Paris–Nice twice during that period, and I'd say he was *the* best one-week stage racer of the recent generation. He was also one of the best three-week racers, but didn't quite get the results to reflect that. One reason for that was that as soon as there was wind, he seemed to have a mental block. Paris–Nice and no wind? He'd walk it. In a Col d'Eze time trial, nobody could get close to him. But if it was windy in the first few days, we'd have a real chance. Heaven for me was hell for Richie.

I should qualify that a little, though. The wind could prove hellish for me as well. If I was racing for myself in a

Classic, I felt like I was carrying no burden at all. On the other hand, if I was in a Grand Tour or a one-week stage race and helping someone else, I did have that sense that there was a lot on my shoulders. If I made it into the front group with Sergio Henao, Geraint Thomas or Chris Froome, then that was what was expected. But if you're in the second group and lose thirty seconds or a minute, like Contador's domestiques did on that first day at Paris–Nice, you'd failed to do your job.

Luckily, during my career there wasn't a big balls-up while looking after a GC guy in the crosswind. I can't think of an occasion when we lost time. On all of the Paris–Nice stages we were always there, on all of the Tour de France stages we were always there. That was down to the make-up of the team. Early on we had myself and Ian Stannard, then Kneesy came in, and after that we signed Michał Kwiatkowski, who's one of the best in the world for sniffing out an opportunity in the wind.

When you get the right combination of riders, it doesn't make riding in the wind easy, but you're so confident that you've got an edge on some of your rivals. You'll be thinking, 'We'll be there. Whatever it takes, we'll be there.' That's the message that your leader wants to hear as well. If you're asking questions and you're nervous, your leader will sense that and they'll be nervous. That's the last thing you want because they're more susceptible to crashes and they'll brake half a second earlier. You want them to have total confidence, even to the level of arrogance. This is where Kwiato, Stannard, Kneesy and those guys were brilliant. We'd be telling our leaders, 'We'll make the front group. Just follow us. We'll make sure we're together. If you lose our wheel, we'll come back to you. We'll always stay with you.' Hearing that, our leaders would be thinking, 'OK, that sounds simple. I'm happy with that.' On some team buses, though, they're all flapping before a windy stage. Knowing that would make us even keener to get going.

6

Sprints

Thinking back over thirteen years of pro racing, the sprint that stands out from all of those that I've played a part in is one that we didn't end up winning, although I'm still adamant that we should have done. I'm referring to the 2016 Worlds in Qatar, where Peter Sagan won the second of his world titles by narrowly denying Mark Cavendish a second rainbow jersey.

We were confident that we could win the race. We'd had a few punts in the years before with Ben Swift and Pete Kennaugh, but that was the first Worlds I'd ridden since Cav had won in Copenhagen in 2011 when we went in with a real favourite. We had a really good group and everyone was buzzing. We all knew that there was an opportunity to achieve something great.

To a large extent that feeling came from the confidence and cohesion that Cav instilled within that team. He was like the glue within any outfit that he was part of. You could see that when he went to Astana right at the end of his career. They weren't a sprint team at all, but he changed that ethos and had all of the guys giving all they could for him there. There's no doubt about it, he was one of the best leaders to work with.

At the World Championships, where you're riding for your country rather than your trade team, he might be racing with guys he'd been on a team with a couple of years before, another who he'd ridden with on the track, some younger guys who he'd never even met, and between the Wednesday when you met and the Friday he'd have the whole team ready to ride and give their all for him. He just had it, and I can't put my finger on what 'it' is. It's partly down to him being a like-able character and a genuine bloke, but he has real charisma too and he was incredible at orchestrating things in those situations, firing everyone up for the job they needed to do.

We had a big fright in the days immediately before the race in Qatar, when we almost lost him as our leader. We'd gone out for a training ride and were lined out with Cav towards the back of the string. All of a sudden he hit something in the road and went down really hard. He was absolutely ripped to bits. We had a bit of an inquest and it turned out that Geraint Thomas had been on the front and hadn't seen this bloody big stone on the road. We all wondered if Cav was going to be OK to race and I remember our coach Rod Ellingworth saying, 'Nothing's broken. It's just skin. He'll be fine to race. I know Cav, he'll be fucking right.'

G got the shit taken out of him all week for that incident. 'What stone?' We still take the piss out of him now for it. Cav still puts on his best Welsh accent: 'What stone you mean?' It's been an ongoing joke that years after you can laugh about. At the time, we were all like, 'For fuck's sake, G!' He made a mistake that day. I'm not one to point fingers because I've made many mistakes in my career, but that one was on G.

We had to get behind Cav a bit after that incident, but as soon as he put that race number on, he was up for it. He's a tough fucker and it was like he hadn't crashed. He put his bandages on and raced like it was nothing. For sure, subconsciously, whenever you crash it does take a few percentage points off, but Cav was so motivated because he knew he could win. He had a team who 100 per cent believed he could win, and the effects of the crash weren't going to deter him.

The race was very difficult, quite complex. We pretty much had 50K in one direction into a block headwind, turned right into a crosswind, then turned right again with a cross/tailwind to go all the way back to the circuit where we had to do seven laps of the marina in Doha. Everyone knew that it initially came down to those two right-hand turns, that it would be full gas with echelons, and the race would be made there because you'd never be able to get a group back from the rear to the front in the cross/tail and tailwind that was blowing all the way back to the circuit. So it was simple, in theory. We had to get good numbers at the front at the right-hand turn. We were coming off a four-lane highway so there was loads of room to move, and pure manpower was going to make the difference into that right-hander.

I was road captain that day and we had a really strong team – Ian Stannard, Swifty, G, Dan McLay, Steve Cummings, Adam Blythe, Scott Thwaites and Cav. Being the World Championships, we didn't have race radios, so that made it more critical for me to make the right calls at the right time, especially going into those key turns.

Steve, Dan and Ian had the job of getting us to the front after 50K and there was a little bit of controversy along the way involving Steve and me. As a rider, he very much did his own thing. He was with some great teams and was an out-and-out winner. He achieved that by racing as a one-man band, looking out for himself, and was extremely successful at it. Every win he had was pretty much off his own bat. Steve would usually be seen at the back of the peloton; if he was at the front it was because he wanted to go in the breakaway. At the same time, though, he contributed very little to anyone else's success. That's not necessarily a negative thing. He was the type of rider who achieved a lot by racing in that manner and was a very valuable asset for his teams.

In Qatar, just like the rest of us, Steve was there purely to support Cav, and he was all up for that job. I was road captain and still quite young to have that role within that squad. I found it quite challenging trying to tell smart guys like Steve what to do. What's more, I don't think he really appreciated the fact that I was making those calls.

When we had to accelerate towards that first right-hand corner, I was perhaps third or fourth in line. I was shouting when to go faster, to go slower, to go left, to go right, and Steve didn't really like that. I thought he was accelerating too soon before the corner and shouted, 'We've got to wait! Stay calm! Stay calm!' We'd said in the meeting before that we had to keep our cool and accelerate late, because on a four-lane highway there's always room to move. If you accelerate too soon, you'll get swamped. So I was, 'Easy, Steve. Easy, Steve. Relax, back off.' But, with still a few kilometres remaining to the corner, he kept on going and going, then swung off the front like he was pissed off.

In the meeting after the race he said to me that he would have got us to that corner, that I just had to let him do it his way. But I wasn't happy with that. I told him, 'If I'm road captain then it's my responsibility and it has to be my way. And if we're fucking up, then that's on me. But I can't have eight

guys doing it eight ways. You have to have eight guys doing it
one way, and you have to do it cohesively.' Rod Ellingworth
and Cav, who was our leader, had wanted me in the road captain's role. I'd been teammates with Cav numerous times and
knew Rod very well both through the GB set-up and from
Sky. They trusted me 100 per cent. Steve possibly didn't feel
the same way, or simply didn't like a younger guy telling him
what to do. After the race we got on well, had a laugh and a
joke, but there was still an underlying tension. After a few
years he joined INEOS as a DS. I was hesitant as to how that
relationship would go, but quickly enough it was as if nothing
had ever happened. We ended up having a good relationship
as DS and rider.

So, after we lost Steve, we used Dan and Ian to get us
into the right turn. Going into it, I was first wheel, Cav was
second. As we started accelerating out of the corner I gave
the twirling finger signal to indicate we should start rotating. We did, and it was perfect, absolutely textbook. We had
myself, Blythe, Cav, G and Swifty in a group of thirty-odd
riders that was chasing behind the early breakaway. We were
really well represented – then disaster struck. Within a kilometre, G, Swifty and me all had mechanical issues. The wind
had blown rocks and sand on to the road and there were a lot
of punctures. In a few moments, we went from having five
riders at the front to just two – Blythe and Cav.

The race had just split and all the cars were behind the final
group, which was where I ended up. Steve was there too, and
Rod came up and told him, 'Steve, I need you to do everything
to try and get Luke back.' He absolutely buried himself on the
front to try to close the gap to the next echelon, and somehow
managed it. It was funny that 10K earlier we'd disagreed, then

a few minutes later he totally emptied his tanks for me. But, as we'd predicted beforehand, once you were behind on that course, there was no coming back. I couldn't get back up to Cav's group and that was the end of my race. When we hit the circuit, we were already that far behind that we abandoned and watched the rest on TV.

It was obvious that Blythe was going to do the lead-out for Cav and he made a really great job of it. But Cav didn't follow him, perhaps because he didn't have full confidence in Adam, who was at the back end of an average year. Cav was so pissed off that he didn't win, because he was the best guy in the race. He could have been a two-time world champion and I think it still pains him now. He doesn't really want to talk about it. But in a race like that where crosswinds are such a significant factor, Adam was still one of the best in the world. You could run that race a hundred times and he would have made that front group a hundred times.

If Cav had followed Blythe's lead-out, I think he'd have won the race. As the road turned to the right, Cav went on the left-hand side because the right-hand side was blocked. Ninety-nine times out of a hundred the door won't open on the right, and that's why Cav went to the left. However, that was the one instance when the door did open. Sagan sprinted through it and won. After the finish, Cav was like, 'Fuck, I could have gone right, but that just doesn't open up. Doesn't happen. It shouldn't have happened, it should have been blocked. I should have gone up the left. I should have won the race.' But someone drifted or peeled off and a gap opened.

We had a meal after and it was a bittersweet occasion, because as a team we'd been good, but we'd had a lot of bad luck in losing guys. I think if myself, G and Swifty had been there, we would have really nailed that lead-out and Cav would have won it easily. But we had some bad luck and things didn't pan out. Being on a team that had won a world title would have been one of the highlights of my career. When you represent Great Britain, it's always a bit different. You're riding with guys you've known for a long time, far longer than you've known teammates in a trade team. It's special.

We said that evening that we'd come back with that group and that it was only a matter of time before we did win, because we were a great team. But we haven't even won a medal since. Ultimately, you've got to make hay while the sun shines, and we didn't quite make hay that day.

As with breakaways, there are two different perspectives on bunch sprints depending on whether your objective is putting a sprinter in the right place to go for victory or your goal is to ensure that your GC leader makes it safely through the chaos. Given the fact that I spent most of my pro career trying to keep the likes of Froomey, G and Egan Bernal out of trouble in critical and often dangerous situations like these, let's start with a look at how we'd go about this on our team.

As the road captain on a team that was focused entirely on the GC, this task would be dictated by the 3K rule, which lays down that all of the riders who are in the lead group 3 kilometres from the line will be given the same finishing time as the stage winner (in some races this is extended to 5K). Introduced in 2005, this rule came in largely because GC guys were realizing that there were splits in the peloton very late on that they could exploit. Consequently, they were staying right in the mix all the way to the finish line and the result was often a horrible scenario where the GC guys would be sprinting

amid the sprinters' teams and lead-out trains because someone might lose the wheel and they'd gain a few seconds as
a result. The 3K rule nullified this eventuality. All that matters now is where you are at that point, bearing in mind that
there's also an additional rule that says that a gap between
riders has got to be more than three seconds in order for it to
count towards the overall classification. Thanks to these regulations, the number of riders who get involved in the action
right at the front of the bunch in the last 3K has been reduced.
It's effectively chilled the GC guys out and I think it was a
great move on the part of the Union Cycliste Internationale
(UCI) to introduce it.

It meant that in Team Sky's glory years the 3K-to-go banner
was our finish line. We'd try to be right in the front until
that point so that our leader would be safe if there were any
crashes. After that, when all the craziness of the bunch sprint
erupts, we'd try to drop back so that if there was a crash we'd
have time to brake, knowing that there's very unlikely to be a
three-second split when you're all racing at 50 or 60kph.

Depending on the terrain, the GC teams – certainly those
I was part of – committed early in going to the front because
they knew they didn't need that final firepower right at the end.
We had a staple tactic of using the big engines – guys like
myself, Ian Stannard, Christian Knees and Vasil Kiryienka
mopping up kilometres, taking wind on the front, with the
focus always on that 3K mark. As soon as we passed that, it
was pressure off and you'd just slip back a little bit. Once we
were dropping back, I'd always tell the GC guys to stay to one
side of the peloton simply because if you're in the middle you
can get hit by crashes from both sides. If you're on the outside
and leave a bike length in front of you, it gives you that little

bit of stopping distance. Most of the time there's a bit of run-off space on the sides.

It didn't take long for the smart sprint teams to realize that they could benefit from our strategy. They'd be thinking, 'If we sit in behind Sky, they're going to take us to 3K to go. Then they're going to drift back and we can get past them. We know that we're safe until 3K to go, and then we'll have three or four lead-out men with our sprinter, which is exactly what we want.'

When Cav was with the Dimension Data team (2016–19), he'd often get his riders to use us. In fact, a few teams would actually jostle and fight for that position right behind us, because they knew exactly what we were going to do. They knew we had the horsepower to avoid getting swamped coming into the finish – that's to say, if it got faster and faster, we could go man and man with any team and hold our position at the front. They also knew that we would always stay on one side of the road, simply because then you only have to defend yourself on one side, whereas if you are in the middle you lay yourself open to rival teams on both sides.

I would try to work out from quite far out which side of the road we ought to be on. Sussing out the influence of the wind is the biggest issue, but you also look at the roundabouts on the run-in. There might be four roundabouts and they're all faster to negotiate on the left side, or three of the four are faster on the left side. So if the wind was cross/tail from the right or cross/head from the right, you'd be looking for the left-hand gutter. But it depended more on the wind direction than roundabouts and other road furniture. If you're on the sheltered side of the road, you're laughing, but that's prime real estate. Most people know that you want to be on the sheltered side, so you've got to get there early. Once you're there, you can stamp your authority and make a bubble. You don't ride single file, but two or three abreast, forming that bubble.

There are pros and cons to being on the protected side. Say that is the left, if you're at the back of a peloton and you want to move up, you always have to move up into the wind, which will be coming from the right-hand side. When you're at the front, the danger stems from the fact that, as the speed increases, everyone's going to push over to the left. So there was always a risk of being swamped. If a swarm did come on the right and you lost pole position, it would mean that you had to drop all the way back and come around on the right. In that situation, you can't batter your way up the left-hand side because very rarely will the door open there. So you have to get there quite early, bubble up, and depend on the person at the back, the gateman or gatekeeper, being able to fend off the swarm.

When we got into the bubble formation, we always said that our leader, Froomey or G usually, could sit wherever they wanted, wherever they felt most comfortable. They didn't even have to ask. They'd just take up the position they pre-ferred, which was normally in the middle of the eight men, in fourth or fifth place in the bubble. As a leader, you don't want to be right at the back because you're further back in the pelo-ton, and if you're second or third wheel you're copping a little bit of wind. So the sweet spot was in fourth or fifth position. However, if you were coming into a real key point, sprinting into a roundabout, a village or on to a climb, they'd probably shuffle up into second or third, so they didn't get caught in the crossfire behind.

The guy at the back, the gatekeeper, would have to stay all the way to the left. So if someone came up on the inside of us, he'd have fucked up. It was his responsibility to keep the gate shut, so he'd be riding all the way into the left-hand gutter so nobody could move up on the inside of us. This wasn't a role that was all that physically demanding, but whoever did it had to be quite switched on. In the later years at Sky/Ineos, Dylan van Baarle did it quite a lot because he was tactically smart. Wout Poels did it a lot before that. You'll get people trying to box up your inside, so you have to be able to shut the door and effectively say, 'Not today, mate.' You've got to stay totally focused if you're the gatekeeper. If you lose concentration, drift right and someone comes up on your inside, it's quite hard to then box them out. If one guy comes in, and then he pushes right, his teammate can come on his inside, which results in you being pushed further to the right as they exploit the chink that's been found in the armour of your bubble.

In these situations, you want to have a good sprinters' team behind you. If we were heading into a sprint finish and, say, Katusha were there with Marcel Kittel, they wouldn't want to come up the inside. I might actually say to them, 'Stay there, boys, you know what we're going to do.' Then, when we did get to that 3K-to-go mark, we might well move a bit to the right so that they could get through on the left. They'd expect that and want it to happen. You also have to be aware that if you don't move and let them through, then the next time they're probably going to box at the inside earlier. There's always a fine balance, complicated by the fact you're often collaborating with different riders and teams every day. But if two teams have the same goal – that's to say, to be in the best position with 3K to go – it suits both to work together to achieve it.

On the flip side, when you're leading out a sprinter, if you're on the front with 50K to go, you can't hope to remain on the front with 500 metres to go, or at least it's very hard to do. Teams used to be able to do this, but the sport's changed. Nowadays, on sprint stages it's like a switch is suddenly pressed and everyone's instantly thinking, 'We're in the final now.' It's a nervous time and everyone's fighting for position. That switch seems to go off earlier and earlier. It used to be the case that you could reach the last 20, 25K before people started jostling for position, now it's 50 to 70K out, and some-times it can be all day long, especially during the opening days of the Tour de France.

For us, as a GC team, the finish was always quite simple, because we didn't need that big explosive kick in the last 3K for a full-on lead-out. We just had to get to 3K to go, which is not an easy task, but it's a lot more straightforward than leading someone out in the final sprint. But when we put our sprinting caps on at races other than the Tour, I would always try and do exactly what other teams were doing and sit second team, saving ourselves as much as possible for the final. GC teams can't gamble in that way. They've got to be at the front, taking the wind. It's hard work, but you do it. Whereas, the sprinters' teams have to gamble a bit to get it right. They can't depend totally on brawn, there has to be some brains.

The tactic doesn't always work out, though. You might sit back, gamble and try and come late, then end up getting blocked and never making it to the front. When that happens, it's very tempting to think, 'Fuck, why didn't we hit the front earlier?' But if you want to deliver a lead-out from 3K out to the finish line, you have to take that risk because the level of sprinting is now so high and the margin between winning and failure is so small that you have to accept the risk of it all going pear-shaped in order to get it spot on.

The days of a nine-man lead-out train dominating, like Fassa Bortolo or HTC once did, have gone. There's just too much strength in depth, too much firepower. You simply can't do it. Even if you're at the front with eight men with 6K to go, you'll still get swamped, because they come from behind with such speed. This happened at the European Championships in 2024 when Italy had a whole squad behind Jonathan Milan, undoubtedly one of the leading sprinters of that season. They had good numbers in the lead group and tried to take it on, but they got swamped and Milan didn't even make the top ten. It just takes one lead-out man with one sprinter to hit you in the last 500 metres, and all your pace-setting comes to nothing.

When you've got a sprinter on your team and you're part of his lead-out train, you have to be prepared to take risks in order to win. You're in that danger zone where there are crashes. Unfortunately, the area in the peloton that's most protected from the wind and the easiest to ride in is also the most dangerous. If you sit in thirtieth, fortieth place in the middle of the peloton – and I've seen the numbers on this because Sky broke them down – that's the best position to be, the sweet spot. But it's also a perilous place to be, partly because everyone wants to be there, but also because if there's a crash, it normally happens relatively far forward in the peloton because that's where there's the most tension. Most crashes take place there or a little bit ahead of that point, and we all know if there's a sudden crash in front of you a body stops quicker than a bike does. When I had the crash that left me with severe concussion and effectively brought my racing career to a premature conclusion at the 2024 E3 Saxo Classic, I was in around thirtieth, fortieth place. A few moves had gone, I was in the middle and was going to follow a rotation back to the front. But I was in that sweet spot – the death zone, as we call it.

If you're bringing a sprinter into a bunch finish, your tactics and thinking are going to be very different from those occasions when you're thinking 'GC'. The critical key to success is simply trust. It's a hard thing to establish, and you have to get a lead-out right a couple of times before your sprinter believes in you. I'd say that with the sprinters we worked with later on, we always lacked the last lead-out man. We had myself, Owain Doull, Swifty, G, Kwiato, Ethan Hayter – these guys were there to help with the lead-out, but none of them was a last lead-out man. We didn't have a top-level guy like Michael Mørkøv, who filled that role for so many leading sprinters, including Cav, Elia Viviani and Sam Bennett. That always made things tricky for us. Unless it was a lower-level race where one of us could act as that last man, it was always a case of looking after the sprinter as well as we could and trying to drop them off on a good wheel inside the last kilometre. So it wasn't a conventional lead-out where the goal is to take the sprinter all the way to the finish line, like Mørkøv or, say, Simone Consonni would, dropping their sprinter off with around 200 metres remaining.

The biggest challenge for a sprint team is developing that sense of trust. When Elia first came to our team in 2015, he was obviously a top-tier sprinter. He arrived from Cannondale, where he'd worked in tandem with guys like Jacopo

Guarnieri and Daniel Oss, and they'd done a great job for him. Then we had to gain his trust. You know when you've managed to do that when your sprinter doesn't talk that much. They're happy to follow. They'll be thinking, 'I'll just stay here and they'll put me in the right position.' Quite early on, we as a team gained Elia's trust.

I'd say he was one of the smartest sprinters I've ever worked with. Most sprinters have got some kind of track palmarès and he'd obviously done that at the very highest level, and became an Olympic gold medallist during his first three-year stint with Sky. He was the type of sprinter who was super fast, but not particularly torquey, like Marcel Kittel and André Greipel. High-torque sprinters can really get on top of a big gear and pound it out. Jonathan Milan is high-torque. Whereas Sam Bennett, Caleb Ewan to a degree and Elia are simply fast, more like pure sprinters. Cav was the full package, because he had the pure speed but you'd also see him win some sprints in a bigger gear, over-geared, slightly uphill. He just had it everywhere that he needed it.

Elia didn't climb particularly well, like a lot of sprinters. His threshold power wasn't that high. He was like a pure-bred sprinter. He could do one thing and do it very well. So he had to duck and dive his way through. To a degree, he was quite similar to me in the way I got the most out of myself during my career, by being in the right place at the right time, by being smart. Elia was very much the same as a sprinter. He had to move around the peloton towards the finish, like Cav did on his last Tour stage win in 2024, riding that last kilometre perfectly. Elia often sprinted in that same way when he was at his peak, switching from one lead-out train to another, using his own guy sometimes, going up the inside when normally he should have gone on the outside. He was very astute tactically and was very easy to work with because he could tell you exactly what he wanted before the stage and you'd just try and replicate his request in the best way that you could.

There was a big difference between him and the younger sprinters we had on the team, guys like Kristoffer Halvorsen and Chris Lawless. They joined us as first-year pros and, on paper, they were both sprinters. But with those guys, you'd just say, 'Stay with us. We'll do the best job we can.' That was because they didn't know what they wanted. They didn't know how to sprint at that level. They'd just been racing in the under-23 ranks, which is a jungle, and they would back you 100 per cent because they knew nothing else. They were buzzing to be there and to have some big names in the lead-out. They just bought in and followed the wheel they were told to. But it wasn't always that easy for sprinters on our team because we were always looking to drop them on to a lead-out man from another team within the final few hundred metres and let them take it from there. Unlike our GC guys, who got backing whenever they needed it, our sprinters usually had to sink or swim.

7

Descents

There's one thing that I must stress about descents and tactics. Our team would never advise one of its riders to attack on a downhill. I don't think the team management, the DSs or me as the road captain would have felt comfortable telling someone to attempt this type of attack. Rider safety overrides every other consideration when it comes to descents, and I don't remember a single occasion when the team suggested that we put security concerns aside and go eyeballs out down a mountain. Whenever a rider did attack in this fashion, it was a spur-of-the-moment decision, like Froomey's raid down the Peyresourde into Luchon in the 2016 Tour de France, or Tom Pidcock's jaw-dropping acrobatics going down the Galibier in the 2022 edition. Both of those were instinctive attacks, and this is almost always the case. It would be very difficult to plan this kind of attack because there are so many variables on the climb to any summit. By their very nature, these offensives have to be opportunistic.

Tom's daredevil drop down the Galibier underlines this. I remember the stage well. The day before, Jumbo-Visma leader Jonas Vingegaard had demolished his rivals at the

finish on the Col du Granon. Tom, who'd been right up in
the GC battle going into that previous stage, had lost a stack
of time and fallen out of the top ten. Given that he was ten
minutes back on yellow jersey Vingegaard, we agreed in the
team meeting prior to the Alpe d'Huez stage that it would be
a good day for Tom to try to get in the break and go for the
win, and that was our plan when we set out from the start at
Briançon.

The road ran north from there in a dead straight line
towards the Lauteret pass. It's really exposed up there and, as
is often the case on that climb, it was a block headwind all the
way up, which I was very happy with because it slowed the
pace down a lot. It's not very often you go up the Galibier and
think it's easy, but that day it was because the wind was that
strong. Nobody could manage to get clear of the bunch.

Towards the top of the Lauteret, when the route turned
right towards the Galibier and began to climb more steeply,
groups started to go away, none of them featuring riders of
any significance to the GC. Tom kept jumping, and Jumbo
would just close him down easily because in a headwind it's
very hard to go clear on your own. It got to the point when
I actually made the call. I told him, 'Tom, you've got to stop,
mate, you're just pissing in the wind here.' He obviously
wanted to be in the break and, even though he was quite far
back on GC, Jumbo knew that they would be able to ride at a
steadier pace if he wasn't off the front.

I told Tom to see what happened later on the stage, that
there might be an opportunity for him to attack on the next
climb, the Col de la Croix de Fer. We didn't talk about the
descent off the Galibier at that point. It was only when we
got about 2K from the top of the pass that Tom asked me,

'What's the descent like?' I know it pretty well and explained that it's quite twisty, that it's a downhill where you could make a difference. Although we didn't talk about him attacking, I knew what was going through his head. But, as I emphasized before, I've never encouraged a rider to attack on a descent because if they crash and get injured then that's on me. In my head, though, I was thinking, 'The perfect thing to do here is for you to go on the descent.' And, actually, when he asked what the descent was like, I think he was kind of sussing out what I thought as well. But, as I said, I would never say to any rider, 'Yeah, go on the descent.'

Even though it hadn't been discussed, it hadn't been mentioned on the radio and we hadn't said anything to any of our teammates, we both knew exactly what was going to happen. I was about tenth wheel going over the top and Tom was just in front of me. And when he started to move right, I was thinking, 'OK, here we go!'

As the yellow jersey group led by Jumbo approached the top of the Galibier, the break was about a minute and a half ahead. Froomey was chasing behind it on his own in no-man's land. As we reached the top and Tom accelerated, Jumbo tried to follow him for a little bit, but that created a few gaps within the team, and they called it really early. Someone clearly sent a message to the effect of 'Leave him – forget about it'. In that situation, Vingegaard and his team did the right thing. It wasn't worth them chasing Tom headlong down a fast and technical descent and risking someone crashing, perhaps Vingegaard himself. He'd already lost time in the mountains and he was only going to lose more time, so they let him go.

The rest is history. Tom did a fantastic descent, captured so thrillingly by the TV helicopters and motorbikes. He got across to Froomey, flew past him and sped on towards the break, which he quickly caught as well. He then went on to win the stage, with Louis Meintjes second and Froomey third. That was only his second victory on the road and a break-through win for him really. He'd performed well in one-day races beforehand, but to do that, especially halfway through a Grand Tour when you're dealing with a lot of fatigue, was a major statement. Of course, there was also all of the coverage about his descent of the Galibier, which made him a sensation on social media and established him as one of the best descenders around.

When we were defending the jersey or targeting victory in a big stage race, the focus on descents would always be to get from top to bottom safely. That was the number one priority. Of course, there were times when you'd be chasing the breakaway, perhaps because there was a dangerous guy in there, and you'd have to pull hard no matter whether you were going up or down. In those situations, I'd regard descents as an opportunity to take back time because I'd be confident that I could go downhill faster than the breakaway. So, at times I'd be going full gas on the front of the peloton, or almost full gas because you've got to think about your team-mates behind you as you don't want to put them on the limit.

The team leader would always pick where they wanted to be in the line. The one certainty, though, was that they'd never be last man because if something happened to them they'd have no teammate behind them to see it. So if there were eight of you, they would be in seventh place at least. It was up to them to sit on whichever wheel they were comfortable. If Stannard and me were leading the way down, they might put themselves on Kwiato's wheel just behind us two because he's a confident descender, or they might want to follow a rider with a bigger build to get a bit more shelter. The only rule was for them never to be last in the line. If they had a puncture or lost control of their bike, crashed and couldn't speak on the radio, you might not hear them. So there was always someone behind them, which was the case right across the board.

We did have one little trick on descents, which was a bit naughty, but still a legitimate tactic. If you're on a descent that's, say, 10K long, you can really stretch the peloton out and there'll maybe be a split or two. But you can do as much or even more damage by taking the descent at a steady speed and then, when you get to the bottom corner, kicking out of it full gas. The guys further back in the peloton won't know what you've done until they reach the foot of the descent, and then they'll have to make a big effort to close the gaps that have opened.

This wasn't something we'd do very often, because you don't want to make the peloton nervous for no reason. If you do that then you're going to end up with a lot of stress and panic at the top of every climb. You'll end up pulling for the whole climb and then having to fight for position at the top so that you can take the descent in the front. But, when we did want to put the pressure on, we would take the descent quite fast, but in control, then kick out of the bottom corner, which would split the peloton into groups. It's a bit of a bugger's trick, and you don't make many friends from doing it, but we were in the business of winning bike races and not making friends.

Just as I would on the flat, I'd always be looking to see who was around me on a descent, primarily with safety in mind. I'd always be thinking, 'Who am I behind? Do I have confidence in him? Should I let a bit of a gap go? Should I let a few guys get in front of me? Or should I get in front of him?' Not everyone is a great descender. Like every other aspect of the sport, the skill is largely innate, and you quickly learn which guys you want to avoid, the ones who don't seem confident, who don't read the road and conditions well, who come into the corners too fast or too slow. There are people in other teams who are like this and there's always some in your own team. It's inevitable.

As with every other part of the all-round skillset each rider has and needs, descending can be worked on and improved. Recent developments in tactics, coaching and marginal gains have led to some riders working with specialist downhill coaches, often guys who've come from downhill mountain biking. I think Froomey, Pavel Sivakov, Magnus Sheffield and Thymen Arensman are among those who worked with a downhill coach on our team. Given the fine margins that races are often decided by, riders do look for any slight weakness in a rival and teams attempt to iron these out, whether it's in time trialling, riding in the bunch, climbing or descending.

I was always pretty confident that, whenever I was leading the peloton down a descent, I could use the motorbikes and the data from the GPX file, assess the roads and the trees, and set a fast pace that ensured that everyone got down safely. At the same time, if I was on someone's wheel, I rarely lost contact on a descent. I always trusted myself to be able to follow anybody, although there were the odd few exceptions.

I remember being in a break in the GP Québec with just Julian Alaphilippe for company. It was late on in the race, with around a couple of laps to go. At that time he wasn't a superstar, although he was clearly very good. I didn't know then, though, quite how talented he was. I remember him distancing me and thinking, 'This guy is killing me because he's physically better than me.' I soon worked that out! He was also gapping me on every corner. I thought, 'He's gonna go sideways sooner or later,' but he was brilliant. He was pushing the limits but always in control of his bike.

Sam Bennett told me a story about the Frenchman that illustrates how good the very best are. At QuickStep, they had a choice between wet and dry tyres. The dry tyres rolled better, but the wets were obviously more grippy in the rain. It was a rainy stage and everyone was on wet tyres, but Alaphilippe said he wanted the dry ones. They pointed out that the conditions weren't great. 'That's not a problem,' he said. When they got going, they were heading down a hill in the rain and Alaphilippe was going around the outside of them on bends, going faster than they were. Now Sam is a brilliant bike handler, and that underlines just how great the very best in the world are. Often, they seem incredible even to their peers.

When there's talk about who are the best descenders, most fans would probably say, 'Oh, it's Vincenzo Nibali or Tadej Pogačar,' or perhaps one of the other GC leaders because there's so much focus on the guys at the front of the bike race. They're the ones on TV. But I can tell you – and this has always been the case in bike racing – some of the guys riding in the gruppetto at the rear of the race would leave them for dead on a mountain descent.

The guys at the back are always going to lose time on the climbs, where they're not as strong, but they compensate for that on the descents and in the valleys. When you're in the gruppetto, there are guys who absolutely hammer down the descents. Not only do they tend to be a lot heavier than the GC leaders battling for honours at the front, they're completely determined to regain time they've dropped on the climbs so that they're not in danger of missing the time limit.

This isn't to suggest, though, that the GC specialists don't look for opportunities to exploit their rivals' weakness or inattentiveness on a descent if they sense there's a chance to gain some time. Froomey's Peyresourde attack in 2016 was a spectacular example of this. When he got a small gap over the top of that pass that dropped down into the stage finish at Luchon, he had Alejandro Valverde and Nairo Quintana behind him, the dual leaders of the Movistar team. If you have one leader in that situation, the other rider knows it's their job to close that gap straight away. But having dual leaders can create some real dilemmas – who does the work in chasing behind and who follows?

Obviously, the big talking point that day was how Froomey sat on his top tube as he dropped down towards Luchon and somehow managed to keep pedalling when he was in that position, which became known as the 'super tuck'. I was riding alongside our DS Servais Knaven, who was driving the second team car, and he was laughing at what was going on. 'Froomey just did some crazy thing on the descent, sitting on his top tube,' he shouted across to me. Everyone was astounded because that tactic was almost completely new. Matej Mohorič had done it when he'd won the under-23 Worlds in 2013, and a few other riders had tried it. But nobody had really done it to any effect at WorldTour level as far as I can remember.

When we got to the finish line and saw Froomey again, we were all asking him, 'Fuck, where did that come from?' Unknown even to us, he'd been practising the technique out on the road on his own for months. He'd been thinking, 'This is going to be my secret little weapon, and at some point when I need to do it, I'll do it.' You did need to do quite a bit of practice, I'll swear to that. I've tried it and if you're not careful your knees hit your bars and push you off. It's one thing being in the tuck on the top tube, but then pedalling is quite an absurd thing to do, especially for him with his osymetric chainrings, but he'd spent time getting used to that. There was a lot of debate about how safe the super tuck was and it was perhaps no surprise that the UCI eventually banned it during the 2021 season.

One other thing stands out from that day. That same evening, when the mechanics were cleaning his bike, they noticed that his top tube was broken. There was a small crack in it. They said to Froomey, 'Please, do *not* do that again.' It was a super light frame, not built to be sat on and certainly not to be used as a cushioning point when you were pedalling at the same time. It doesn't bear thinking about what could have happened given the speed he was going, the vibrations that would have reverberating through the bike, because he was absolutely hoofing down the Peyresourde.

He's probably not given the credit he deserves for this, but Froomey was quite a thinker. In general, he didn't have to think that much, because Sky's strategy was simply to make the pace as hard as we could, then, when the GC contenders reached the steepest point on the final climb, he'd attack, and most of the time no one would be able to follow him. If they did, then he'd go again and finish them off. So, more often than not, racing at the Grand Tours was quite simple for him. From a tactical point of view, he didn't have to be that switched on because he was the best.

Tadej Pogačar's a bit like that today. While Pogi is tactically very good, he actually doesn't have to be. He just picks the hardest point and goes. It doesn't matter whether there's 100K or 20K left, when he goes nobody can live with him and nobody can bring him back. Like Pogi, though, Froomey did show he was the fastest thinker at times and he did produce moments of tactical brilliance. That descent into Luchon was one of them.

8

Tour preparations

GC riders are a special breed. Talk about don't judge a book by its cover. Some of them are high-50s, maybe 60 kilos and look like schoolboys. But they're so hard. People think the Classics specialists are the big tough guys, but they're not. It's the GC guys. At the Classics, you turn up one day, lay it on the line, win or lose, pack your bags and go home, then come back a week later and do it again. But the GC guys are wired differently; they have to be able to mentally hurt themselves that much for twenty-one days. They can never have a day off, and all the pressure's on them, perhaps even the future of the team or the commitment of sponsors. OK, they're also paid the most, but with the big salary comes responsibility. Their mindset is one of 'I have to deliver for this team'. I think that's even more the case now as a result of the focus on the UCI points system. It's all on those guys. They're the warriors.

I could relate any number of anecdotes to back this up. This one involves Sergio Henao, who epitomized the grittiness and toughness that are fundamental to GC success. We were at the Tour of Switzerland in 2014, doing the recon for the time trial. They told us, 'Just be aware that the roads have only just closed, but how well closed they'll be, we don't really know.' Anyway, we were riding the course and he went through a crossroads and got T-boned by a car. He was obviously pretty badly injured, but he stood up and was stumbling around. We were asking him, 'What are you doing? Sit down, chill out.' And he was like, 'I've lost my phone. It fell out of my pocket.' It turned out that his patella had been smashed into forty pieces, and he just stood up and looked for his phone. Grit takes you a long, long way in this sport. Sergio had it in bucket loads, as did every other GC rider I rode for.

While fundamental to success in any three-week Grand Tour or week-long WorldTour stage race, this tenacity and singlemindedness can only take you so far. There are endless things that you need to get right and countless things that can go wrong. For a decade, Sky and Ineos were the masters of this process. I want to offer a road captain's perspective on those years, explaining the details that enabled our team to win eleven Grand Tour titles with five different riders and examining why we've been knocked off our pedestal in recent years.

Let's start by rolling back to my Grand Tour debut at the 2013 Vuelta a España. Everything had gone so well in my career until that race. Over a season and a half as a professional, I'd taken a step upwards at every race I was put into. I was coping and confident. Then came my first three-week test, which ultimately only lasted two. I didn't really know what to expect, but I just wasn't at the required level, it's as simple as that. There's always talk about riders turning pro too early, riders doing big races too early, and, for me, that was a Grand Tour too early. From the get go I wasn't comfortable racing at that level.

Like any young pro, I was excited to be riding my first

Grand Tour. Sky went in with two leaders, Rigoberto Urán and Sergio Henao. My role was to do what I could for them and to gain experience. You've got to make mistakes to learn, and I ended up with two weeks' worth. My biggest error was not listening to the advice of my DSs, specifically before the stage to Valdepeñas de Jaén at the start of the second week. In the meeting before the stage, they told us that Katusha were going to ride hard as the finish was perfect for Joaquim Rodríguez and Dani Moreno. It was pretty much flat all day with a vicious final climb, super steep up the town's main street. They told me to try to use the day to recover a bit. However, when four guys jumped at the start, I just couldn't help myself and joined them. It was an amazing experience to be in a breakaway at a Grand Tour, but it was stupid. I never recovered and soon paid the ultimate price.

The end came after a really tough day in the rain in Andorra. The next day, another wet one, we went straight up the Port del Cantó from the start and I was dropped at kilometre zero with two other blokes. A team car came back and one of them latched on to it and disappeared into the distance. Then another car came back and the other guy went off too. Nico Portal was our second DS at the race and he came up to me. He wouldn't have let me hang on, but I said, 'I either go out of the race or try to finish.' We got to the top of the climb and I was minutes behind. That was the end of my race. I sat in the back of Nico's car crying. My career had gone so well and it was the first major setback I'd had. I was ashamed, so much so that when we drove past my wife, her sister and their dad, who were standing at the roadside like three drowned rats waving a Welsh flag, I didn't acknowledge them. I felt like I'd let them, the team and myself down.

What came next was extraordinary. As I sat there in the pits of despair, Nico said to me, 'Luke, the Vuelta isn't the race for you. The Tour de France is the race for you.' I couldn't grasp what he was saying. I didn't know if he was trying to be nice. All I could think was, 'The Tour de France is another level again. I haven't finished the Vuelta, and you're saying that the race for me is a level above the one I haven't finished?' He went on to explain that the climbs at the Tour would suit me a lot better because the gradients are a lot more consistent, very different from the crazy steep ascents you often encounter at the Vuelta. Nevertheless, I was still thinking, 'This guy's nuts.' The Tour de France seemed like a million miles away, especially after jumping in the team car 25K into a stage. But, as was usually the case with Nico, he was absolutely right. He could see when I was still twenty-three that the Vuelta wasn't for me. I rode it the following year, completing it on that occasion as Froomey finished second to Alberto Contador. Yet, from 2015 the Tour became the principal goal of my season.

Going into that 2015 season, I was told that I was on the long list for the Tour, but it still felt quite distant. The Tour de France was still this giant beast of a thing that I'd never had anything to do with. What's more, when I looked through the roster of riders at Team Sky in 2015 it was so stacked that part of me was wondering why they would take me over some of those other guys. My doubts were heightened when I raced the Critérium du Dauphiné in early June and got very ill, so bad that I didn't fly home on the day I pulled out of the race because I couldn't get out of bed. I remember thinking 'Have I just fucked this?' because there was such strength in depth within our squad.

Once again, it was Nico who buoyed me up. He came to see me in my room while I was laid up and told me not to stress, that I'd be going to the Tour as long as the illness was just a two-day thing. Even though it was a short illness, I still wasn't sure I'd be starting until Nico called me a few days later and said, 'Congratulations, Luke, you're going to the Tour de France.' When the call ended, my wife Cath and I started jumping around our apartment because it was such a mammoth thing to be doing, especially as I'd be racing as road captain in a team that had the favourite for the yellow jersey in Froomey.

In the end, I knew I'd deserved my place. I'd been good through the first part of the season and also at the Dauphiné until I fell ill. I'd also had a really good altitude camp in Tenerife with the other guys on the long list for the Tour. Nowadays, almost every team does this kind of training. However, when Team Sky first took to the road in 2010 only a handful of riders did it. It's impossible to overstate the role that Tim Kerrison, our head of performance, played in changing this and many more things relating to preparation for the season's biggest races, above all the Tour.

A bit of an unsung hero in the team, Tim was our conductor. He was waving the baton and we were all out there playing his music. When he first joined the team in 2010, he didn't do a lot for the first six months. He essentially watched and learned, about the individuals, the team, the sport, the training. Once he'd taken that time to figure it all out, he knew where the weaknesses were, what the strengths were, what needed to be done to raise the team's performance to a higher level, and then went about implementing his initiatives and innovations.

Above: A family sport. With my brother, Matt, as juniors (left), and together with our parents (right).

Above: Besting Geraint Thomas and Rhys Slack at the Penarth Criterium. I still had some growing to do (left). As a young lad at the Tour de France. My first taste of that magical race (right).

Above: As a new pro (*right*) posing alongside world champion Mark Cavendish and British champion Bradley Wiggins at Team Sky's 2012 season launch in west London.

Above: Celebrating my debut victory as a pro after outsprinting Boy van Poppel to win the opening stage of the 2012 Tour of Britain in Norwich.

Left: Topping the Paterberg ahead of teammate Salvatore Puccio during the 2013 Tour of Flanders. Having established myself as a dependable team rider I quickly became a member of Sky's Classics squad.

ight: Chatting with Bradley Wiggins in the aftermath of the 2015 Paris–Roubaix, where I finished in what would be a career-best eighth place.

Below: Checked over by ky DS Brett Lancaster and ace doctors after crashing at Paris–Roubaix in 2018, after returning from my 017 leg break. The Classics are always punishing.

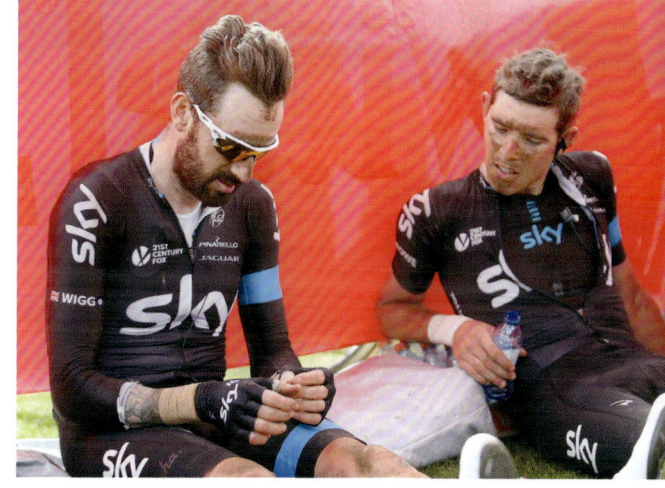

Above: In team time trial mode. Setting the pace on the front of the Team Sky line at the 2013 Tour of Qatar.

Left: With Great Britain teammates Geraint Thomas (*left*) and David Millar (*centre*) on the presentation podium before the 2014 Road Championships in Ponferrada, Spain.

Below: Taking the wind for Sky teammates Gerain Thomas and Ben Swift during the 2015 edition of Milan–San Remo.

Right: A proud moment after retaining the white jersey for best young rider at the 2015 Tour of Qatar.

Left: Congratulating Chris Froome as he secures his 2015 Tour de France victory in Paris.

Below: Time for a beer. With Ian Stannard and yellow jersey Chris Froome, toasting back-to-back victories on the final stage of the 2016 Tour de France.

Left: A few months earlier, with Niki Terpstra waving at photographers during the snow-hit Paris–Nice of 2016.

Above: Riding with one of my best mates has always been a pleasure. With Geraint Thomas at the 2016 Tour of Flanders, where I finished a career-best fifth.

Left: It doesn't get any better. With G waving a Welsh flag on the road into Paris as he claims his 2018 Tour de France victory.

Above: A road captain's duty. Keeping G, our Ineos Grenadiers team leader, well fed during the 2022 Tour de France.

Above: Conferring with the race commissaires during the 2022 E3 Saxo Classic.

Above: Dylan van Baarle, Wout Poels and I lead the peloton into the stage 12 finish at the 2019 Tour de France that would be won by teammate Egan Bernal. Our fifth consecutive Tour victory and the end of the Sky/Ineos era of dominance.

Above: On the tarmac after crashing at the 2024 E3 Saxo Classic, which would prove to be the last race of my pro career.

Right: Family time. With my sons Alfie (*left*) and Ollie after the finish of Milan–San Remo in 2023.

His coaching was revolutionary. As part of this, he introduced a whole load of 'efforts' – gruelling training sessions. It makes for pretty dull reading to go into exactly what they were, but their names are permanently etched into my brain, primarily because of the pain I still associate with them. There were EPDs, noodles, torque sandwiches, SAPs, SLITs, weird and wacky names that now every pro cyclist is familiar with. They still use them across every team, although they've evolved over the decade or more since Tim came up with them.

Thinking back to that period, I am sure we trained harder in 2015/16 as a team than we did in my final years at Ineos, and I think that was part of the reason for our decline. We simply weren't training hard enough. When we were in Tenerife with Kerro, the guys would be close to breaking point. We were given efforts that we just couldn't finish. Tim's philosophy was 'more is better'. So if you did five hours and you could physically do six, then do six. If you could do seven, do seven. If you had an effort at maybe 300 watts or 400 watts and you could manage it at 310 or 410, do it. It was more, more, more.

When you're the best, like we were then and UAE and Visma are now, your rivals wonder what you are doing in terms of training, camps, ketones for performance and recovery, tyre pressures and so on. Other pros would always be asking 'What efforts have you got today?' or 'What camps are you going on?' and we'd just play it down. We didn't want to give anything away. In fact, we used to mess with them a bit. Once, Cath did an online order in France where she tried to buy two red onions, but instead received two boxes of them. So we had probably a hundred red onions. I thought, 'Right, we'll get some of these boys going now.' We met for a group ride, eight or ten of us – me, G and Froomey from the team and seven other pros – and I filled my pockets with onions, six or eight of them. I texted G and Froomey and said, 'Whatever happens with the red onions today, just go with it.'

G and Froomey were on the front of the group and I was at the back with all these other pros in the middle. I rode up next to them at the front, pulled an onion out of my pocket, gave it to Froomey, pulled another onion out and gave it to G, then went to the back of the group again. All these guys were like, 'What the fuck's that?' We could see them talking between themselves. When we got to the café, halfway through the ride, someone asked, 'What's with the red onions?' I told him, 'Ah, I can't really say.' Froomey and G were right on my wavelength and one of them said, 'It's the onion diet.' They were like, 'What's the onion diet?' We told them we couldn't really say too much, that we were eating a lot of onions, that they were good for this, good for that. 'Once a week, we try to have an onion day. We eat onions all day. I had a few spare and I know G and Froomey haven't got so many, so they'll have that onion when they get back home.' We were, of course, talking absolute bollocks.

Months later, guys who weren't even on that ride were asking me about the onion diet. We still laugh about it now. Because it didn't stop there. A couple of weeks later I went on another ride and took more onions. We kept this going through a whole winter. The local Americans would be like, 'Oh my God, man, you just eat onions for a day?' We'd just shrug and say, 'That's what you've got to do, mate.'

They all knew, though, that Sky were ahead of the curve. Kerro's main focus every year was the Tour de France, his baby. He'd prepare the guys and he had the budget to get us anything we needed. Prior to us, pre-Tour de France camps would be, say, Alberto Contador going away with his wingmen, Dani Navarro and Jesús Hernández. We might see Vincenzo Nibali in Tenerife with maybe one of his teammates, or Dani Moreno on his own. All of the superstars went on camps, but nobody went as a team. Sending a big guy who would be working on the flat was not a thing. It was Tim who decided that if it was beneficial for a GC leader, it was equally so for the whole squad. He made those camps work for everyone. When we got there, the first thing he'd do when we started climbing would be to strap one of those wrist or ankle weights to the back of Froomey's bike. He'd get to the bottom of a two- or maybe two-and-a-half-hour climb and Tim would attach the weights to his bike. 'Right, that levels the playing field doesn't it,' he'd say.

I remember him telling me and Stannard that the most important part of winning the Tour de France was Froome being the very best version of himself that he could be. 'The support you guys provide is massive, but unless you've got that one guy who can win, we're fucked.' He then went on to say that neither of us could ever slow the group down. So on the effort days, we'd do our efforts, but on the general days when we did no efforts, we'd still effectively be doing them because we'd always be riding a zone above Froomey and the other GC guys simply because they were stronger than us. It was just a case of suck it up and say nothing, and never hamper Froomey, G and Richie's training.

Tenerife was a horrible place for training camps when we first went there, although it's changed now. There was no phone signal back then, no frills or home comforts, nothing to do but ride your bike. As brutal as it was, you just had to go with the right mentality. I'd always take a poker set, and we found other distractions too. One year, we couldn't stay in the main hotel on the Teide volcano because it was full. We were lodging at two houses in the middle of nowhere instead. There were geckos everywhere. Being African, Froomey would capture these small lizards and hide them to freak us out. It was horrible.

One evening, we had a massive food fight. Me and Stannard were in a little house on our own down at one end of the road and all the other lads were in the other one further up. The generators for all of the buildings went off at ten o'clock, so there was no light, no internet, nothing. It was a proper back-to-basics camp, and brilliant because of that. Anyway, one night at about eleven or twelve o'clock, the other guys were obviously bored and came down to where we were. One of them climbed on our roof, then someone else knocked on our door. When we opened it, they poured flour, eggs and yoghurts on us. Kwiato was at the back with a drone, filming the whole thing from the sky. Me and Yogi went to our fridge and started pelting stuff back. It was absolute carnage. But it was just an example of how to make it fun.

We also had this crazy hot chilli sauce that was like rocket fuel. I think Froomey had brought it from Kenya, and it became a thing trying to trick each other by getting it in someone else's food or drink. At one point I ate this dried apricot that, unbeknown to me, they'd cut open and put this sauce inside. They'd stitched the thing back together, and when I bit into it my head just about blew off. Silly things like that kept us busy, and helped us come together as a team. These camps were brutal physically and if you didn't do stuff like that they could be really hard mentally as well.

Kerro would always find ways to spice up the riding too. He used to love his shortcuts, but they were always steep. He'd always say, 'That's the normal way, that's the shortcut, you choose which one you want.' Tenerife has got some of the steepest roads in the world, 30 per cent a lot of them. When we were staying in those houses, the staff hotel was on one of his shortcuts and it was ridiculously steep, like a wall. Our South African mechanic Gary Blem, renowned for his long, scruffy hair, reckoned that it was so steep that nobody could ride up it.

'I could get up it in the big ring, Gary,' I told him.

'No, honestly, it's impossible for anyone to ride up that hill in the big ring.'

'What if I ride up it in the big ring? Can I cut your hair?' He'd had his hair really long for years.

'Yeah, if you can ride up it in the big ring, you can cut my hair. But it's impossible.'

The next day I told Kerro to plan the route so we went up that hill. He loved the challenge of doing that. It was harmless fun and wasn't hampering training – it was maybe even enhancing it, for me at least. Anyway, long story short, I got up there in the big ring and was let loose on Blemski's hair. When the other guys came back in, I was there cutting and blow-drying it. His missus sent me a message later saying, 'Thank you so much. I've been wanting to do that for ten years.'

Those camps fitted the old cliché of train hard enough and racing becomes easy. To be honest, it didn't, but it almost did. I used to dread those Tenerife camps, fucking dread them.

I never let on that I did, because if you get in a grump, it's like an illness that spreads through the team. Everyone gets a bit grumpy. It only takes one person. We all knew how hard it was, but nobody whinged. Kerro wouldn't allow it. It was a no-whinge culture, one where we had to stay positive and keep focused, because success at the Tour depended on it.

9

The Tour

In the 2010s the Tour was the only race that mattered to the team, and they did everything they could to ensure the riders were as well prepared for it as they could be. This also included taking one race off our programme because of what happened there the weekend before I made my Tour debut in 2015.

That season the British national championships were held in Lincoln and just three other Sky riders lined up with me – Ian Stannard and Pete Kennaugh, who were also heading to France, and Andy Fenn. The course comprised a few big circuits in the countryside and then smaller laps based on the steep cobbled climb of Michaelgate in the city centre. On a training ride the day before the race, I noticed that after 3K or so the route turned left into terrain that was very exposed to the wind. I told the other three that we should sling it in the gutter at that point and we'd probably all end up in the front group and might catch some of the other pros out. It sounded a bit mad to attack so early, but if the tactic paid off it would simplify the race for us.

The next day, we reached that point, put the plan into

action and the race split to bits, with maybe twenty to thirty guys in the front echelon. The likely candidates such as Adam Blythe and Cav made it, but we caught out the Yateses (Simon and Adam) and a few others. It triggered an absolute war of a race. In the end, Cav, Pete, Ian and me were left at the front, then Pete and Cav got away, with Pete going on to take the title. That left me and Yogi racing each other for bronze. Going into the final right turn with just a few metres to go, we were literally shoulder to shoulder, like he was trying to ride me into the barriers and I was getting stuck into him. He edged it.

Although Rod Ellingworth wasn't at the nationals, I knew he would be pissed off with the way we'd been having a go at each other. Perhaps Rod thought there was an issue between Yogi and me, but we were just giving our all. We paid for that, though. When we got to Utrecht a few days before the Tour got going, we were still battered because the Nationals had taken so much out of us. The team was royally pissed off and promptly introduced a new rule. From 2016 onwards, no Sky or Ineos rider has ever ridden the British national champs and the Tour in the same season, simply because the Nationals is always a smash fest. Nothing could be allowed to distract from the Tour.

That 2015 race started in the Netherlands with a shortish time trial in Utrecht. I cruised around, saving everything I could for stage 2, which went out on the dykes right on the edge of the North Sea. The organizers were obviously hoping for the weather to have an impact, and they got exactly what they wished for. A huge storm blew in off the sea. We were racing through the outskirts of Rotterdam when it hit.

We'd been well primed by Nico Portal before the stage. There was a succession of roundabouts, and QuickStep, as we expected, hit the front going into them. They were on the right-hand side going through them and one of my jobs that day was to ensure that we were tucked in behind them. We managed to get into the position we wanted, then it began to rain torrentially and things became chaotic. We got a bit split up in the mayhem and I ended up on the left-hand side, where there was a big crash that delayed most of the peloton. While that meant I didn't feature in the final, Froomey, G and Yogi made the front group that gained almost ninety seconds on most of our GC rivals, notably Nairo Quintana.

While there's an element of luck in situations like this when shit happens on one side of the peloton and you avoid it, pre-stage preparation and communication play a much more significant role. The DS is the boss and they're responsible for putting together the tactical plan for each day of racing. This work begins almost as soon as the Tour route is announced in Paris in late October. By the time they go round the rooms the night before a stage, they'll know the next day's route inside out. They would usually see each of the riders when they were on the massage table. For most of them the conversation probably wouldn't go too far beyond two basic questions: 'How was the day? Good for tomorrow?' With me, though, they'd always go through what lay ahead in quite a bit more detail.

We'd run through any small issues together, assessing the team as a whole and the riders individually, giving a bit of feedback, not all of it positive – 'So-and-so was good but he fucked up at one point and got us in the wrong position.' We might talk about the opposition, the fact that one of our rivals looked a bit weak. Once we'd gone through these details, the DS – and it was always Nico at the Tour until 2019 – would say, 'Right, this is what I'm thinking for tomorrow.' I would already have looked at the following stage and would have my own ideas. The DS would say something along the lines of 'This is how we're going to use the guys, him there, him there, and him there. We want to go in the break / stop the break / open the race here [whatever was the case] . . . what do you think?' Then I'd give my input. As road captain, you can suggest tweaks to the plan – 'Actually, I think it should be done this way' – but the DS always makes the final call. Nevertheless, your input is valued and considered because you see and hear everything first-hand, while they're picking everything up second-hand.

They don't see the intricate details of how the peloton moves, evolves, the little things that riders do wrong or right, their strengths and weaknesses. But, as the captain in the middle of your team, you see everything and know everything. In feeding information back, you're not bad-mouthing anyone, you're just trying to get the most out of your resources. You've got to be honest, even about yourself. I might well have said, 'Nico, I've had three hard days here. I'm pretty fucked, mate. If we can use so-and-so a bit more tomorrow and save me a little bit . . .' Or tell him, 'Stannard did most of the work today. He got quite exposed early on and had to do most of it. I think I should try and do a bit more tomorrow.' You're trying to stop anyone on your team from digging themselves into an early grave.

After the road captain and the DS have conferred, the rest of the team will probably find out more in the meeting on the team bus the next day. Nothing's kept secret – if you're talking, you're talking – but the actual battle plan isn't presented to the whole team until you're all on the bus the next morning. One key reason for this is that you don't want your riders to have anything too heavy to focus on each evening. You want them to switch off, zone out, forget about bikes and watch some Netflix or something.

Every bit of stress or thinking that you can remove from a rider is energy saved, and this applies most significantly to your team leader, especially when racing. I always found that the best leaders to work with when racing were those who don't think and say too much, but just go with the flow. That's when you know that you've got them, when they're riding exactly as you want them to. Chris Froome was like that, and Tom Pidcock is definitely like that, although they weren't like that from the off. You've got to earn their respect. But once you'd got that and their complete trust, they often wouldn't question anything.

They both had 100 per cent confidence in me and would follow me blind. Once I'd gained their trust, which was the hardest part of this process, they wouldn't query what I was doing or why. If, say, we were drifting back in the peloton, they wouldn't ask, 'Should we move up to the front? Are you sure this is the right place to be?' They'd just be thinking, 'I'm with Luke and I'll just follow him.' That's what they'd been told to do and they'd stick to this unquestioningly. They would have known that there was probably a good reason for me easing off. If, for instance, we were on a three-lane highway, I wouldn't want to be taking wind or fighting for position. I'd want to sit back and then move up at the last minute when we approached a one-lane road.

I've got a good example of how much trust Froomey had

in me, one that still makes me wince a bit. He would always want to sit on my wheel, not only because he had that faith in me keeping him where he needed to be, but also because I was usually the biggest guy, the one who provided the most shelter. On stage 19 of the 2017 Tour, we were racing out of the Alps to Salon-de-Provence, a bit north of Marseille. There were rumours of crosswinds towards the end, and, with Froomey safe in yellow, we were happy to let a twenty-strong break go clear, letting Vasil Kiryienka and Mikel Nieve ride on the front that day in the event there were crosswinds later on, saving me, Christian Knees and Michał Kwiatkowski for that possibility.

Anyway, Kiry and Mikel were riding, controlling the break, doing a brilliant job, while I sat in front of Froomey. The following stage the next day was a time trial in Marseille so we needed him to be as fresh as possible. We got around 50K into the 222K of stage 19 and we knew the wind had died down. I was like, 'Right, how can I save Froomey the most energy?' I decided I would try to sit as bolt upright as I could for the rest of the day. I didn't use my drops at all. I'd either be on my brake hoods or on my tops, attempting to make myself as tall as possible, literally trying to stick my head up all the way into the finish.

I knew this was the last chance I had to help the team with only the time trial and the stage into Paris to come. Towards the end my back was hurting from sitting in this unconventional position, but I stuck with it because the faster you go, the more benefit the guy behind gets. At the end of what was an easy stage, my back was completely fucked. In the time trial the next day it was still sore, and so were my legs because I'd been riding in this stupid position. In Paris I finally asked Froomey, 'Did you realize how upright I was on stage nineteen?'

He looked at me a bit oddly and said, 'No, what do you mean?'

'Fucking hell! I rode 200K like an absolute melon to try and save your energy!'

He hadn't even twigged. He was in his own world, sitting on my wheel, trusting that I'd get him to where he needed to be, not thinking about how I did it.

It was always interesting to see how riders who were new to the team would adapt to this style of racing. When, for instance, Adam Yates joined Ineos in 2021, he had a reputation for always sitting at the back – in fact, both of the Yateses do. I realized I had to be careful how I handled this issue, because our team generally try to keep a good position quite far forward in the peloton. I couldn't dive right in and say, 'Right, Adam, this is how the team ride. This is how I want to do it.' I'd have lost him within a month.

I remember going into the UAE Tour, the first race I did with him, and saying to him, 'Mate, I'm going to try to keep this as chilled as possible. We'll sit where you want, sit at the back, but on those few occasions when I say "Right, it's game time!" we've got to be in the front. Whenever I say that, commit to me.' And he was absolutely fantastic. In fact, it's always noticeable that the Yates brothers do tend to be at the front when they really need to be. They don't often get caught out when it splits.

Ethan Hayter, on the other hand, would always sit in the back and frequently missed the splits. You could clearly see how physically good he was when he came to the team – what I'd have given to have his legs for just one day! The Classics should be his bread and butter when you look at his numbers, but those races aren't simply a physical challenge. As well as being able to ride your bike, you've got to know the roads and be in position – you need to be strong on the tactical and technical side of things too. Physically, Ethan's the whole package. He knows the roads pretty well. But can he be in position at the right time? No.

I really tried to be patient with him, to be aware that it wasn't going to happen overnight. He did respond to a certain extent, but I often felt that he lacked a little bit of commitment. I think he trusted me, but not completely. Some riders are like that, they see the dangers a bit more. I feel like I failed with him to some extent. I don't mind working with someone, investing time in them, if they come out the other end a better rider or accomplishing what you wanted them to do. But he never quite got there. I still feel that he can do it, though, if he gets his head around it, and I really hope that it works out for him now that he's moved on from Ineos.

You do have to adapt to different leaders and be careful not to piss people off. You've got to get them onside, and the best way to do that is simply to do your job to a very high level over an extended period of time, and they'll buy in. Of course, with this came responsibility, because if there was a crash, they missed a split, or were out of position, they'd say that they'd simply been following me. I didn't mind this because it was my job to get them where they needed to be. Nine times out of ten I'd get it right, and that's about as much as you can ask for really. Nobody's perfect, and I was far from that. I made plenty of mistakes.

However, as long as you're making the right call on where to be in the peloton most of the time, where to save energy and when to sit back, you are doing the job expected of you. It would be the easiest thing in the world to think 'I'm going to stay in front all day' and tell your guys to take the wind for 200K. You can do that for a day, for two, but try to do it for three weeks and you'll all be fucked. You often see teams fall into that trap, of deciding to stay at the front all day every day, but they end up lacking punch. When you're carrying fatigue, you can keep your steady diesel engine rolling, but you will find that you lack explosiveness because you're running at the same intensity. There's no extra power.

This underlines why you've got to use your team's resources in the right way. Your collective energy is a very valuable asset, one that's not limitless. Every time you do a micro acceleration, or a big acceleration, you take the wind; it's like putting a needle in your bag of sand, gradually reducing your reserves. So, you want guys to follow you without question, almost to the point where if the race goes straight and you turn left, they'd follow you. The main fundamental is for them to preserve as much as they can for the moments when those reserves are needed.

The most renowned tactic associated with this harnessing of resources was the Sky train. Riding on the front of the bunch at critical points of a race not only allowed us to keep our leader out of trouble and, largely, out of the wind, it was also a means to control and intimidate our rivals. It was based on a very simple premise: if the strongest team with the strongest individual rides hard from A to B and then, a few kilometres before the end, the best guy attacks, they will win. It was highly calculated, although we never really got given instructions like 'Luke, you do twenty minutes at 420 watts, then someone else do X minutes at 400 . . .' Instead, we all knew what power we could hold and for how long, and our objective was just to ride 'a solid pace', almost like a team time trial.

We grasped the fact that the train had become a significant asset for us because it was given that name, 'the Sky train'. The whole peloton referred to it that way, as if it were a fearsome force that couldn't be stopped. We realized that when we had between seven and nine riders on the front – the number varying depending on the size of the race – the other riders and teams would be thinking, 'Fuck me, we've got to let them burn some matches before we move.' They knew that if they attacked, we wouldn't react impulsively, but just keep that paceline moving in time-trial fashion and gradually reel them in. Meanwhile, Froomey would be sitting on the wheel of his domestiques, waiting for the moment he planned to move. It was so easy to work out where he'd attack as well. He'd examine the stage map beforehand, look at the final climb, locate the steepest point, and say, 'I'll attack there.' It happened time after time. The success we had with the train not only filled us with confidence, but also a certain degree of arrogance. We were the best, and we knew we were the best.

Focusing on the Tour specifically, we aimed to keep that train running with as many strong men as possible, thereby reducing the chance of our rivals attacking. When we had the yellow jersey, we wanted the racing to be nice and calm. Our aim, particularly on big mountain stages, was for our rouleurs – myself, Stannard, Kiry, Kneesy and, later on, Gianni Moscon – to remain on the front for as long as possible, so that when the race hit the penultimate or final climb, we'd be left with five relatively fresh blokes, who we'd have been saving for as long as we could.

Consequently, our mantra was 'Whatever speed we have to ride, it's important that we never lose a man'. So, if someone was having an off-day, it wouldn't be a case of them saying, 'I'm going to pull the pin and drop back to the gruppetto because I can't give any more.' We would just tell them to give less but stay within the train. So I might have been on my knees, incapable of pulling on the front for another 100 metres, but I would sit third wheel, thereby keeping the collective together. As a result, when any of our rivals looked up, they'd be thinking, 'Fuck me, they haven't even lost a man yet.' However, if they'd done a micro acceleration, we might have lost three and suddenly become very vulnerable.

Never losing a man became our thing, something that everyone on the team clung on to, so that we looked like this impenetrable force and left the rest thinking, 'What the fuck are we supposed to do? It's best to attack when their leader's only got one or two helpers, but they've got eight guys there with Froomey.' We really mastered the art of getting as many guys as possible as far into the race as possible. Speaking to riders who joined us from other teams, they confirmed that seeing so many Sky riders at the front was always quite daunting. It got into their heads. We had them exactly where we wanted them, on the back foot, thinking they were beaten because we not only had the best guy, but we could also back this up because we had the numbers to do so.

A big part of my job as road captain was to make sure that no one did too much on any stage, particularly early on in the day, because if you overdid it you'd be fucked for the next stage. If, for instance, I pulled for the first 100K of a stage, then I'd be cooked after it. But if I shared that workload with Kiry, Kneesy and Stannard, then we could all make it a lot further. So every day I'd be gauging who was weak and who was strong. Who'd done more the day before? Who should do more the day after? What's the terrain like that's coming up? How can we get as many men over that climb as possible? Sharing the workload and riding at our speed would then enable us to achieve the daily goals we set, making it look like we were stronger than we sometimes were, deceiving our rivals. As I said, even a small acceleration could at times have put us in real difficulty. It was a mind game, one that we kept on winning.

A good example of how this intimidatory aspect of the Sky train worked was the Peyragudes stage of the 2017 Tour. Froomey was in yellow at the start of a day that went over the Port de Balès and the Col de Peyresourde passes before the steep climb up the airport runway at the finish. Froomey always had a bit of a habit of under-fuelling because he didn't want to put on weight during the Tour de France. He hadn't fuelled enough that day and I remember him telling us early on, 'I don't feel so good today.'

We decided that we would have to ride in the same way that we always did. If we rode easier, other teams would sense it and react, so we stuck to our usual pace. He just had to grin and bear it. We had to bluff because once you're in the race and you haven't fuelled enough the night before or that morning, it's impossible to come back as you're burning more than you're taking in as it is. Matching input against output is really hard to do, especially in the most demanding race of the season. But if your tank's not full to start with, trying to make up that deficit is impossible.

Froomey had to fuel as well as he could, while we just rode our line and tried to sandbag the lot of them. We did it right the way through the stage. He was suffering from the off, but we did all we could to keep his morale up and nobody had a clue. If they'd lit it up on one of the earlier climbs, he could well have lost minutes. But the battle between the GC favourites came down to the very last kilometre of the stage, and with numbers on hand we were able to limit our losses. In the end, Froomey only lost a handful of seconds to a few guys including Fabio Aru, who took the jersey. Two days later, Aru was caught too far back on a tricky finish and Chris got the jersey back again.

After that latter stage, Michael Valgren, who was a teammate of Aru's at Astana, responded with the comment 'Ah, good' when he was told by a reporter that his leader had lost the jersey. Unsurprisingly, that didn't go down very well, but what Michael meant by that was that he was happy Astana didn't have to control the race any more, that the responsibility would be back on us. Obviously, the yellow jersey is massive, but defending it takes a huge physical and psychological toll. We were prepared for that in a way that other teams simply weren't, partly because most of them were used to sitting in behind us and letting us get on with the hard work, as Michael's comment underlined.

Giving guys on the team a 'day off' was all part of the strategy designed to cope with this. I'd have a say in this, as would the DS, but it essentially came down to numbers. I was never privy to this information at the time, but I've subsequently seen some of the files. Say we'd completed three days of the Tour de France. They'd analyse what the nine guys had done and realize that, for instance, the mountain guys had done very little, or perhaps that the mountain guys had really struggled on the flat, and they'd try to balance the workloads.

Take Wout Poels, for instance. His job was clearly to perform in the mountains at the Tour, but he had to help as much as he could on all twenty-one stages. On the flat stages early in the race, he'd have to help with positioning the leader. But if there was a mountain stage coming up late in the first week where we knew that we would really have to depend on him, we'd organize his workload so that we only used him sparingly on the opening days, when guys like Stannard and me would carry much more of the burden. On the flip side, when we got to that mountain stage, I'd just have to survive it, to go as far as I could with the team then simply get to the finish, whereas Wout would need to be all in. So, the key was to find that balance, ensuring that every rider contributed, but to the right degree given the profile of the stage.

During those flat stages, it would be partly down to me to assess how much we needed Wout. We'd make a bit of a plan in the pre-race meeting, but I'd have a big say on the road in deciding how long he contributed to the work, which depended on how stressful it was, the speed of the peloton, if it was windy, whether we were chasing the breakaway full gas or it was quite a relaxed day. I was the one who'd tell him when his job was done and he could go and chill further back in the pack in order to save himself for the days ahead.

I'm convinced that they cut the number of riders in teams at the Grand Tours from nine to eight as a direct response to the Sky train. As a team, we had the biggest budget and the greatest all-round quality of rider. Our third best guy at the Tour de France was maybe slightly better or similar to someone else's third best guy. But, because we had so much talent, our ninth guy was very close in terms of performance to our third guy and substantially stronger than their ninth guy, so taking a guy out hurt us more than the other squads. Also, as a team that's controlling, you need the numbers much more than in situations when you're sat on the wheel and trying to be the aggressor, going for stage wins and breakaways. So, having fewer guys impacted the stronger teams who were winning and having to control a race more than the rest of the teams. Ultimately, the Sky train got boring – and it was definitely boring – and they tried to clamp down on it.

Of course, even we couldn't keep all eight or nine riders together all day on every key stage. On the big mountain days, we'd each be allocated our scheduled work, which for the bigger guys like Ian Stannard and me meant grafting early on and then dropping back into the gruppetto, the group at the back of the race that has the sole target of finishing within the time limit on tough days like that. The first thing to say about the gruppetto is that it's not the happy, joyful place it's often presented as. It's not the so-called laughing group. Even if you know you're going to be dropped, even if you're a sprinter, it's still not a nice place to be. You're there because you have no other option. It's fucking horrible.

It's got that easy-going image because you sometimes see some funny footage from there, guys doing wheelies or grabbing beers from fans. The TV also often shows that moment when everyone's crossing the finish line and they're delighted to have made it, tapping each other on the backside in congratulation. In reality, though, you're in there because you're suffering, or you're ill or you're injured, and a lot of the time you're fighting to make the time cut. What's more, most people don't realize how hard you have to ride at times within the gruppetto. It's not like you're tapping away on a Sunday club run. You'll still be riding up the climbs at 350 watts.

On any stage where there was even a chance that I might be in there after it split and the time cut was an issue, I'd definitely make sure I knew the time limits. They're calculated based on average speed, and the final figure could fluctuate quite a lot depending on how quick the race had been. If it had been full gas at the start, for instance, the time limit would be lower. As a consequence, you'd be riding with a few different figures in your head and would only get the final time limit once the winner had crossed the finish line and your DS had then done the maths. You might have twenty minutes to finish, thirty minutes, or even more, but I'd always have a very good idea even before that point what the time limit would be on any particular day. Other riders would even ask me what I thought it would be because I got a reputation for being pretty accurate with my estimates.

The gruppetto used to have a reputation for togetherness, a place where team differences didn't matter. Dubbed the *auto-bus* in French, it would have a 'bus driver', an experienced pro who would organize a pace that would ensure the gruppetto finished within the time limit. I think I caught the back end of that early in my career, when somebody like Bernie Eisel would know what the time gap was and know how hard to ride, and you respected that.

Over the years, though, the gruppetto's become a place where there's increasingly less cohesion. At the 2022 Tour, I can remember seeing Dylan Groenewegen with all of his BikeExchange train, Caleb Ewan with all of his Lotto train, and Fabio Jakobsen with all of his QuickStep train, all of them riding separately. Traditionally, those three groups would have come together and ridden as a unit of three teams with three sprinters, with perhaps twenty guys in the group, which would enable them to get up to hellish speeds on the descents and in the valleys, where they could make up some of the time they'd lost on the front of the race. But, from my position just ahead of these groups, I could see that there was a minute in between each of them. They seemed to want to outdo each other, to avoid being the last ones to finish, or perhaps even to force a rival out of the race altogether. This kind of attitude nullifies the power of the gruppetto, which is strength in numbers.

My sense of the modern gruppetto is that nobody listens any more. There are too many people who think they're clever and they'll be saying 'We're going too fast' or 'We're going too slow'. Nine times out of ten, they will be going too fast. I often found myself urging them to 'Go easier. We've got 10K to do and they've only just finished,' but it would usually fall on deaf ears. The next morning, I'd see those same guys trying to get into the breakaway and exploding, and I'd be thinking, 'Why didn't you ride easy yesterday, you knobhead.' It's all about self-preservation, about trying to avoid stabbing too many holes in your bag of sand.

Sometimes in those situations I'd even drop out of the gruppetto and leave them to it. I'd make full use of the time limit if I was on the final climb and roll in five minutes after everyone else. That's the one occasion when the gruppetto is a nice place to be, when you've got to that point on the final climb where you know that you're going to make it safely inside the time limit. I finished dead last in the 2017 Tour, Froomey's fourth and final win. That was one of my best Tours from a performance perspective, but I deliberately lost time on some stages to preserve energy, coming in a couple of minutes behind the gruppetto.

One other aspect that's critical to success in the major races is time trialling. I very rarely looked forward to these days because I've never been any shakes as a tester. My goal in any individual time trial was to get round as best I could and, above all, preserve resources for the days ahead. As a consequence, I can't legitimately offer any insight into tactics for a TT. Team time trials are a different matter, though. I always had a role to play in these, because you've got no option. They were always the days I feared the most, far more than the big mountain stages or even those when you go up a long climb from kilometre zero. I always backed myself to get through those TTT days relatively OK, but I hated them because I knew I was out of my comfort zone and, this being the case, tended to think that it was inevitable that I'd let the team down somehow. How I performed depended on how good my level was on the day. Usually, though, it was difficult for me to have much of a positive impact.

From the road captain's point of view, there's not a lot to do in a TTT because the specialist time triallists will conduct operations on the day. Geraint Thomas, for instance, was super strong in them, so he'd have a lot to say. Essentially, though, it's all pre-decided. It's all about preparation by the staff pre-race, and everything follows from there. With regard to the line-up, they'd try to spread the weaker and the stronger guys throughout the team. So, they'd make sure that we didn't have two strong guys or two weak guys next to each other.

Once you start a team time trial, pretty much everything comes from the car, because the riders are wearing aero helmets and travelling at such speeds that they can't hear anything. At Sky, we had our own little language, extending to just three words. They were: hold, squeeze, in. Because you can't really hear anything, we picked three that don't sound similar. The rider who dictates the speed is the second in line because he's got a good feel of it, whereas when you're on the front it's difficult to know what's going on behind. The second guy has also got the best line of communication to the first guy. So if the front guy starts to slow down, it's 'squeeze' – go faster. If he's accelerating too much, it's 'hold'. And the third word is 'in', which is only used by the rider on the back if he wants to miss a turn. So if someone comes to the back and you have to let them slot in ahead of you, it's 'in'.

The key to success in team time trials is maintaining speed, and the only variant for each rider is how long you sit on the front. It's all very well explained in advance. They'll tell you how long your turn should be. I might be doing eight- to ten-second pulls, while someone stronger, such as Kiry or G, could be doing twenty- to twenty-two-second pulls. It would all depend on how strong you were, how aero you were, how fatigued you were. Guys had different ways of measuring their turn on the front, but I would do a countdown in my head, backwards from ten, then I'd pull aside and the rider behind would come to the front for his stint. We'd stick to those pre-set pulls for the first half of the TTT, maybe two-thirds, then it would become more of a free for all. You'd just give what you'd got, which for me wasn't much.

Back in the team car, it's all very methodical and thought out, and they're quite chilled on the radio because it's such a stressful day. They're not bellowing 'Come on! Come on! Come on!' at us. As with any other aspect of racing, calmness is key.

That first Tour of mine in 2015 featured a team time trial in

Brittany and the staff had put together a clear battle plan for it. There was a climb in the middle and another right at the end. Ian Stannard and I had to get most of the way up that first climb. After that, the rest of the team had to go all of the way to the base of the final climb, then try to stick together on the hill. However, we lost Pete Kennaugh, one of our stronger team time triallists, really early as he was starting to struggle with illness. Yogi and I did what was required of us and then we were out of the game.

Nico Roche was struggling a bit and I remember G told him to sit on, but he kept going through in order to keep contributing where he could and then cracked a bit on the final climb. I'm not blaming him, because he lasted a lot longer than I did. That meant they had to wait for him and, at the finish, BMC beat us by a second. Although I was a little bit gutted to end up so close to being part of a Tour de France stage win, the most important thing that day was that we pumped a lot of time into Nairo Quintana, who was Froomey's main rival for the yellow jersey.

BMC beat us narrowly again in the TTT at the 2018 Tour, which once again took place in western France, four seconds the gap between them and us that time. The month before, we'd beaten them easily in the same test at the Dauphiné. I'd put on a pretty good show and was quite happy at the end. We were absolutely flying that day and were confident we could repeat our performance at the Tour. However, and I don't know why, I had an absolute stinker. I got dropped maybe two-thirds of the way through as we went up this drag. Obviously, racing down the other side of a drag is one section where having more men can make a bigger difference, and I wasn't there for the other side. It's a horrible feeling when you're dropped like that, before you're expected to fall back. All you can do then when you're on your own is keep the chain tight and not lose too much time on the way in as you still have to finish inside that day's limit. After beating BMC by thirty-eight seconds at the Dauphiné, we lost narrowly to them when it really mattered. I really feel like I let the team down that day.

Having analysed how good we once were as a team at the Tour de France, I should also reflect on where I think things have gone wrong for Ineos at the race in recent seasons. We made the yellow jersey our own thanks to seven overall victories in eight years, but the team has now been knocked off its pedestal by UAE and Jumbo-Visma (now Visma-Lease a Bike), collecting just a couple of third-place finishes since Egan Bernal won the 2019 edition.

To a significant extent, this drop-off in performance was the result of losing big personalities from the set-up. Froomey had a horrendous crash at the 2019 Dauphiné that ended his days as a Grand Tour contender, while Egan had a near-fatal crash in January 2022 that he's courageously come back from but which has left him below his previous level as one of the very best racers in the peloton. In addition, Nico Portal, one of the great DSs in the sport's history, died in March 2020, while Dave Brailsford and Fran Millar, who were behind the team's foundation in the first place, have moved into new roles. At the same time, Tadej Pogačar and Jonas Vingegaard have emerged as the Tour dominators, leaving everyone else racing for third.

But Ineos have also made a lot of mistakes since Egan won the Tour. I think they signed the right riders to remain contenders, but haven't deployed them in a way that has allowed this. There was nothing they could do about Egan's back issue that totally scuppered his defence of the title in 2020, but I think we got it really wrong as a team in 2021. We realized that we'd struggled to go man-on-man with Pogi and Jonas, so we tried to go in with numbers. On paper, we had four leaders: Richard Carapaz, Richie Porte, Tao Geoghegan Hart and Geraint Thomas. The theory was that if we could get to the mountains with four leaders still in contention, we could play the numbers game. I said that this could work, but the danger was spreading ourselves too thinly and coming away with nothing. I also suggested that it wasn't realistic to have Jonathan Castroviejo, Michał Kwiatkowski, Dylan van Baarle and me looking after four riders. You can't have four protecting four when you're competing against teams with seven looking after one.

I wasn't alone in thinking this strategy could very quickly go pear-shaped. Even the four leaders didn't think it was viable. You can get an awful lot out of a team if all of the riders have belief, but if they don't buy in to the staff's plan, you're likely to lose them and end up talking to yourself. And that's precisely what happened. The management, the DSs, lost the bus, they lost the riders. We didn't think it was possible for the strategy to succeed. None of the leaders was happy about being one of four. They were always looking at each other. When they were heading into a key moment, they'd be thinking, 'Where do I stand in the pecking order? Do I get to sit directly on the four domestiques? Or am I the eighth guy who's effectively acting as the gatekeeper who might lose the wheel and get lost in the peloton's washing machine?' In short, we had no belief and the plan to have four leaders went tits up.

As it turned out, Carapaz was third, the best of the rest behind Pogačar and Vingegaard, but we didn't win a stage. Lots of teams would have been happy with that, but we definitely weren't. And it all came down to the fact that nobody on our team believed in what we were being told to do. Tao didn't, G didn't, Richie really didn't. He'd finished third the year before, but needed a lot of support to get through the flat days. He was an incredibly talented climber, but depended on the full backing of a team because of his stature. He'd got that at Trek, but finished more than two hours down on GC with us.

I spoke quite vocally about all this and ended up getting myself in the shit with senior management after the Tour.

Chris Froome on Luke

There are countless stories I could recount about Luke, about the times he saved my arse when we were caught up in difficult situations, particularly at the Tour de France. From the outside, it's not easy to see how vital he was to me, both as road captain and as my protector on the road. I went wherever Luke led me in the peloton and I never doubted that I'd end up exactly where I needed to be, although sometimes that did ruffle some feathers. One good example of that occurred in the opening days of the first Tour we raced together, in 2015, when we had a fall-out with one of our rivals that resulted in Luke getting a new nickname.

After two stages in the Netherlands, stage 3 took us into the Ardennes for a finish on the Mur de Huy, the super-steep climb that's the traditional finale for Flèche Wallonne. The roads are narrow, and it's constantly left, right, up, down, and once you're in position you don't move from there. But we'd missed out on the rush to get into position coming towards a key climb, and I think there was a risk of crosswinds as well. What I do remember clearly is that it was a freaking stressful day.

We needed to get back up to the front, and Luke basically said to me, 'OK Froomey, get on my wheel. I'm taking you to the front.' I got on his wheel and we started creeping up the left-hand side of the peloton. Progress was slow – we were moving up literally one rider at a time. As soon as a little gap opened, he'd take it, and make space for me to come through and follow.

Then we came up behind Katusha's Giampaolo Caruso, who was holding tight to the left. There was no way past him. But then he moved slightly to the right, just a few centimetres, but it was enough for Luke to figure out there was enough of a gap to squeeze his handlebars through and then push him out of the way. So he squeezed in, took the gap and – I think in an absolute panic to close it – Caruso then went left really hard. I braked because I immediately realized he was going to take me straight off the road if I tried to follow Luke. As I braked, the Italian over-corrected and went careering off into the ditch. We weren't racing at a massively high speed, but I think we were probably doing a good 40, 45kph.

We then carried on working our way up to the front and made it up there, which was freaking incredible. Soon after, there was a big crash on the right-hand side of the bunch, which took out around sixty guys, and the race was then neutralized. We were at the front, but we weren't next to each other when the race stopped, and this guy came straight at me and was demanding in Italian, 'Dovè, Robbie? Dovè, Robbie?' ('Where's Robbie?') I was like, 'Mate, there's no Robbie in our team.' But he was adamant: 'Sì! Sì! Sì! Robbie! Robbie! Robbie!' I just shook my head. 'No, no Robbie here, mate.'

I can't remember exactly what happened next, whether he spotted Luke or Luke rolled up next to us or something. But I do remember he lost his shit, saying how dangerous that move was up the side and that it had basically caused him to crash into the ditch. Safe to say that after all that, you were known as 'Robbie'.

There was another day really early on in the 2018 Tour when I think Greg Van Avermaet had yellow and we had a stand-off with Movistar because they weren't in yellow and we weren't either. The break went, I think Greg was in there again even though he was in yellow, and Movistar didn't want to help us pull. They said they would come later, and we ended up in this huge stand-off. The gap got to like ten minutes and it was so tense. We were waiting, waiting, waiting, and then eventually they caved in and agreed to ride with us. At moments like that we really had to keep our wits and stick to our plan, and be like, 'No, we're not going to fucking pull. End of story.' There was a lot of negotiating, a lot of talking backwards and forwards with the car. Luke was crucial to the team in that sort of situation.

10

Froomey

I've already remarked that GC riders are the real warriors of the pro peloton. During my time within it, few riders epitomized that to the same extent as Chris Froome. He was an absolute pit bull on the bike, as I quickly realized when I was one of his domestiques at the 2014 Vuelta a España. He came into that race slightly fatigued and a little underdone, having crashed out of the Tour de France a few weeks earlier with a broken wrist.

On one of the early mountain stages to the Valdelinares ski station, he was riding in that yo-yoing way that we all became familiar with. He got dropped by the likes of Nairo Quintana, Alberto Contador and Joaquim Rodríguez on a steep section, then he came back, then he got dropped once more and came back again. He was battling away, trying to stay with riders who were stronger than he was at that moment. He ended up losing a handful of seconds.

As soon as we got back on the bus, he told us not to lose belief in him. We'd set the pace for him that day on the final climb and it hadn't worked out as we'd hoped. But he urged us not to let our heads drop. 'I can do this. I had a bad day today, but don't panic. Just back me. Don't lose belief.' It was exactly the right thing to say at that moment, to tell us that he was up for a fight. As it turned out, he pushed Contador all the way to the end of the race. On the penultimate day, when Froomey stood little chance of overturning his deficit, he was still giving it everything and we were still backing him. I remember saying that we needed to throw the kitchen sink at Contador, and then having to explain what this meant to some of our guys. They soon got the message, and we did give everything. We had total belief in Chris.

When it comes to working out what made Froomey so good, you have to take into account his route into the sport. I don't mean to suggest that he's had a particularly hard life, but his upbringing was unconventional – brought up in Kenya, boarding school in the UK, home in South Africa – and as a result of that he had to find his own particular path into the pro peloton, which included a spell at the UCI academy at their HQ in Switzerland. It's an indication of his determination that he stuck at this quest and it illustrates what a tough bugger he is, both on the bike and off it.

When he was racing, he could really hurt himself mentally, and was probably the strongest of all the riders I've worked with from that perspective. He was fixated on his weight and took dieting to the limit too. He used to get into shape by starving himself. Seeing what he was eating – or not eating! – I'd be thinking, 'He's going to keel over dead one day. How's he doing it?' He'd have this weird green tea for breakfast and go and ride his bike for five, six hours. He was always on that line where he ate just enough to get through a stage when racing. If it was a flat, easy day, he sometimes wouldn't take anything in the feed zone. He was always on the limit because he didn't want to put on weight.

He really had that Kerro mentality that I described in an earlier chapter in relation to training – to get fitter, you simply had to train more and more, and to get leaner, to eat less and less. The approach worked, because he won a lot of races, but we've all learned over time that it's not the way to do it, that there are better and healthier ways to control your weight. But that's the way it was back then and a lot of people had that same attitude towards nutrition.

As was the case at the 2014 Vuelta, he also had the ability to rally his teammates around him. He's a got a lot more character than he lets on in the media, where he could come across as a bit dull and earnest. But he's not like that at all. He's a real character and was always very good at getting the group to believe in him, to buy into his goals. At the start of the year, he would look at the thirty riders on the team and think to himself, 'Which eight do I need to be at the top of their game at the Tour de France?'

He was a bit like Cav in the way that he could create a strong group around him. He'd gather us together and tell us, 'Come on, boys, we're on a mission,' and you really felt like you were on a journey with him. We'd be at the December camp and he'd already be talking about and focusing on the Tour. I remember there was a cobbled stage in the 2015 Tour, the day when Tony Martin won and actually took the jersey from Froomey, and Chris had been talking about that stage in December and January. 'How are we going to enter the first cobbled section in the front?' We'd give some insights, and he'd say, 'I want more detail. How do you do it in Roubaix?

How do you stay in the front? How do you ride the cobbles?'
He'd really quiz you.

The best insight I can give on this comes from the cobbled stage to Roubaix in 2018. It was my responsibility to be
with Froomey that day and someone else, Kwiato I think,
was designated to be with G, because we had two leaders.
Obviously, in the thick of the action it gets very hectic on
a stage like that, and we were getting close to the first section of pavé and it was so sketchy. At times, when you're
staying with a leader like Froomey, you'll be in front of
them and you try moving up, but if a gap opens, you'll let
them through, then you'll be behind them for a bit. As we
approached these cobbles, I was behind him and I could see
that he was taking huge risks. He was going left, right, braking on his front wheel, skidding.

I remember Mark Renshaw once saying that in order to
win the Tour de France you've actually got to get to Paris, and
at that instant I thought there was a real chance that Froomey
wasn't going to get there. I needed to calm him down because
he was about to crash. I told him, 'Froomey, just stay with me.
We don't have to hit this in the front.' If he'd gone down on a
cobbled stage like he did in 2014, his race would have likely
been over. I could see the same thing happening. I was like,
'Listen, just fucking chill out. We have to stay on our bikes.
Chill out! We'll be all right.'

We went into the first section of cobbles in fiftieth or sixtieth position and I remember G was up towards the front,
very well positioned. That was a situation where I made a call
like any good road captain would – sacrifice position and stay
on the bike – because there were crashes. Then there was a
kind of lull on that first section of cobbles and we actually

moved up, and by the time we exited the pavé we were quite close to the front and it calmed down a bit.

There were fifteen cobbled sections in all that day. Sky then took it on approaching the fifth. We managed to split the race, and there was a group of no more than twenty guys in the front part of what had been a big peloton. As well as me and Froomey, we had Gianni Moscon, Kwiato and G. So we had three domestiques with two leaders and the three of us were pulling. Normally in that situation the commissaires would create a barrage so that the convoy of cars can't get up to the front group. But they never pulled the convoy from behind us, so while we were going full gas, groups were getting back up to us in the shelter provided by the cars. It would split again and groups would come back in the convoy. It was an absolute joke.

Actually, that's one of the few occasions I look back on and feel pissed off at the way a race was run, because we raced perfectly from a tactical point of view and could have taken a lot of time out of a lot of people. We committed totally and they were all just coming back with the cars all the time. If you look at the final result sheet, nobody lost time. Nobody. Romain Bardet had an absolute nightmare that day, with three or four punctures, but managed to limit his losses to just seven seconds against the other GC guys, including Froomey and G. I'm not having a go at him, because if the cars are there you use them. But if you have three or four punctures, you should never, ever come back from that in Roubaix. You should be losing time. But Bardet hardly lost any.

In the end, it all went a bit to shit for us coming into a later section. Going into a 90-degree left-hand corner, I was second or third wheel. Dmitriy Gruzdev from Astana led in.

It was so dusty because it was the middle of summer and you couldn't see a thing. I knew the corner was coming, but Gruzdev overcooked it and went down. Kwiato crashed as well. I managed to hold it up, but broke my bike. And then in the very next section, Mons-en-Pévèle, Gianni crashed on the entry to it along with Froomey. So we went from having five guys in a group of twenty to having just G. Froomey got back into that group eventually, and the main thing in the end was that our two leaders were there.

Thinking back to that stage, I also recall that I'd asked the team if they could adapt my bike a little bit in the event that Froomey had some kind of mechanical issue on the cobbles. There were several reasons why I'd act as his guardian angel on flat stages, particularly complicated ones like that Roubaix day. As well as being confident in my ability to place him where he needed to be in the peloton and my position as road captain, we were also a pretty similar size. If he'd punctured, crashed or whatever and needed a new bike, I could hand mine over and he'd be able to get quickly back into the race.

Prior to the 2018 Tour, I'd noticed that Danilo Wyss, who rode alongside Richie Porte at BMC, had a seatpost that had been modified slightly. About an inch up this old-style circular seatpost, the team's mechanics had fitted another clamp that was set to the height that Richie would want it. So if he had an issue, they could loosen the skewer on Wyss's bike, drop the seatpost and then secure it with that second clamp.

I went to the team a few months before the Tour and asked them whether it was likely that I'd be riding with Froomey on that cobbled stage. They told me that was set in stone, so I said to them that we should look at doing the same thing, using a quick release so that we didn't need an Allen key in order to lower the saddle. I thought it would be well worth it just for that one stage, but suggested it might even be useful on the sprint stages. They definitely looked into it, but it never came to fruition. I don't know if that was because we used bladed seatposts which made that adaptation impossible.

I did ride Froomey's bike a couple of times, and it felt really weird with those osymetric chainrings, but I only ever handed my bike over to him once in a race. That was in the 2015 Tour, two days after Tony Martin had taken the yellow jersey from Froomey on a cobbled stage to Cambrai. The race was still up in the north and finished up a climb about a kilometre or so in length in Le Havre. There was a crash halfway up it, and Chris and Astana's Vincenzo Nibali, who was the defending Tour champion, both went down, as did Tony Martin, who broke his collarbone and couldn't start the next day.

Ian Stannard and I had led the team into the climb and then dropped back, so I reached the riders on the floor a few seconds after this had happened. As Nibali stood up, he took his bottle out of its cage and launched it at Froomey before riding off, because Nibali thought he was to blame for bringing them down. There were photographers all around us taking pictures of Froomey and I said, 'Listen, mate, just take my bike and get to the finish.' He had no concerns in terms of time because the 3K rule meant he would be awarded the same time as the winner. I told him, 'Just get away from the riff raff.' I could see as I gave him my bike that he was fuming.

I sorted out Froomey's bike, got the chain back on, and got to the finish as quickly as possible. David Rozman was the soigneur at the finish line, ready with the post-race drinks for the riders. I asked him where Froomey was and he said that he didn't know, that he'd just ridden straight past him.

I was like, 'Oh, fuck. I know exactly where he's gone.' I went to our bus and asked if Froomey was there. Once again I was told that he'd gone by without stopping, so I sprinted up to the Astana team bus, leant my bike against it and started to climb the stairs on to it. As I did so, Froomey was coming down them.

'Are you all right?' I asked him.

'Yeah, all good. Let's go.'

We made our way back to the Sky bus, and when we were on it I asked him what had happened. Froomey simply stated, 'He won't be fucking with me for a while.' It turned out that he'd got on to the Astana bus and grabbed Nibali by the scruff of the neck. The footage of the crash was on TV, and Froomey said to him, 'Show me how I caused the crash,' although he wasn't quite as polite as that. Although Nibali had blamed him for the incident, you could see on TV that it wasn't Chris's fault. Nibali, meanwhile, went as white as a ghost and didn't know what to say. Froomey told him never to fuck with him or the team again, or words to that effect, and then stomped off the bus. Both Sky and Astana had a few Slovenian staff on the teams, including Rozman, and we subsequently heard through them that Nibali was shitting himself after that encounter. Like I said, Froomey had some dog in him and that was one moment when it came out.

That's an example, I guess, of how we were prepared to do anything to back each other up and be together as a unit. I didn't know what I might be walking into on the Astana bus, but that didn't matter. If Froomey was going to get on their bus, then I was going to follow him. I knew that he was pissed off and that he'd be outnumbered. Cyclists aren't boxers, we all know that, but I was set on backing him up.

However, as I've already said, Froomey can handle himself so there was never really an issue. In fact, that incident turned in our favour a little bit later in the race. We were riding on the front and Astana started coming up the outside on a climb as we were pacing. It pisses you off when guys come up alongside you like that. But as they did, Froomey looked across at Nibali and went 'Fuck off!' and they dropped back again. We had him by the balls.

People talk about the likes of Bernard Hinault or Lance Armstrong being the peloton's *patron* at the Tour, the rider who basically decides who does what and when, and Froomey had that about him as well. He could not only impose himself physically, but also bend most situations to his will. He demonstrated that on the Tour's Ventoux stage the following year, before the mayhem that eventually ensued on the final climb that none of us will ever forget.

One memory stands out before that point, though, one that highlights why we always gave everything we had to support Froomey. The 2016 edition started at Mont-Saint-Michel in Normandy, just a few weeks after he'd won the Dauphiné. Ian Stannard (Yogi) and I had ridden with him in that race and were roommates for the Tour. We were lying on our beds a couple of days before things got under way when Froomey came in and put a box on the end of each bed. 'Just a little something for you both. I just want to say, whatever happens over the next three weeks, thank you for the Dauphiné and – win or lose – over the next three weeks, thank you for your support here.' He'd bought us Rolex watches, each of them engraved. On the back of mine it said 'Luke Rowe Team Sky Tour de France 2016'. Even now when I put it on I feel incredibly proud. One thing that struck me at the time was the fact that he could have crashed out on the first day, or not had the legs to compete for the yellow jersey, but still made that very touching gesture. Anything could have happened – and in fact it did, on the stage from Montpellier to Mont Ventoux.

It was a crazy day almost from the off. The Mistral was blowing strongly and we got a bit found out early on in the wind as the route crossed the flatlands in the Rhône valley. QuickStep – who else? – went in the wind. They were riding for Dan Martin and caught us napping a bit, although we did all make it into the front group. The wind, of course, was already wreaking havoc on the Ventoux, forcing the organizers to move the finish down from the summit, which is totally exposed, to Chalet Reynard, at the top end of the forest about 7K from the top. We were all well aware of how fierce it was too. It made the peloton a lot more nervous than it would usually be on a stage halfway into the Tour.

There was only one climb before the Ventoux, a third-cat, so the peloton was still together coming off that. We were riding on the front with Orica-BikeExchange, who were looking after Adam Yates, and, as we went round a corner, his teammate Simon Gerrans high-sided in the wind. Yogi was right behind him and went down, Kiry was next and he went down too. I was fourth in line and got tangled up in it, although I managed to stay upright.

When you're the road captain, the onus is on you to react instantly in situations like this, because the DS can't do anything – they won't even know for a few seconds that there's anything wrong. Instinct kicks in because you can't think things through. I could see Yogi bent over a guard-rail, screaming in agony, that Kiry was OK but had some bike issues, and knew that both I and my bike had escaped unscathed. My thought process was: 'Yogi, you're in a lot of fucking pain, but you're not unconscious, the doctor will be here soon. I'm OK, but Kiry is more important than me on this stage so the first priority is getting him back on his bike.' I sorted that out, and he got going again. I then jumped on my bike and said 'See you later, mate' to Yogi as I left him to it as there was nothing I could do for him. This may seem harsh, but all any rider would think about in this situation is defending the yellow jersey. Of course, by this time the peloton had passed us and team cars were starting to arrive, meaning Yogi received medical attention very quickly.

Meanwhile, up at the front, Froomey took advantage of his status as the race leader. He signalled for the peloton to slow, then stopped for a piss. The unwritten rule is that no one attacks the yellow jersey when he does this, although the race leader would usually only stop when the racing wasn't as full on. Froomey's decision to do this enabled Kiry and me to get back in position for the final kilometres into the Ventoux, and was a really smart move on his part.

When we reached the climb, the peloton was already a bit split up, but I was at the front as we went on to it. I soon drifted backwards, and didn't really know anything about what had happened further up the climb until I got to the finish line. A few guys in the gruppetto had been saying that something crazy had happened, that Froomey had been running, and I was thinking, 'What the fuck are they talking about?' I had no clue.

I got to the finish and made my way to the bus and it was total pandemonium on there. I asked the guys what was going on and they were all looking at the TV screen. I then saw what all the fuss was about: Froomey had indeed been running up the Ventoux without his bike. Some were saying that he'd lost the jersey, others were going through all the rules and regulations, trying to work out what applied in a situation like this, which was completely without precedent as far as I can remember. Everyone was talking at the same time. 'Let's do this!' 'Ring them!' 'Speak to him!' 'How can they do that?' It was chaotic.

It was at moments like this that Dave Brailsford was really good. He said something along the lines of 'Will you all chill the fuck out, boys! I'll deal with this.' He left the bus and spoke to the powers that be, pointing out that the incident had resulted from mistakes made by the race organizers and that there was nothing Froomey could have done.

Dave got his point across, but one very crucial aspect when it came to the decision to award Froomey and Richie Porte the same finishing time as Bauke Mollema – whom they'd both been riding with when the three of them ploughed into the back of the race motorbike that suddenly came to a stop in front of them – was the response of the Orica team management. They were set to be awarded the yellow jersey, which would have gone to Adam Yates as Froomey had eventually finished more than a minute behind him, but they were brilliant. I'm not sure whether it was Brent Copeland, Jerry Ryan or Matt White at Orica, but they were adamant that they weren't prepared to take the jersey in that way. The UCI and the race organizers were apparently quoting some rule that you have to be with your bike at all times, and they might well have been able to take the time off Froomey, but Orica insisted that Adam wouldn't have taken the jersey if it hadn't been for this freak accident. So we held on to yellow.

While that issue was more or less sorted on the day, there

was another significant and extremely ugly aspect to that afternoon that we had to deal with over the next couple of seasons, something that few people were aware of at that time. In the midst of the mayhem that followed the crash into the motorbike, Froomey was getting hit and punched by spectators. He said afterwards that his overriding thought was 'I just have to get out of here – if I keep standing here, I'm just going to get battered.' Fearing for his safety, he started running. It was after that he got on a Mickey Mouse neutral service bike with the wrong pedals and the wrong saddle height, before eventually getting a spare bike from our team car and battling to the finish line. It was pointed out to the race organizers that not only had the official motorbikes caused the crash, they'd also been unable to protect us from being attacked by people in the crowd.

A few days later, we had an uphill time trial into Megève in the Alps and that was the first time I saw Froomey get nervous about his safety. If there was a single stage where he would be most vulnerable, it was that one with the long climb up to the finish where he'd be on his own. So the team spoke to the UCI and the race organization about how to play things. They ended up putting two motorbikes in front of him and getting them to ride wide so that fans had to move back out of the road. There were two more motorbikes closer to him, who were told to ride a bit wider in order to ensure people stayed at a good distance from Froomey. The team car stayed close behind him, to prevent anyone coming in from the rear. It worked without a hitch, but did make us think about how easy it would be for a fan with a grudge to attack a rider if they wanted to.

By that point, Sky had won three of the previous four Tours

and were heading for another victory, and some fans were getting pissed off with it. They didn't want to see the same winner from the same team riding in a boring fashion. It was clear that a growing number of people hated us, especially in France. To an extent that's the curse of winning every year, no matter what the sport. Cycling's seen it before with the antipathy towards Eddy Merckx, Lance Armstrong and even home favourites like Jacques Anquetil and Bernard Hinault, when they were dominating the Tour. We were a British team, relatively new, big budget, riding in boring fashion, riding conservatively, and winning France's big race every year, and people weren't happy, which meant that the hostility towards us was increasing.

By that time, if I was in the gruppetto, I wouldn't ride on the side of the group, next to the fans, as it went up a climb at 10kph. I'd always be in the middle. If I was ever caught on my own, I'd either try to catch up with the group in front or slip back to the one behind. I'd never ride on my own. When you're at the front of the race, you've got all the motorbikes, the race marshals, you're followed by team cars, and they're on TV, so anyone who tries anything is likely to get caught. At the back of the race, though, it was a jungle. Me, Yogi and the other guys out the back were the most susceptible to abuse and aggression. It was horrible.

Froomey, of course, won that 2016 Tour and went on to take his fourth overall title the year after. Going into the 2017 edition, Geraint Thomas was better than he'd ever been. He'd won Paris–Nice the year before and won the opening TT at the Tour in Düsseldorf. From the outside, it might have looked like Sky had two leaders, but that wasn't the case at that point and there were no complications within the team at all. It was still clear cut that Froomey was number one. There was a very big drop-off to number two. What's more, G knew the extent of his ability. He enjoyed his days in yellow, which were fantastic for the team, but there was never a question of him being a co-leader that year. Obviously it was a bit different a year down the line, though.

The thing that stands out most about that opening stage in Germany that G won was that we had four riders in the top eight – G, Kiry, Froomey and Kwiato. There was a bit of controversy about that TT because we had a new skinsuit, the Vortex, with pimples on the sleeves that were designed to improve air flow, and there were claims that we were cheating, including from other teams. It was one of our marginal gains and perfectly within the rules, at least until the UCI changed them a year later. In fact, the weather was a lot more significant than our skinsuits. It was pissing down, and a few of the GC guys crashed, notably Alejandro Valverde, whose race ended almost as soon as it had begun.

Froomey ended up winning that Tour pretty comfortably and then went to the Vuelta in August and won that. Then, right at the very end of that season, the news came out about him having a positive test for the asthma medication salbutamol. In between those events taking place, Sky had held its usual meeting in October, when we'd always be told what the implications of a positive drugs case would be on the team. They'd tell us that this was the one thing that could bring the team down. They'd stress that all the individuals in the room – and there were around 120 of us – plus our families would be impacted. If you're thinking of doing something, they'd tell us, if you're on the edge, just remember this: 500 people's lives will be affected and the team will fold overnight.

Obviously, there was a lot of speculation swirling around us simply because of our performances, and we just had to ignore that. But when that news about the salbutamol case came out in December 2017, everyone was shitting themselves, myself included. We'd only recently been reminded what something like that could mean for the future of the team and everyone associated with it, and we were in a state of limbo for a few months until Froomey was cleared of any wrongdoing by the UCI. However, we were all certain that, despite him being exonerated, we were going to face even more hatred at the 2018 Tour.

As we headed to the race's Grand Départ in the Vendée, over in western France, we were saying to each other, 'If it was bad last year, God knows what it's going to be like this time.' We drove into the team presentation and actually had no clear idea what we were in for over the three weeks. However bad we thought it was going to be, though, it was set to be ten times worse. As we rolled into the parking area, they were already giving us the finger. People had made banners, and the two words that I heard for those three weeks ringing in my ears were *dopage* and *tricheur* – cheat.

Just before we got off the bus to ride down to the team presentation, we had a little talk from Dave. He told us: 'Whatever happens, boys, whatever happens, we can never react, we CANNOT react. If we react we'll be going home. It's as simple as that.' We knew the race organizers were aware it could get a bit spicy and they were on our side. But, as Dave had underlined, if we reacted at all, if there was any confrontation, we'd be out of the race.

As we rode through the streets to the Tour presentation podium, we passed between two walls of people shouting abuse. You couldn't fail to notice the hatred. There were even a few fans who were spitting. When we got to the foot of the stage, G did react. This was a surprise as he's the most relaxed guy. He can get shaved by a car when he's out training and won't get riled. He started to square up to a guy in the crowd who'd grabbed his arm. 'What the fuck do you want?' he yelled at this bloke. I think we were more taken aback by G's anger than anything, but I grabbed him and pulled him away before it could develop into something more serious.

When we got up on the podium, it was nuts. Just about everyone who was there booed – kids, pensioners, all jeering at us. It was that bad that we just started laughing. We couldn't help it. It was one of those situations where if you don't laugh you'll cry. The organizers then made the silly mistake of trying to interview Froomey. He couldn't hear the questions that he was being asked, so when they held the mic to his lips he just started talking, making up his reply off the cuff, saying those things you'd expect the defending champion to say just before the race starts – 'Great to be back', 'Looking forward to it', that kind of thing. But even on TV they couldn't hear what he was saying. Then we got the same treatment after we came off the podium and rode back through the streets to the bus.

We were all pretty horrified when we got on the bus, Egan Bernal most of all. Our Colombian climber had had a great season up to then and was making his Tour debut and he'd had no idea how bad it would be because he'd not seen what we'd had to deal with before. It was kind of up to you where you sat on the bus. Some of the guys had their particular seats, but if there were, say, two Spanish-speaking blokes on the team, we'd put them together. So Jonathan Castroviejo, for example, would be next to Egan in order to keep an eye on him. Anyway, Egan's seat was on the front row, which meant he could see everything that was going on as our bus edged through the crowds. All of the colour went from his face. He clearly wasn't enjoying what he was seeing. 'What are we going to do?' he said to me. I told him, 'Don't worry, mate, it's OK.' One of the directors clearly clocked what was going on: when we went down to the bus on the morning of the first stage, they'd moved Egan to the back so that he couldn't see the fans and witness the abuse they were giving us.

When stage 1 got going, the team started riding for the bunch sprint at the finish. We were sat second team, bubbled up in our little pod. There was an ever so slight bit of wind, but there was no pressure at all. We were to one side of the road as usual. As we were racing along, Egan came up to me and asked, 'Can we ride in the middle of the road?'

'What do you mean?' I said to him.

'Well, get some of the guys, maybe you or one of the other big guys, to ride down the middle of the road so we're not close to the fans on the side because the amount of shit we're getting is scary,' he explained.

'Mate, if a team is riding in front of us, we can't just plough our way through the wind to the middle of the road. Right now we're doing 40K, 50K an hour past the fans. They can't do anything much. But I think what you have to realize is that in a few days' time we'll be going up mountains at 10K an hour next to these people.'

I could see his face just drop as the reality of that hit him. 'Right, OK,' he said.

As the days passed, we raced in our normal fashion, right at the front but to one side of the road. There was still plenty of abuse, but we just got stronger off it. We developed this kind of us-against-the-world mentality. Fuck them all. G took the jersey on the first big day in the Alps and we were determined to keep it. Whatever they were going to throw at us, we were going to keep the jersey all the way to Paris. The funny thing was that the hostility worked to our advantage in a way. That was the closest group I've ever been part of and it was because of the circumstances we found ourselves in. Each morning I'd say, 'We're leaving the bus now. Whatever happens at the end of the stage, the yellow jersey stays on this bus. There'll be no confrontations, just let it all go past us. The best way we can stick two fingers up to the lot of them is to keep the yellow jersey on this bus.'

There was just one hiccup in the end, and that was down to me. The abuse was at its most intense early in the race, to the extent that it became laughable. But I lost my sense of humour one morning. We were on the bus having the team meeting before a stage start and there was an old guy outside with a sign saying 'Sky Go Home'. Seeing him out there just pissed me off. When we went to sign on, I clicked my pedals on and as I went past him I quickly grabbed the sign out of his hand and shoved it up my jersey. When I came back to the bus, I showed the boys what I'd got and then threw the sign in the bin and thought nothing of it.

Nobody ever wanted to interview me at the end of a stage. They were always after the superstars. But when we got to the finish of that stage, three or four press outlets came up to me: 'Luke, Luke, can we have a quick word?'

I thought it was a bit strange. 'Yeah . . . what's happening, boys?'

Then I realized what they were after. 'What happened with

the fan at the start? The confrontation over the sign, the confrontation with the Frenchman?'

Right on cue, our press manager came over and I rode off
before I said the wrong thing. I did do an interview a bit later,
and the inevitable happened. I got slammed by the media.
They tried to make us out to be the bad guys, and that got the
fans going even more. When we were in Carcassonne on the
rest day, for instance, there were cars coming past our hotel
at night beeping their horns, doing laps around the block,
waking us up every time we dropped off to sleep.

We had a bigger security presence around us during that
race. Froomey had a security guard, an ex-military guy who
never left his side. Even when he was in massage he would
be outside his room. Even in a time trial this guard would
follow him.

I'll go more deeply into events at that 2018 Tour in the next
chapter, although I won't be giving anything away by saying
that Froomey didn't win it and that the 2017 yellow jersey
would prove to be his last. In early June 2019, I was heading to the Tour de Suisse when the news came through about
Froomey's awful crash during the recon of the Dauphiné TT,
and I was told it was really bad. At that point it was never
about 'Oh no, he's not going to be OK for the Tour'. We were
concerned about how he would be as a person, what it was
going to mean for him in the long term.

I went to visit him after Suisse and pre-Tour in the hospital
in Monaco. Beforehand, I'd been wondering what I could take
him to cheer him up a little. I didn't want to take him food
because I knew he wouldn't eat it. So I googled sports stories
about comebacks and bought him a book about that. Inside
it, I wrote something like: 'Enjoy this story about a comeback.

In three years' time, you'll be writing your own story about your own comeback. You'll fucking smash it, mate!'

When I visited him, he was a hell of a mess. He looked like a decrepit old man, battered, a huge bruise on his hip like a rainbow. His leg looked horrific. Having seen the state he was in then, the injuries that he had, it's astonishing that he managed to make it back to the Tour at all, even if he wasn't anywhere near close to the level he'd been at when he was at his peak. As I said at the start, the guy's an absolute pit bull.

Geraint Thomas on Luke

The first thing to say about Luke as a road captain was that even when we were just kids he always wanted to organize stuff, whether it was devoting money or time to something designed to help the group, or arranging some sort of activity with everyone. That was the case when he was fourteen and remained so when he was thirty-four. He always had that sense of leadership.

When it comes to racing, I think two things jump out. Obviously, the Tony Martin incident is one of them. While it probably wasn't one of Luke's best moments, I think it showed his commitment to the team. It showed the extent to which he – and Tony as well – were doing their job for their teammates and leaders. They weren't thinking about themselves at all. It showed the lengths he'd go to for the boys.

The second thing that stands out – and I don't know if Luke will remember this – took place on a Tour stage in one of the very early years. He was just starting out as a road captain in races of that stature, and I remember that a break had gone away that was quite dangerous. The race had been hard and I remember Luke saying something like, 'Oh, it's OK. Let's let it go.' But I was like, 'No, maybe we need to just close it down now, because otherwise it's going to be a tough day.' It was a lumpy stage and we would have had a long day riding behind the break, so we ended up closing it down and a smaller group then went away that was easier to control.

It was a moment Luke definitely learned from and he never did anything like it again, which I think is another key characteristic of his. I think he was always willing to take on board other people's points of view, to learn from them and absorb that lesson so that it became part of his own thinking. I see that as a big strength, one that's underestimated by a lot of people.

11

Me and G

No matter what their favourite sport, kids will always imagine playing it at the highest level. Young footballers dream of Wembley, cricketers of Lord's, and for budding cyclists like the ten-year-old Geraint Thomas and the seven-year-old me, it was the Tour de France. It still seems incredible that we both ended up not only riding it but doing so multiple times, and for the same team. It's absolutely mind-blowing to think that one of us ended up winning the greatest bike race in the world and the other was at his side crossing the line on the Champs-Élysées in Paris.

I've already highlighted the warrior trait that's a fundamental part of any successful GC rider. G has that in spades. I could always see it, right from those early days together in Cardiff. But it became very apparent as he rose through the hierarchy at Team Sky. My first race as road captain, the 2014 edition of Paris–Nice, was also one of the first stage races in which G was the leader, alongside Edvald Boasson Hagen, who was our main man for the sprints and stage wins.

I don't remember having any particular emotions going into the race. Being road captain was never a nerve-racking experience, because it just came naturally to me. I'd probably been playing that role on occasions before then, sometimes taking over and making calls without even realizing what I was doing. The first part of the race went well for us. G took the lead halfway through, held the jersey for a couple of days, then lost it to the Colombian climber Carlos Betancur on this wall of a finish in Fayence, not far from Nice. The next day, on the penultimate stage, he was in second place, just a few seconds down, when he went down in the rain. He slid underneath a crash barrier and his back was cut to bits.

We were roommates for that race and, as is often the case with cuts and abrasions on your back, you'd have initial treatment from the doctor and then clean them again in the shower at the team hotel. Obviously, he couldn't see what he was doing, so he asked me to give it a scrub. His wounds were horrific, with bits of gravel still in them in places. I had this gauze-like sponge and started rubbing his back with it and he didn't even flinch. I'd have been bent over in agony, but it suddenly made me think, 'Right, now it makes sense. You don't feel pain.' He just braced himself and took it. That's pretty much G in a nutshell. When he's racing, he doesn't feel pain, or more precisely he can ignore it to a ridiculous extent. This gives him quite an advantage when it comes to winning big bike races.

One other thing that makes G stand out is the amount of respect everyone has for him, both on and off the bike. He's earned that in two ways: firstly, with his palmarès, which include an Olympic gold medal in the team pursuit and victory in most of the major one-week stage races on the international calendar; and secondly, with his work ethic, which you can't fail to be impressed by.

He's one of the hardest-working guys in the peloton, if not *the* hardest-working. He's quite old school in his approach to losing weight, too. I don't want to say that he starves himself, but it's pretty close. If you look at Jonas Vingegaard, he's a natural GC rider who I imagine gets down to his race weight fairly comfortably. Tadej Pogačar and Primož Roglič are similar. Of course, they have to be super careful about what they eat, but G's natural weight is significantly higher than what he has to be at for a Grand Tour. If G was a normal bloke, he'd be 82 kilos, but he has to get down to 67. If Vingegaard didn't ride a bike for ten years he'd probably still only be 62, and he needs to be 58. There's not many GC guys like G. Brad Wiggins was like that, then you have to go back to maybe Miguel Induráin to find the last Tour winner who was a comparative heavyweight. Froomey was different again, because he's just a skeleton of a bloke and lean anyway.

When the team were in Majorca for training camps, you'd see G at breakfast and then again at dinner. Everyone else would come back after their five hours' training, but he'd be out all day. He'd ride super slow, but for as long as he could. He did a forty-two- or forty-four-hour week. During those camps we did a three-day block of training, had a rest day, then another three-day block. Even on the rest days, he still did four or five hours. The way he saw it, he was there to work and there wasn't much else to do. Although he rarely lets loose, he goes big when he does, no doubt because he spends so much time being hard on himself and his body. For the most part, though, he's the ultimate professional.

When it comes to racing, G's a bit of a silent assassin. He won't really ask much or even say too much. He's like that too in team meetings, preferring to have conversations on a one-to-one basis rather than holding court in front of every-one. I don't think he likes to talk in front of a group. He'll chat to the DS and to me, and sometimes I'd propose something on his behalf. Yet, when he does talk, everyone listens. He tot-ally commands the room.

His breakthrough success as a stage race leader came at Paris–Nice in 2016. He'd already won quite a bit before then, both stage and one-day races, but that was a signifi-cant step up. He was the quickest of the overall favourites in the prologue on the opening Sunday. Then we tried to shake it up in the crosswinds on the first stage with QuickStep's help. The peloton did split but all the favourites were in the front group, so it didn't make any significant difference to the standings.

The clearest memory I have of that stage was giving Richie Porte a bit of support. He'd won the race the year before for Sky and had moved on to BMC at the end of that season. After it split, I was next to Richie, who was a bit isolated. He'd been wearing a jacket, had taken it off towards the end of the stage and was trying to shove it up his top, but couldn't manage it. He had it clenched between his teeth for about 500 metres, trying to work out what to do with it, when I called across to him: 'Richie, pass it here, mate.' I took it and shoved it up my back, and I remember thinking, 'I don't want my team to see me with his jacket when I get to the finish.' So I went straight to his bus and gave it back to him.

After that day in the wind, the race was very close, partly because the third stage to Mont Brouilly in the Beaujolais region halfway down the east of France was taken out because of snow. G took the lead on the penultimate stage after going clear on the Madone d'Utelle climb with Alberto Contador and Ilnur Zakarin, who won there. That meant that we went into the last day with G leading Contador by fifteen seconds.

We then faced what's become the traditional finale at Paris–Nice, running over some smaller climbs inland from the Côte d'Azur initially, then returning to the coast via the Col de Peille, before tackling the finishing circuit in Nice with the Col d'Eze as the final ascent. We suspected that Contador would attack on the Col de Peille, which is a tough climb, and he went full gas right from the bottom. That was effectively the end of my race, and I dropped back close to the second team car to follow what was unfolding ahead of us.

Sergio Henao did a great job that day, keeping the momentum going in the chase group behind Contador, who had Richie and Tim Wellens with him. It went right down to the wire, Wellens outsprinting Contador for the stage win, with G in the group that came in a handful of seconds behind them, which meant G won the race by four seconds overall. I remember I was halfway down the Moyenne Corniche just heading down into Nice when I heard that he'd hung on and won the race.

It was a big stepping stone for G. I remember him saying, 'If I never win another big stage race, it doesn't matter. I've won Paris–Nice.' He couldn't quite believe it, and it was a really strong field as well with Contador pushing him all the way. He'd prepared incredibly well for it and it could have been the biggest win of his career. 'It's fucking Paris–Nice, man!' he said to me that evening as we celebrated his victory in Monaco. G's always been good at finding that balance between setting a target and knowing when it's the right time to kick back, and that night we had a good few drinks along with his wife Sara and her parents, who were over. Although we had some big races in front of us, he wanted to mark the fact that he'd won one of the most prized races on the calendar.

Winning Paris–Nice was big, but it didn't alter the fact that G was still well behind Froomey in the pecking order within Sky. His TT win on the opening day of the 2017 Tour didn't change that either, and he knew that better than anyone. The shift in status really began when he won the Dauphiné in 2018. Like Paris–Nice, that's usually a very closely fought event, but he cantered to victory after Sky creamed everyone in the TTT. He was the strongest rider on the four mountain stages that followed as well. Froomey had just won a very taxing Giro d'Italia and still had the salbutamol case hanging over him, which could have resulted in him missing the Tour. So the team were glad of a strong, dependable back-up option in G.

Going into the 2018 Tour, there was a really strange dynamic within the team. It was a shock for everyone that G had performed so well at the Dauphiné, but we were still very much focused on Froomey. They weren't co-leaders. G was still the number two, and we all backed that decision I think, even Geraint. He'd won Paris–Nice, he'd now won the Dauphiné, and they were incredible victories. But the Tour, as they say, is the Tour. It's a different beast entirely, and it was still the Froomey show.

I'd say that the first questioning of that pecking order arose on the morning of the stage 3 team time trial at Cholet. It was partly triggered by events on the Tour's opening day, which is guaranteed to be one of the most nervy of the season. There'd already been a couple of crashes in the final 20K, with Egan Bernal and Wout Poels caught up in one incident. With 5K left, Froomey was the next victim. As the peloton barrelled around a sweeping left-hand bend, a Katusha rider inside him was forced to the right, clipping Froomey and sending him somersaulting off into the roadside field. Although he got a soft landing, came out of it OK and was then paced into the finish by Kwiato and me, he finished fifty seconds behind the sixty-strong front group, in which G was the only representative from Sky.

In the meeting prior to the team time trial, you always discuss the strategy if any mishap happens to befall your protected riders. That day, they told us that if there were any issues with Froomey in any part of the TTT we would wait for him, even if it was with a kilometre to go. Then they added that if G had any issues over the first half of the course, we would wait. After that, he'd be on his own. We were all a bit surprised by this. I felt, because we were only at stage 3, that it was too early to write off one of our strongest guys by effectively saying that if he punctured a kilometre beyond the halfway point, we wouldn't wait for him. He'd lose two minutes and almost any chance of contending for GC. It didn't add up to me.

I said in the meeting that I thought it would be sensible to give Froomey and G equal billing for the day, and that if anything happened to either of them at any point we would wait. I pointed out that there were eighteen days of racing still to go and asked whether we should be ruling one guy out so early on. Although there's actually only a very small chance of some kind of issue affecting your leader in a TTT, as road captain I felt that was one moment where I needed to query the team's strategy, or at least say that I wasn't too sure about it. However, the buck stops with the DS, and Nico said, 'No, we only wait for Froomey for the whole course, and for G it's to halfway.' In those situations, you have to accept what the DS says as he's the boss. G was a little bit pissed off and that was the first moment where there was, not friction exactly, but a feeling of 'OK, let's see how this develops'.

As it turned out, neither of them had any issues during the TTT and the next key stage came three days later with the short but steep finish at Mûr-de-Bretagne in Brittany. Dan Martin won the stage with the GC favourites close on his heels. However, Froomey, who'd adopted his usual tactic on the climbs of pacing himself, lost five seconds when the riders in front of him failed to stay with the strong guys at the front, including G. It wasn't much over the course of a Grand Tour. He'd just shown in winning the Giro that he had the capacity to overturn significant time deficits. The Tour, though, is a big step from the *corsa rosa*.

Coming out of that Mûr-de-Bretagne stage, G, who was second on GC behind Greg Van Avermaet, was fifty-nine seconds ahead of Froomey and looked a tad stronger. As a result of this, the team's strategy was tweaked. Even before we got to that cobbled stage into Roubaix where we should have taken time but no barrage was put in place behind the peloton when it split, we were more focused on looking after both G and Froomey.

I'd found the whole leadership situation very tricky since the beginning of the race. As road captain, I'd been told we needed to protect both guys, but that Froomey was still number one. G had been my friend for a long, long time, but I was very close with Froomey too, and I had to make a conscious decision to put friendship to one side and accept that I was doing a job. I had to be professional, and there couldn't be any favouritism. I had to do what was best for the team.

Then we got to the first big mountain stage to La Rosière in the northern French Alps.

That year, the UCI had cut the number of riders on each team, so we'd had seven instead of eight at the Dauphiné and other week-long races, while there were eight instead of nine at the Tour. This was designed to improve safety by lowering the size of the peloton and to reduce the grip the strongest teams could have on races, but it made no difference at all. Anyway, Castro and I had done our bit as the favourites went up the Col de Pré, leaving Egan, Kwiato, Moscon and Wout with Froomey and G. As they led what was left of the peloton on to the foot of the final climb, which was close to 18K long, Alejandro Valverde and Tom Dumoulin, two of our GC rivals, were about forty seconds ahead of them.

Moscon, who'd been dropped on the previous climb and had then descended like a demon to get back up to the group of favourites, gave all he had left early on the climb. After Gianni swung aside, Wout took over, then Kwiato did a really long pull, which whittled down the group of favourites and ended Valverde's hopes. When Michał ran out of gas with 5K to go, G, taking advantage of the fact that we had strength in numbers, attacked and quickly bridged up to Dumoulin, leaving Froomey twenty or so seconds behind with the likes of Romain Bardet and Dan Martin.

The final few kilometres underlined how difficult it was for Nico Portal to work out the balance of power between our two leaders. For me, G was the strongest and the final kilometres were the first time that he clearly showed that. Having jumped across to Dumoulin, he sat on him, then jumped again in the final kilometre just as Froomey was closing in behind having gone clear of his little group.

Until G's final attack, it had looked like Mikel Nieve, who'd been in the breakaway all day, would hang on to win. If anyone deserved to have a Tour of France stage victory it was Mikel. He'd joined Mitchelton-Scott that season after spending so much of his career committing himself to others at Sky, where he'd been on three Tour-winning teams. I felt a real mixture of emotions when I heard that G had caught him 300 metres from the line, a touch of sadness to go with the elation of knowing that one of my best mates had won the stage and taken the yellow jersey.

This was where things became really tricky for the team. G winning the Dauphiné was one thing, but he'd now ridden everyone off his wheel on the Tour's first big stage in the Alps. He had the best form. Froomey, though, was the defending champion, the superstar with four Tour wins to his credit. He looked very strong too. Before that La Rosière stage, everyone, even us, had been wondering how it would play out, and that day gave us the answer. We had two legitimate leaders, filling the top two places on GC.

On the team bus the next morning prior to the big Alpine stage to Alpe d'Huez, Dave made the point that we were in an incredibly strong position. We were only halfway through the Tour, but it was already ours to win or lose. The Alpe d'Huez stage underlined that.

Froomey had asked on the bus if he could attack 5K from the top of the climb. In the end he made a dig a kilometre or so after that, quickly gaining 20 metres on the yellow jersey group, but was unable to stretch his advantage beyond that as he would have done when at his very best. Bardet, Dumoulin and G bridged back up to him. There was some cat and mouse between them leading into the resort of Alpe d'Huez, allowing Mikel Landa to reel them in and, as he reached them with 700 metres remaining, attack. G was first to respond, the only one to do so. He swept around the roundabout at the bottom of the drag up to the line and powered away to win.

It underlined that he was the best guy in the race. We were twelve stages in and he was leading Froomey by one minute thirty-nine seconds, with Dumoulin third, another eleven seconds back, and the rest slipping out of the picture. When I spoke to Nico over the course of those days in the Alps, we were both of the same mind: it didn't matter who won the race as long as they were in our team. Dave was saying the same. 'Who gives a fuck if it's G or Froomey?' was his perspective. As long as one of them wins – happy days. But, obviously, G was now our best prospect. The only doubt was his ability to keep hold of the yellow jersey for another ten days. It's one thing leading the Tour during the first week, as he had done the year before, but it's a challenge of an entirely different level managing that over the race's final week.

The next test came at Mende, a favourite finale for the Tour with a 3K climb averaging 10 per cent that leads up to a finish on the runway of a small airport. We controlled it really well early on. There were almost thirty guys in the break, but we'd been careful to make sure that none of them were a threat to us on GC and were happy to let them go and sweep the bonus seconds at the intermediate sprint and the finish. I led the peloton into the bottom of the final climb, then Wout, Kwiato and Egan controlled on the steeper ramps, before G and Froomey went on to the finish together.

This might make it sound like our progress towards Paris was pretty serene, but I should point out that we were still getting plenty of abuse hurled in our direction – and worse!

Twice during that race I had piss thrown at me, and on that climb at Mende I got off my bike and confronted a bloke who spat in my face. My job was done for the day and I was going up at my own pace. Stupidly, I was on my own. In those situations, where you're riding slowly and trying to preserve as much as you can for the days still ahead, I always tried to be in the middle of a group so that the fans couldn't get close to me. You knew that when you were dropped you were susceptible to idiots at the roadside because there are no cars or motorbikes around you to fend them off.

Mende was such a short climb, though, that I thought I'd ride it on my own. It was a dumb move. This guy started running next to me and was shouting right into my face. I was looking forward, hoping that we'd reach a policeman on the side of the road or that the bloke would get bored – not reacting, not reacting. And then he hawked and spat straight into my face. I felt it hit me and instinctively stopped and got off my bike. He took a few steps backwards and I said, 'Get over here, you fucking prick! Come here!' I took a step towards him. He took another step back. Then every time I stepped forward, he stepped back, mimicking me. I glanced around and realized that there were quite a few people around us and none of them were on my side. I was in a very vulnerable position, so I got back on my bike and carried on up.

When I got to the finish, I was worried that someone might have got some phone footage, but nothing ever surfaced luckily. I was worried because we'd been told that if there was any aggression at the race, we should never bite back. However, I don't regret confronting someone who spat in my face.

One thing I should stress is that it was very much a minority of fans who were giving it out like this. But, of course, you never knew where the next clown was going to be. As road captain, it was important to ensure that no one's head dropped, in the way that we did for Egan in the first few days. After a few stages we became quite numb to it, but that didn't make it any less horrible. We were being sworn at, punched and had urine thrown at us, and we couldn't react. You'd be riding along stinking of sweat and piss. It didn't feel like sport, a day for fans to enjoy bike racing. The way we were treated was absolutely disgraceful.

As I said before, that was the closest Tour de France team I was ever a part of. All that aggro brought us closer together. I lost count of the times I said on the team bus: 'Fuck them all. All that matters is that we take the jersey to Paris.' Most other riders and teams were on our side too, including the French ones. I had French riders coming to me and saying, 'I'm sorry that you're having to put up with this,' because they could see how bad it was. I think they were shocked by it. I'd ride up next to someone, and say, 'Can I ride in the middle of you guys?' They'd think I was being silly. I'd tell them, 'You watch what happens.' Then they'd witness the abuse we were getting. Honestly, it almost felt like it was us against the world.

After Mende, we headed towards and then into the Pyrenees, where we arrived at the one point in the whole race when I absolutely didn't agree with what was discussed on the Sky bus. This took place ahead of the very short stage to the Col de Portet, the one that began with the top riders on GC starting on an F1-style grid in Luchon. Froomey was always straight when it came to saying what he wanted and he asked, 'Am I allowed to attack on the final climb?' They said he could as long as Egan was able to stay with G.

I remember thinking, 'This is bullshit.' While we'd been

saying that it didn't matter who won the race for us, our strategy had always been to protect the top guy. Now we seemed to be playing our top two riders off against each other. We had strength in numbers, riders in first and second place. It wasn't up to us to attack. I said something like: 'Shouldn't we all stick together and if G cracks, then Froomey carries on and takes over the lead? If G doesn't crack, he wins the race.'

By this point, G was really confident. He knew he was the best, so he played it quite cool. In fact, I reckon he handled the situation really well. He could have thrown his toys out of the pram, but he dealt with it very professionally. Only when the two of us spoke together after the briefing on the bus did he admit how pissed off he was. There didn't seem to be a plan for the last climb. Froomey had a free role and it appeared the management were happy to see how that played out.

When the yellow jersey group got on to the Col de Portet, I think Froomey attacked largely to show that he could. He responded to a move by Primož Roglič, even gave a brief pull, his move prompting Nico to tell him to sit on Roglič's wheel and use him. But when Dumoulin surged to the front of the chasing group, they were quickly reeled in.

G, tucked in behind Egan, who was having another super day, never really looked like he was going to crack. Froomey, though, was starting to struggle. As they approached 4K to go, he went on the radio: 'I'm not feeling super. Slow down a bit.' When Roglič attacked again soon after and G followed him, Froomey was done. In the end, after Nairo Quintana had taken a solo win ahead of Dan Martin, G rode clear of the other GC guys to extend his lead, while Froomey was shepherded in by Egan and dropped to third overall behind Dumoulin.

Credit to them both, really, because they handled it well. It could easily have boiled over, but I do think Froomey was genuinely happy for G. It also helped that one of Dave's strongest assets was man management. He sat down with both of them to discuss the situation and did speak to us all on the bus. The management team could clearly see that there was the potential for conflict, but put out the fire before it really got going.

What swayed it in the end was the simple fact that G was the strongest rider in that Tour. The way he performed over those two stages in the Alps gave him immense confidence ahead of the Pyrenees, and he retained that all the way to the finish. He didn't get carried away, though, and allow himself to think that he had the race won. I remember saying to him with just a few days to go, 'You're going to win this Tour, man, you're going to win it.' But he didn't want to contemplate that, to curse his hopes in any way. Even going into the time trial on the penultimate day, when he was two minutes clear of Dumoulin on GC and pretty safe, he wouldn't talk about the prospect of winning. 'I don't want to jinx it,' he told me.

It was pretty wet that afternoon and I couldn't control my nerves. I was all over the place. I was thinking, 'If there's one person in the whole peloton who's going to high-side this, it's G.' I wasn't the only one thinking like that. The whole team were jittery. G's calmed down a bit now, but back then he had a reputation for being upside down more than he was the right way up. He did crash a lot, but that day he did exactly what he needed to, as had been the case all the way to that point. He stayed out of trouble, took the opportunities when they were available, and no one could argue that he didn't deserve to win the yellow jersey. He'd won two of the toughest mountain stages, including Alpe d'Huez. He'd been fucking awesome.

The next afternoon on the Champs-Élysées did feel different from the other times I'd ridden up there as part of a winning Tour de France team. We had the team photo taken at the back of the peloton early in the stage, and then loads of people wanted pictures with G so I moved up through the bunch. Then he came up and called me to the back again. He'd got a Welsh flag from somewhere. 'Just hold this for me,' he said as we had pictures taken. That was such a classy thing to do and was one of the proudest moments of my career. When you think that we go right back to a seven- and a ten-year-old riding around the streets and the track at Maindy, it's an incredible story. I don't know of another one like it in the history of cycling, of childhood mates who rode right to the very top.

He gave me a signed jersey, which said: 'From the bright lights of Maindy to the Champs-Élysées, we fucking did it!' It was pretty special and it's something I'll never forget or take lightly. We went all that way together and then spent a full three months partying to celebrate that we'd managed it. Mission accomplished.

12

Egan's rise and Ineos's fall

While my knowledge of the sport's history isn't anywhere near comprehensive enough for me to assert definitively that we were the first team in history to win the Tour de France with four different riders, I can't think of another squad that has achieved this remarkable feat. After Brad in 2012, Froomey in 2013, 2015, 2016 and 2017, and G in 2018, Egan Bernal continued that incredible run of success in what turned out to be one of the most astonishing races I've ever ridden.

The 2019 Tour was the first we rode in Ineos colours, after Sir Jim Ratcliffe and his company bought out Sky to become our primary sponsor on 1 May that season. That big story was followed by another the following month when Froomey had his awful crash at Critérium du Dauphiné, which ended any hopes he had of joining the exclusive list of five-time Tour winners – Jacques Anquetil, Eddy Merckx, Bernard Hinault and Miguel Induráin.

Going into that Dauphiné, Froomey was at his best level ever, according to what we were being told within the team. They were always quite up front and wouldn't have been bullshitting us. Tim Kerrison said Froomey's training numbers had never been as good, and if that was the case, I don't think there was any reason why he couldn't have won the Tour. Froomey himself was really confident that he could do it and I'm sure he would have been right up there.

That year we were in a fortunate position as we were heading into it with three potential leaders – Froomey would probably have gone in as our main guy, even though G was reigning champ and Egan was the peloton's most exciting up-and-coming rider. So even when we lost Froomey, our prospects only dimmed slightly, from amazing to great. We still had two very strong options and were confident that we would win it. Like the previous year, we didn't care who led the race into Paris as long as they were wearing an Ineos jersey.

Losing Froomey did change the dynamic, though. As I said before, I've never been a fan of having three leaders because it stretches a team's focus too much – more work has to be taken on by fewer people. It never worked for Movistar, who tried a number of three-leader combinations, and it definitely didn't work for us when we tried it later. You spread yourself too thinly and end up on your arse. Consequently, Froomey's absence simplified things for the team because it would have been really tricky going in with a trio of protected riders.

Thinking back to that period, it's interesting to recall how Sky were ahead of the curve in recruiting Egan. Nowadays, all the top teams are chasing young talent, trying to find the next Grand Tour winner-in-waiting. However, back in 2017, when Sky began their pursuit of Egan, GC riders were expected to advance step by step, with most reaching their peak in their late twenties. Egan was the first to break that mould.

He emerged from the Colombian mountain bike scene.

The late Gianni Savio, then manager of the second-division Androni team, was tipped off about his ability and brought him over to Italy when he was nineteen. Egan won a stack of races over two years with Savio, who got a good return from Sky when they bought him out of his contract to ride for us in 2018. He wasn't fazed in the slightest when he joined us, quite the opposite in fact. He won a big stage race in Colombia early in the year, was lying second in the Volta a Catalunya when he crashed out on the last day, then finished second in Romandie and won the Tour of California, which was a really big target for Sky because the company was part of Los Angeles-based 20th Century Fox. Then he was huge in the Tour.

He became one of the heartbeats of the team from very early on. He'd only just turned twenty-one and almost immediately established himself as a leader at WorldTour races. He spoke pretty much perfect English, which helped him to fit in, he's a very likeable character and, like Froomey and G, he has that pit bull mentality.

This was apparent even in his first few races with us, above all when he got into a ding-dong with one of the big sprinters one day. The guy threatened him when they were jostling for position in a race, telling Egan he'd crush him and ride him off the road. Egan fired right back, telling the guy he wasn't in the least bit scared. 'You don't know where I've come from. You think that scares me? I don't give a fuck.' He told the other guy that he'd ride him off the road if he tried to do that. He wasn't intimidated in the slightest. I fucking loved that. He's got balls the size of watermelons, real *cojones*.

Going into the 2019 season, I don't think the team were considering Egan as a Tour prospect. He'd done great things already, finishing fifteenth on his Tour debut despite losing a lot of time on the cobbled stage into Roubaix and then tirelessly working for G. But leading a team in a Grand Tour is quite different from riding it as a mountain domestique. Froomey was supposedly in his best shape ever, G was Mr Consistent – you knew, race in, race out, exactly what you were going to get from him. However, when Egan won Paris–Nice, his status began to change. He got nearer to those two. As I've described already, you've got to be a complete rider to win that race, and he absolutely was during that week.

He started off by showing he could cope in the crosswinds. He was brilliant in them. Egan, Kwiato and I obliterated the field on the second day. Although he wasn't like Sergio Henao, who had no clue about how to ride in the wind, Egan was still pretty green. We talked through the tactics with him and he grasped them straight away. He knew exactly what to do and the right place to be. What's more, and without wanting to sound like I'm blowing my own trumpet, he had in me and Michał Kwiatkowski two of the very best in that racing environment. As a core of three riders, we moved together in perfect unison.

Kwiato took the lead on day four, Egan moved up to second behind him in the time trial the next day. On the penultimate stage on the Saturday, we finished up the Col de Turini, the big climb behind Nice that's famed as a key location in the Monte Carlo Rally. When they got to that climb, we had Iván Sosa, Egan and Kwiato left in the yellow jersey group and they were under threat from Philippe Gilbert, who was in the breakaway. He'd started the day quite a way back, but had played his hand really well and was the virtual race leader on the road.

The two Colombians were riding at a solid speed, trying

to control the peloton and reel in Gilbert, while also being aware not to go too fast and drop Kwiato, who was starting to struggle. In the end, Michał told them, 'Listen, guys, I'm pretty cooked. I can't go any faster, but you have to catch him. Just go!' Egan turned to Sosa and went, 'OK, let's go,' and they both got out of the saddle and just flew off – bam! They didn't catch Gilbert in the end, but Egan regained more than enough time to take the leader's jersey. Unlike Sergio and G, who'd had to battle right to the wire to win Paris–Nice, he had enough time in hand to have a relatively comfortable final day and, with that victory, take another step up. That's one of the hardest races to win and he never really faltered or put a foot wrong.

I thought then that Egan was ready for the Tour, and that feeling was backed up when I next raced with him at the Tour de Suisse, three weeks before July's main event. It wasn't the most stacked field. It was one of those years when almost all the big GC hitters had opted to ride the Dauphiné, which does tend to attract a stronger line-up. We rode in our stereotypically conservative style, regularly telling Egan that he didn't have to attack and risk blowing up. He took the lead on the first big mountain stage, won the next day on the famous Gotthard Pass and then held his own in the time trial. He won the race at a canter. Rohan Dennis was the only rider within sniffing distance of him, the rest were three minutes and more back.

At the end, I asked him how he felt the week had gone for him, and he said to me, 'I don't feel like I've got out of first gear all week.' He'd wanted to be let off the leash. He's got that Colombian mentality where they just want to race. On the stage to the top of the Gotthard, which is cobbled for the last few kilometres, he was told, 'Just stay with the team, use them and just finish with Dennis, no stress.' He pretty much did that, but said it was easy. I remember thinking, 'Fucking hell, now I can see the type of rider we're working with.' OK, it wasn't a star-studded field, but if you win the Tour de Suisse, a race that is nonetheless packed with world-class bike riders, and you barely feel like you've broken a sweat, then you're clearly very special.

From there, we went into the Tour thinking we had two cards to play. G hadn't had a great season, partly due to the demands brought about by winning the Tour. He'd also crashed out of the Tour de Suisse halfway through. But we knew that we could count on him finding his form at the right time. We also knew from the way he'd performed in 2018 that Egan had the ability to last the pace over three weeks at the Tour, and he clearly had the form to be a GC contender. We went into the race really confident of our chances.

Yet again, we ended up in second place in the team time trial, this time in Brussels on the second day, when Jumbo-Visma beat us. After that it turned into the Julian Alaphilippe show, and that ran for a lot longer than we or anyone else was expecting it to. The organizers had introduced these extra time bonuses which were always on little punchy climbs with 5 or 10K to go. He'd dart off and claim them, then keep going. He won on the third stage and went into yellow, lost the jersey at La Planche des Belles Filles (stage 6), where G especially looked good, then took the lead again on a really tough rolling eighth stage into Saint-Étienne.

Alaphilippe had produced some great climbing performances in previous Tours, but he'd never managed this on long climbs and had never been consistent through the mountains in a Grand Tour. To us, and everyone else I'm sure, he was a great one-day bike racer, a great one-week bike racer, but three weeks were beyond him. We were thinking, 'Have your glory for a week and we'll have the jersey when you finish with it, mate.' We weren't nervous at all in the first half of the race.

The race reached the Pyrenees, where there was a time trial in Pau. Alaphilippe had ridden some great time trials over the years, but we thought we'd take the jersey that day. G went into it a minute and twelve seconds down, with Egan another four seconds back in third. It was quite a long TT, just over 27K, very rolling and with a final kicker up to the finishing tent in the last kilometre. We expected G to gain around a minute on Alaphilippe, and he was doing well until that kicker up to the line, when he wilted a bit. Pretty much every rider slogged their guts to get up, then Alaphilippe came along and sprinted up it like it was nothing, before finishing with a big heroic skid beyond the line. As I said, he was putting on quite a show, and the French fans were lapping it up. He not only held the yellow jersey, but won the time trial and extended his lead. Suddenly we were worried.

Next up was a summit finish on the Tourmalet. Everyone was saying that Alaphilippe didn't go well at altitude, that he didn't like long climbs. Now he faced a 19K climb rising to more than 2,100 metres. The racing didn't follow the usual pattern when the GC favourites started up the Tourmalet. No one team managed to impose itself. It was almost as if everyone could sense that they had an opportunity and went for it, particularly the French. They not only had Alaphilippe in yellow, but Thibaut Pinot was right up there too, the pair of them seeming to feed off the euphoria among fans at the roadside.

In the final few kilometres, Alaphilippe looked like he was done at long last. He was on the back of the yellow jersey group, apparently set to crack at any moment. But he never did. Instead, when Pinot attacked in the final few hundred metres, Alaphilippe found another gear from somewhere and chased after him. They finished in that order. G lost time but stayed in second on GC, two minutes back. Egan lost a bit too and ended the day three minutes back in fourth.

By that point we were two-thirds through the race and there wasn't a crack in Alaphilippe's armour. We just stuck with the process, though. That basically boiled down to no easy kilometres and keep chipping away. We didn't believe that the Frenchman had the same engine strength and endurance as Egan and G over the course of three weeks. We figured that after two weeks the accumulation of fatigue would catch up with him.

That process also included the latest of our marginal gains. We were right at the cutting edge when it came to nutrition. A few of the guys on the team had started weighing their food, making nutrition really specific to each individual – a major step on from the starvation diets that had previously been adopted by the likes of Froomey and G. I'll confess that I wasn't one who went down this path. I never weighed a meal, even in my last couple of seasons when there was some real pressure to do it because a lot of guys were. I wanted to retire and be able to say that I'd never weighed a meal in my life. Maybe this was stupid, but one of the things you can enjoy during races is your food, because of the calories you're burning. I always seemed to get my fuelling just about right and never really dealt with a nutritionist.

We were using ketones as well by then to improve

performance and recovery, as were a lot of the other teams. We kept thinking, 'We're doing everything right. We're looking after ourselves. We've got the best of everything. It will pay off.' We just had to keep the chain tight, keep applying pressure on Alaphilippe, and not let him off the hook at all.

Finally, the day after he seemed to come back from the dead on the Tourmalet, he did crack. It was at the end of a long stage through the Pyrenees that finished up the Prat d'Albis climb above Foix. Jumbo-Visma were pulling for Steven Kruijswijk, Groupama-FDJ were pulling for Pinot, and Alaphilippe eventually lost ground 5K from the finish after Pinot and Egan attacked. With the yellow jersey struggling, the other GC contenders all piled in. Alaphilippe retained the lead, ninety seconds or so ahead of G, with less than thirty seconds then covering G in second and Egan in fifth, with Kruijswijk and Pinot in between.

We then had a couple of transition stages to the Alps, where the race finally swung in our favour, although a moment of stupidity meant that I ended up having no part to play in this after I got myself kicked off the race. It all happened when we were coming into the bottom of the final climb on the stage into Gap. I was trying to bring G up to the front on the outside, got blocked by Jumbo riders and then elbowed my way into their line. As a result of that manoeuvre, the kind you see all the time in the Classics, Tony Martin took umbrage and we ended up in a bit of a shoving contest. It was handbags really, nothing more.

The finish line was on the other side of that hill and when I got there our media officer, George Solomon, came across. He said he didn't know exactly what had occurred, but that

I should go back to the team hotel, which was close by. Not long after I arrived there, Nico Portal came into my room and explained that we had to go back to the finish area to see the UCI commissaires. 'Am I in trouble?' I asked him. He nodded.

Nico, Dave B and I made our way back. I knew there and then that if you go into that UCI video room it's only for one reason. If they're going to fine you or hand out some minor penalty, they don't summon you before doing it. But when you go in there, you're pretty much fucked. We were in that room for more than an hour, watching the incident through with the commissaires. It's unbelievable how many cameras they've got beyond what we see on the television. They had every angle of the brief bust-up, some that I've never seen since. We tried to fight our corner, insisted that the dispute didn't amount to much, but they weren't having it. I was disqualified.

They had Tony Martin in there as well, although separately from me. He was kicked off the race too. Afterwards, Dave, Jumbo team manager Richard Plugge and the media guys decided that Tony and I should do a video together and bury the hatchet. It's still on YouTube. Give it a watch, because it's the cringiest thing ever. We're like two primary school boys who've been told off and are being forced to say sorry to each other. We were both sat there thinking, 'Just get me out of here.'

When I got back to the hotel, I went to see all the boys to say how sorry I was. My mind went back to the year before when Gianni Moscon had been disqualified from the Tour after a similar altercation. We all knew that he was well aware that he'd let us down, but there's not much that you can do or say about it. It's not the time to say 'Bloody hell, mate, you messed up!' It was one of those moments when you try to console them.

The next morning, the show rolled on. Everyone got up, had breakfast, got in their cars and buses, and went on their way. I was left at this Campanile hotel, in the car park with a rucksack and a suitcase, waiting for a taxi to take me to the airport. I was old news already. I'd said the night before that if there was anything I could do to help if I stayed on then I would – handing out extra feeds or anything like that. But the incident with Tony had generated quite a lot of heat in the press and it was decided that it would be better if I went home. I could have been a distraction.

My overriding feeling leaving the race in that way was disappointment, not for myself, but because I was letting the other guys down. I'd given them an extra workload. It was my job to be solid and reliable, and I'd left the boys in a situation where they had to pick up the slack. The only silver lining was the fact that I would have had minimal impact on the four stages that were left. There were three big days in the Alps before the finale in Paris, and the last day I could have had an impact was the one on which I was disqualified. Knowing this didn't make me feel a whole lot better, but it was something.

When I got home I decided I wasn't going to watch the race, but I couldn't stop myself because I knew that Alaphilippe was going to crack. Sure enough, Egan gained some time on him the very next day over the Galibier into Valloire. On the stage after that, Egan attacked once more on the long climb of the Col de l'Iseran, where the Frenchman was dropped again. They were heading for Tignes that day, but a freak mountain storm blew in, bringing torrential rain that caused a landslide on the descent off the Iseran, forcing race officials to end the stage at the summit of that pass. Having been the first rider to reach it, Egan was declared the stage winner and leapfrogged Alaphilippe to take the yellow jersey. The next stage was shortened as well because of the freak weather conditions, and that ended with G moving into second place overall.

The team always had a big party in Paris after the Tour finished on the Sunday, and on the Saturday morning Fran Millar, the team's CEO, called to invite me over for it. I told her I wasn't interested. I just wanted to stick my head under the bed covers and not come out. I tried to brush her off, but she wouldn't have it. 'You're coming – I'll book you a flight,' she insisted. I told her that I didn't want to be there. I didn't want to see the rest of the team because I felt like I'd let them down. She wasn't having that, though. 'You did seventeen days of this race and they won it. You should be here. They want you here. They said they want you here,' she said, so I agreed to go over.

I flew out on the Sunday morning, helped some of the staff to prepare for the party and sat down at lunch to watch the race with Jim Ratcliffe and his family. I knew that I'd fucked up big time, that what I'd done didn't reflect well on the team, that it was embarrassing for the team and for me. But they weren't ever going to let me stay at home. It was a classy move on the team's part, backing a rider who had fucked up. I'd done my seventeen days. I'd done the Tour de Suisse. I'd done my altitude camp. And I did the right thing in the end by going to Paris. It was a very memorable moment celebrating the yellow jersey with Egan and the other guys.

That was our seventh win in eight seasons, but everything was about to change, initially in a wholly unexpected way thanks to Covid. As the pandemic spread and lockdown became inevitable, racing gradually closed down. Paris–Nice just about ran its course, but for some months it looked like it would mark the end of the 2020 season, and that the Tour and every other major race on the calendar would be postponed. Thankfully, though, as restrictions started being lifted, the UCI and race organizers managed to salvage the season by rescheduling most of the postponed events.

The Tour got a new slot in September. Heading into it, we were aware that the odds of defending the title were against us, but I still had this belief that we'd keep the yellow jersey, simply because we always had on the five occasions I'd ridden the Tour. We had a good leader in Egan, the defending champion of course, but he was having back issues and his preparations didn't go smoothly. Despite this, I still had this core belief – it's our fucking race! We'd win it somehow. But it didn't happen.

Egan had some good performances in the run-up to the Tour but started to struggle at the Dauphiné, which he was forced to quit halfway through. Come the Tour, he was well in contention for the first half of the race but began to lose ground on the climbs in the Massif Central. He then cracked on the hairpins leading up the Grand Colombier in the Jura. When we got to the hotel that evening, he was limping and in a lot of pain. He'd done all that he could that day to try to limit his losses, but had really suffered. He managed one more stage, then abandoned. The race then turned into a battle between Primož Roglič and his Slovenian compatriot Tadej Pogačar. If Egan had been fully fit, he could have challenged them. He was right at their level, but his back issue prevented him from doing that.

It was such a different feeling when we reached the Champs-Élysées at the end of the race. Every previous time I'd ridden on to it I'd had a hint of yellow in my kit because we were about to win the Tour. That year, though, it was Pogi and his UAE teammates who had the yellow trim, and that fucking hurt. It used to be us.

Right then I realized that I'd taken winning the Tour for granted. We'd achieved greatness and I'd been too laid back about it. I hadn't realized how special it had been to be on a Tour-winning team five years on the trot. Somehow it became run of the mill. We followed the process, turned up and we won. We were always in control as well. There hadn't been a moment when we'd thought, 'We're X minutes behind and we're not going to win this.' Not even the year before when Alaphilippe had given everyone the run-around. We were always confident that he'd crack.

That 2020 Tour was the turning point for Ineos. Coming out of it, there wasn't much of a gap between Ineos, UAE and Jumbo-Visma. The three teams were pretty much at the same level. Since then, though, year by the year the gap between Ineos and those two has kept getting wider. Ineos has dropped back into the pack chasing those two teams, perhaps third best but, sadly, not really in the hunt for the yellow jersey.

I do think we got complacent. We started to fall into a rut, allowing ourselves to think, 'Let's do what we did last year because it worked.' But even if what you did last year worked, you still need to keep tweaking, evolving and improving. You can't stand still and ever think, 'We'll stick to what we're doing.' Even if you only improve 1 per cent, that's progress. You're still moving in the right direction. But we just copied and pasted, because it was so successful. The sport was evolving, but our

approach wasn't. In addition to that, we lost a lot of key personalities from the team – Dave, Nico, Fran, Kerro – people
who'd had a fundamental role in our success. They were all
ground-breaking in their different fields and just as hard to
replace as a Tour-winning rider.

On the racing side, meanwhile, Ineos have been set back
by factors beyond the team's control. In cycling, a significant
part of a team's budget goes on salary to one, perhaps two,
maybe even three leaders. Like you do at the racecourse, you
back your horse. You stake a lot on those riders, but there's
no guarantee that they will be able to deliver, perhaps due to
injury, lack of form, a loss of motivation. Ineos backed Egan,
and it was absolutely the right thing to do, but it hasn't paid
off in the way that they hoped, due to circumstances beyond
anyone's control.

In 2021, Egan won the Giro d'Italia, which underlined that it
was the right thing to do. Then, in January 2022, just a month
into a five-year contract, he crashed into the back of a bus
when training in Colombia and almost died. Like Froomey,
his comeback has been nothing less than extraordinary. He's
worked incredibly hard, shown endless courage to get over
horrific injuries. If he keeps getting better, that's great. If not,
he's already done amazingly well. For the team, though, it is
extremely difficult to replace a rider like Egan. There aren't
that many like him or Froomey or Pogi or Vingegaard in any
single generation. Ineos do have the resources to find the next
rider in that mould, but it will probably take years.

13

All for one

One aspect of bike riding that often gets overlooked when analysing what drives performance and success within teams is the atmosphere behind the scenes. As a result of there being so much focus on racing, it's easy to forget that professional riders actually spend most of their time in non-race situations – training, resting and recovering, sometimes for weeks at a stretch when there's little to distract. Bingeing on Netflix is one way of fending boredom off, but I've always been an advocate of trying to bring a group together in these moments, by playing cards, having a quiz, having a laugh in the right way, even partying when the moment's right. I'm absolutely certain that if you enjoy yourselves off the bike, you'll be successful on it.

I've already described some episodes where having fun during the down times from racing resulted in the group being more cohesive and successful when we were back in the saddle. One of the most enjoyable races I've ever done was the 2012 Tour of Britain, because of what we did off the bike as well as on it. I believe there's a direct correlation between those two things. It can't be forced, though. It's got to happen authentically and naturally, and almost always comes from the riders. The food fight at the Tenerife camp and me earning the right to shear Blemski's flowing locks after riding up an absolute brute of a slope in the big ring were good examples of this.

As road captain, I always felt that one of my roles was to encourage a good atmosphere within the team, which is why I'd go to races and camps with a poker set, or organize a game after dinner – anything to get the guys together. This would start in December when the team gathered at a Majorca hotel for its first pre-season training camp. From the outside, the focus might have appeared to be on getting the miles in. That was important, of course, but it was also the first time all of the riders, including the new signings, were in the same place. So it was the perfect moment to build a strong bond between the riders, between the staff, and obviously between those two groups together.

As part of that, I'd organize a dinner for all the racers – no staff allowed, just the riders. Before we went, someone would always tell us, 'Whatever you do, don't get drunk!' Of course, that's precisely what we'd do. There'd be all kinds going on. For instance, we did a credit card lottery, where one card got picked out and that rider had to pick up the tab for the entire evening. It was all pretty stupid stuff, but it created that critical feeling of togetherness.

There was similar stuff happening on the training rides too. I can remember we had a bit of fun at Leo Hayter's expense one year. Each morning, we'd roll out of the front door for a five-hour training ride and after fifteen minutes he'd say, 'Can we have a piss stop?' We'd all pull over and someone would tell him, 'Leo, have a piss before you leave your hotel room, otherwise we'll end up being out for seven hours rather than five.' But the next day he'd do it again, and we'd all have to stop and wait for him.

So one morning I told him, 'Leo, if you want to piss, just stop. We're not going that hard. You get in behind one of the cars and chase back on.' Sure enough, he stopped, and as we continued on I said, 'Right, boys, let's push on now and then hide.' Every club team will have done something similar, holing up down an alley. We got ourselves out of sight and Leo came past doing 6okph on the bumper of a DS's car. The DS, of course, was in on it, and although he spotted us, Leo didn't because he was right on the bumper giving it full beans.

On these group rides, we always had our live location on in a WhatsApp group so that we could see where someone was if they happened to get lost. So we started riding again, and as we were mincing along we were watching the live location. Leo was going further and further into the distance, and didn't twig the fact that he hadn't caught us despite the fact we'd only been riding at 3okph and he'd now been going at 6okph for twenty minutes after his brief stop. The DS just kept driving and driving, and we could see this pin of Leo's getting kilometres and kilometres ahead of us.

A little bit of harmless fun like that would have everyone in stitches – you'd be talking about it at dinner and it would help to build camaraderie. Of course, when we did finally catch up with Leo, the first thing we did was stop and have a piss right next to him. I can also add that I don't recall having to wait for him again after that.

Boosting this cohesiveness became even more essential during Covid, when everyone became cautious about the contact they were having. At the December camp in 2021, all the bars and restaurants in Majorca were closed, so while I was travelling out there I'd bought a magnum of red wine. On the first evening, I said to a few of my closest mates on the team to come to my room for a glass of wine. Then whispers began to spread about this and more of the boys were asking me about it on the bike the next day. On the first night there'd been four of us. On the second there were ten, and the numbers kept escalating and pretty much everyone was there. At that point I started a drinks club group on WhatsApp. Each day I'd nominate someone to host us and get the wine, which they had to try to smuggle in. We then tipped the cleaner 50 euros to get rid of all the bottles for us.

Inevitably, we got caught in the end, but not in the way we were expecting. The team used a bedroom on the ground floor for storage. They put the excess kit bags in there and all kinds of other stuff. One of the staff had her suitcase in there and when she opened it one day loads of things were missing and they realized that the room had been burgled. They checked over the CCTV and saw the guy who'd done it jumping over the 6-foot fence to break into the room. However, they also noticed that twenty minutes before the burglar had done his dirty deed, Andrey Amador had climbed over the fence with two shopping bags full of red wine.

Of course, as soon as the first gathering had taken place in my room the team knew exactly what was going. In fact, Rod had said to me, 'Listen, we've got no problem with it. Just make sure it's not cliquey, that everyone's invited, and you wake up the next morning and do your training 200 per cent and we'll turn a blind eye.' He told me that on one of the first nights, so while most of the guys thought we were being sneaky, the managers knew what was happening and I was playing along with it. It can't have been too difficult for them to twig what was going on because we had thirty blokes in one room in a hotel where we were the only guests.

I think if we'd crossed the line even once that would have been the end of it. Say one morning we'd woken up and a couple guys were hung over and didn't ride their bikes, or didn't do the efforts, or didn't do the correct training, or missed a meeting, then we'd have been fucked. They would have come to me or another senior rider and said that it had to stop. After all, full-time athletes don't need to be drinking wine, but most nights it was just a glass, maybe two, and a lot of banter.

Having that drinks club was ten times better than going to a nightclub or going karting to team-bond. The fact that we thought we were being sneaky, that we were the only ones in on the ruse, brought us together. It was just the riders. We didn't tell anyone else. And all we did was sit in a hotel room, play some music and have a laugh. I think it paid off, too. We really made a good group in that 2022 season, partly on the back of that.

There was mutual respect between riders and staff because we all wanted the same thing – to be successful, to win bike races. I'm totally convinced that moments like that did help us towards that goal because it brought the riders closer together and did the same for the whole team. This was vital because, as I've already mentioned, we're competing in a sport where you're losing far more often than you win. When you lose, you need to do it in the right way, thinking that you and your teammates gave all that you could.

As a direct consequence of this, I've always been an advocate of the adage that any win is a big win in pro racing. If a rider is first over the line on a stage of the Coppi e Bartali or the Tour du Poitou-Charentes, it's a major success because you've beaten 150 or more blokes who devote their lives to cycling. I'm not saying you have to go and have ten pints and swing from the chandeliers. Marking that success might involve nothing more than sharing a couple of bottles of wine between the riders and staff, and a pat on the back for everyone's efforts, because we're in a business where you're losing substantially more than you're winning.

Whenever I was part of a winning team, when you've contributed to that success, I always felt I'd won too. I know the staff on the team felt exactly the same. They're as invested as the riders are. They're the heartbeat of the team. They work so hard. When you wake up and look out of your window, the mechanics' trucks are open and they're already at it, the swannies (as the soigneurs are often known) too. They'll be preparing musettes (shoulder bags with drinks and snacks) and all kinds of other bits and pieces. When you get back to your room at night, the trucks are still open and the swannies are still running around. The staff are doing everything they can to ensure that pretty much all we have to think about is racing our bikes to the best level we can.

There's another aspect to this sense of unity. I always felt, and I'm sure most of my teammates would agree, that the team were fully committed to us. Being paid well is part of this, but there were other reasons why so many riders have spent multiple years racing in Sky and Ineos jerseys. I'll illustrate this by describing the backing I got from the team when I went through one of my lowest points as a racer. It's the story of how I smashed my right leg to pieces during my brother Matt's stag do in Prague, which was just a few days after I'd helped Froomey win his fourth Tour de France title in 2017. I'm telling this tale because I've heard and read several different versions of it and none of them are right, some ridiculously wide of the mark. So here's what actually happened.

As best man, I arranged this trip for Matt and his mates. After a big night out on the first evening, we were going white-water rafting the next afternoon. We all had our wetsuits on, walking along the riverbank towards the boats, and we were playing this odds game, daring each other to do dumb stuff basically. So I might say to someone, 'What's the odds of you necking that pint?' They'd weigh it up and maybe reply, 'Ten to one.' Then we'd go, 'Three, two, one,' and both say a number between one and ten. If it was the same number, they'd have to neck the pint.

So Matt said to me, 'What's the odds of you jumping in that river?' The rapids machine wasn't on and the water wasn't moving fast, so it looked fine. I said, 'Ten to one.' But what I didn't know is that the bed of the river was painted black and you couldn't actually gauge how deep it was. I could have jumped in at other points and I'd have been OK, but where we were there were just a few inches of water. We both went, 'Three, two, one . . . seven!' Without a second thought, I jumped in.

My leg was straight as I went into the river and it exploded. They quickly got me on to the riverbank and I told them to crack on with the rafting, that I'd be fine. At that point it didn't hurt that much because there was so much adrenalin pumping around my body. The instructor said that I must have sprained my ankle and he wanted his wetsuit back. By then I was thinking, 'Fuck you and your wetsuit, mate, this feels pretty bad.' He wasn't too fussed, though, and started pulling this wetsuit off my leg. I pointed out that I didn't have anything on underneath it as we'd gone there dressed in our civvies and had taken them off in the changing room, so I was bollock naked. That didn't stop him either. He peeled the wet-suit off and, as the boys swept by on their rafts, I was starkers as I waved and cheered them on from the riverbank.

By then, an ambulance had been called. Wondering how bad it was, I tried to lift my leg and my foot stayed exactly where it was, my skin stretching under its dead weight. It was a clean break, and at that moment I went from 'I've messed up a bit here' to 'This is very fucking serious'. They got me in the ambulance and I asked for some painkillers. 'Just give me anything,' I urged them. They gave me a paracetamol and I was like, 'This isn't going to work for me, mate.'

The hospital was an absolute hellhole. I was wheeled in on a bed that was like something out of the Second World War, with big cowboy wagon-style wheels on it. There were four of us in this awful room. It was like going back in time. I was lying there with every kind of thought going through my head. What's my career going to look like? How is the team going to take this? I was shitting myself.

I called Dave Brailsford because I knew I had to tell him what had happened. It turned out that he'd already found out from someone else. I said, 'Dave, I've fucked up here, I'm not in a good way—' He cut in on me, and this is exactly what he said in response: 'Luke, let me stop you there. You're one of our own. We always look after our own. Whatever you've done and however you've done it, I couldn't give a fuck. We're going to get you back on your bike and you're going to be OK.' In that instant I sank into the bed and felt relieved. That was a huge weight off my shoulders. He never once asked me what had happened. As I said, I heard all kinds of stories, the craziest one being that I was drunk and I'd jumped off a bridge, but I wasn't drunk at all. We were just messing around, no more than that.

A team doctor, Richard Usher, flew out that same day. Sadly, he's passed away since, but he was a hell of a man. They wanted to operate on me in Prague, but he could see how poor the hospital was and he told me that they were going to fly me home on a private air ambulance. They booked it for an hour later, but there was a problem because we were going to fly into Cardiff and the airport was set to close for the night before we landed. So the team said that they would pay for the airport to stay open longer in order for us to be able to fly in that evening.

When I was taken on to the air ambulance, a guy got this briefcase out and it was full of every type of medication. I told him, 'Just give me the strongest painkillers you've got.' My leg still wasn't stable because it hadn't been operated on, and I was on morphine and all sorts, so drugged that the flight home was, thankfully, all a blur.

I should add too that I didn't have to put my hand in my pocket once. They never docked my salary. I think the total bill from the start to the end of my rehab was about £300,000, including that air ambulance. I'm not sure many other teams would have done that for me.

I quickly had my rehab mapped out. As part of that I worked with a physio, Nathan Thomas, who lived in Wales and was with me every day from quite early on. When I was still in hospital, Fran Millar, my agent Andrew McQuaid, Nathan, Richard Usher, my wife Cath and me talked through the injury with Dr Anthony Perera. We made the 2018 Tour de France the end goal of my treatment. The plan was for me to be physically better than I'd ever been before.

Nathan told me to regard the lay-off as an opportunity to work on my physiological weaknesses. Early on, I wasn't sure about being able to get back into racing, let alone be a better rider if and when I managed it. But they planned it all out week by week, month by month, and I just stuck to what they wanted me to do. I'd never been as devoted to anything like that before, I'd never even followed a training plan as strictly as I did the various parts of my rehabilitation. I even focused more on the nutritional side of things.

My rehab started with a simple task – going to the swimming pool and walking neck high so that there was no weight on my leg. I'd walk lengths of the pool for hours. I'd go back two days later and try to repeat this a step further up the pool in slightly shallower water, progressing very slowly. I used an Alter-G machine, a zero gravity treadmill. We transformed one of our bedrooms into a gym, and then did all the rehab in there. I was in there for hours with Nathan. I also put my spare time to good use by employing an Italian teacher to come to the house three times a week as I'd always wanted to learn the language but had never had enough time to devote to it.

All of the way through this, Cath was incredible. I was useless in the first few weeks, couldn't do anything. She nursed me like a baby through that period, helping me to the toilet, to get dressed. We had a bed put in the lounge because I couldn't get up the stairs. Very, very slowly, I started to make progress. I was able to ride the turbo, with the good leg doing the work and the injured one propped up on a stool.

The first time I rode a proper bike was on the velodrome,

because there were no bumps and only a very small risk of crashing. There was a derny session going on, riders being paced by a motorbike around the track. The derny was going round the whole time and you could jump on and off when you wanted to. They said to me, 'Stay out of the way at the top. That's the plan, no risk of any crashes.' I got on and did that for ten minutes, then I was bored. So I jumped in behind the derny and did the session. After that there was 'go till you blow' behind the derny – you do one lap, change, and keep going like that till you blow. There was me, fellow pro Tom Moses, semi-pro Steven Bradbury and a few others. We didn't actually go until the final person blew, but we went to the final three and I was one of the three, although I was fucking swinging by that point.

When I could train on the bike, I was more devoted to it than ever before because my career had flashed before my eyes. The thought had gone through my head that the leg break could have been the end of it, especially after Dr Perera had done the operation. He was the first person who came to see me after the op and I asked him what the prognosis was at that point. 'Do you really want to know?' he said to me. I told him not to sugar-coat the situation. 'OK,' he said, 'there's a good chance that you'll never ride a bike again.' After he left the room, I burst into tears, but I remember thinking, 'I'll fucking show you. I'm not having that.'

I was determined to find a way back to racing. I decided that if my right leg wasn't going to be as strong, I'd compensate with my left leg. I got so stuck into the training that I stopped thinking that I wouldn't get back. Then, in December, I went to the team camp in Majorca. The initial plan was for me to be with the boys in a supportive environment and try to do maybe an hour a day or so. But the team structured things so that I ended up doing three hours with the boys some days, then one of our soigneurs – a Polish guy called Jacek Walczak who I became very good friends with – would meet me and drive me back to the hotel in what became known as 'the Polish ambulance'.

Early in 2018, my first race back was the Tour of Abu Dhabi. The team told me that there was no pressure on me at all, I just had to ride round – and it's actually quite an easy race on which to get from A to B each day. The first stage was a sprint and we had Kristoffer Halvorsen primed for it. With about 10 or 15K to go, I said to him, 'I'll give you a lead-out, mate,' and I did a really good one, dropping him off in a decent position. The next day, we woke up and it was crosswinds. I was thinking, 'Oh, fuck! Here we go.' It's dangerous racing in those conditions, as well as being physically demanding. It split multiple times and I was in the front group all day, and at the end of it I thought to myself, 'Right, now I'm back.'

I'm sure that I did come back better than ever, and the proof of that was the 2018 Tour, which was arguably the best one I ever did. I think I was better than I'd been before and not as good in the ones that came after. I think the rehab that I went through post-injury in the back half of 2017 and into 2018 made a big difference. I sacrificed everything, which I didn't really do very often. I was always a committed professional, but maybe didn't do everything right. But once I got taken out of the sport and understood that my career was in jeopardy, I realized how much it meant to me and I gave it everything. It didn't make much difference in terms of personal results because I was always working for our leaders, but I did notice the effect that going through those processes had on my sensations and feelings on the bike, which is the main thing. Throughout the course of the Tour I felt solid, robust, and I finished it on good form. I probably could have had a good end to the season at ENECO, Hamburg, maybe Canada, if it weren't for the fact that G won the thing and we ended up on the piss for four months.

One thing that I'm really concerned about as I swap racing for directing is that the pressure on riders is now so intense – not only when it comes to performance, but also with regard to training, nutrition and the psychological aspects of competition – that there's no room for fun, for larking about, for doing the kind of stupid stuff that we sometimes got up to at Sky and Ineos, which helps bring riders together. We're hearing a lot more about burn-out, about young riders turning their backs on racing because they're getting over-whelmed by it. Obviously, I understand that riders need to act professionally, but it's not healthy to expect them to be switched on 100 per cent of the time. Riders need the opportunity to kick back, to enjoy their poker schools and food fights. They feel better for them and, crucially, race better too.

I think Ineos and Sky got the balance right on this. From the outside, those teams have been seen as having a very rigid approach and robotic culture, but that couldn't have been further from the truth. We had a good balance between work and pleasure. I should stress too that 'pleasure' didn't mean we were always drinking and getting pissed. There were times when you'd drink a lot and have a laugh. But letting your hair down doesn't necessarily always mean getting drunk. We'd go out for dinner, do some go-karting, whatever we wanted really. I think the sport in general has lost this, and it's taking a toll on riders.

14

The Northern Classics

When I properly started on the rehab from my leg break my long-range goal was the Tour de France, but I knew I'd need to be well raced if I was to get selected for it. Consequently, I set myself a target earlier in the season. When I first began walking in the local pool, I worked out that there were 200 days to Paris–Roubaix. I wrote that figure down on a whiteboard and every morning I'd wipe it off and put in the new one – 199, 198, 197 . . .

I always felt most at home in the Classics, particularly the northern ones that begin with Het Nieuwsblad and Kuurne–Brussels–Kuurne, which usually take place on the last weekend of February, and conclude with Roubaix on the second Sunday in April. Although there are some exceptions, Tadej Pogačar being the most obvious one, these races are tailor-made for the peloton's bigger units, the heavyweights, riders who are 70 to 80 kilos and more.

Unlike lighter guys, who'll often give you the wheel they're on, the Classics specialists don't yield to anyone. It's a completely different game, one where you have to be prepared to get physical. As a result, I always reckon the level of bike handling is higher compared to the mountain climbers or the GC guys. You see riders bouncing off each other, but you know that they're unlikely to crash. Everyone has confidence in everyone else's ability, despite the fact that some of the manoeuvring might seem dodgy.

What's more, I always felt confident on the cobbles at Roubaix and the Tour of Flanders, both with regard to my equipment and myself. The Classics are races where you shouldn't be starting if you're not self-assured. If someone had said to me, 'Luke, you've got to do the Tour de Suisse,' but I didn't fancy it for some reason – the route, how it fitted on my racing programme, form, whatever – I'd go with it and get it done. But if someone says to you that you've got to do Paris–Roubaix and you don't want to, then you absolutely should not be there because you've got to be 110 per cent committed. If you feel even a slight hint of hesitation, a touch of nerves, you're fucked.

Coming back from that injury, I knew the Classics would provide an acid test of my rehabilitation and state of mind. So every day I wrote a new number on that whiteboard with Roubaix in mind. Ultimately, though, my leg healed and form returned quick enough for me to line up at Flanders the Sunday prior to it. Mission accomplished. However, neither of those two Monuments went the way I was hoping.

At Flanders, I was disqualified for riding on the pavement. It happened as I was descending the highway that reaches the sharp right turn that leads to the foot of the Oude Kwaremont climb. I was on the right-hand side of a group of fifteen, maybe twenty riders, and someone flicked right, creating a wave that forced three or four guys on to the pavement. I was the furthest across and had to brake to avoid some fans. Up to then I'd finished Flanders every year, and I reckon that it's tougher to finish than Roubaix. It was like a little badge of honour, and I felt hard done by after what I'd gone through to get there.

I was told via the radio: 'Luke, you've been disqualified, pull out of the race.' I asked why, heard the reason and carried on riding. There was radio silence for a few minutes, then the DS came back on and said that the UCI commissaire had told them that if I didn't pull out of this race immediately the whole team's results would be void. So that was it. At that point I was only the third rider to be disqualified for that offence after James Lowsley-Williams and Bryan Lewis at the 2017 Tour of Britain. Since then, the only other rider I know of to suffer the same fate was Marlen Reusser in the 2024 edition of Gent–Wevelgem. I guess my DQ stopped everyone riding on the pavement in the intervening years.

At Roubaix a week later, I was in a good position again. Then, 300 metres before we turned on to the cobbled section at Mons-en-Pévèle, there was a flick in the line and I went down. From the TV motorbike that was behind my group, you could see me on the floor with my gammy leg sticking out and then Edvald Boasson Hagen rode right over it. Cath said she was watching at home and shouted out 'Oh no!' when it happened. I didn't finish Roubaix either, although my leg came through the Edvald test with flying colours.

I'd had a pretty good run there too up to that point, riding every year from 2012 and finishing every time up to 2017. Thinking back to those editions of Roubaix and looking over the results, one thing that stands out is how close it all was – and by that I mean that the race exploded so much later than it does now. Back then, you'd still be fighting for position going into the cobbled sections after the Arenberg Forest, which is itself about a dozen sections in of the twenty-nine or so in total. There'd be big groups still together late in the race, but these days it's in bits by that point.

Before I go into why the tactical approach to 'The Hell of the North' has changed, I'm going to go back to the first few editions I rode, starting with 2014, when Brad and G were our leaders for the race. At that time Brad was getting towards the end of his career and, after winning the Tour, had publicly said that his next major goal was to win Roubaix. There was quite a push from the team with the equipment. They tried suspension bikes, put quite a lot of time, money and energy into them, but I don't think that investing in that kind of innovation for the Classics was really part of the team's DNA. In the end, we didn't really do much more than say that we wanted to up our game. We didn't recruit Classics specialists. We didn't really do any additional recons or test other equipment. As for the suspension bike, it barely worked and was next to useless.

I was Brad's wingman in that 2014 Roubaix, and Bernie Eisel was the road captain. Our approach with Brad that season and the next was to get him through Arenberg, which has always been and still, I think, remains the tipping point where you get rid of a lot of the peloton's cannon fodder. Beyond there, it becomes a lot less tactical – less of a shit fight and more of a physical contest. If you have the legs to move up, you can at that stage.

We thought that if we could keep Brad in contention past the Arenberg, then he could take care of himself. We'd encourage him to go early and go long. Because of who he was and what he'd achieved, we knew that as soon as he attacked he'd be surrounded by motorbikes, and they play a huge role in racing. If he could get ten seconds clear, he'd be gone. He'd have a lot of motorbikes in front of him and could just chase them, benefiting from the draught. He was Olympic time trial champion, and they'd never see him again. However, no one was prepared to give him an inch.

The plan was for the team to hit the front going into the section at Haveluy, the one before the Arenberg. The cobbles run due east initially, then at halfway there's a 90-degree right-hand turn. The wind was from the left, a headwind. As we went right, we'd string it out. From there, it's 5 or 6K to the Arenberg, and Salvatore Puccio and I were instructed to keep the pressure on there so that we'd go into the Arenberg on the front and Brad would be safe. We burned a lot of riders doing that and I recall G going away with Tom Boonen, Bert De Backer and another guy. I can also well remember how it really hurt me riding that 5, 6K towards the Arenberg.

It's worth adding that tactic of getting into the Arenberg in the front and the rest taking care of itself is pretty much the same approach we had with Pippo Ganna in recent seasons. I actually remember having the same conversation with Pippo that we'd had with Brad, that if we could get him to the point where it's man-to-man and physical, beyond the shit fighty bit, he'd be fine. But we had to get him past the crazy bit.

G, Boonen and De Backer's little group was fifteen, twenty, twenty-five seconds ahead – never very far away. They were almost in sight for 50K, but the advantage they had – and this is crucial at Roubaix – meant they got a clean run into every section of cobbles, while we were all fighting behind, going fast sometimes, then slowing. Eventually, though, they were reeled in. Brad managed to get up to that group and went with a full gas attack about 8K out from the finish, but they brought him back too. As soon as they'd done that, Niki Terpstra countered and he won it, with G seventh and Brad ninth in the group that came in just a few seconds behind him. Brad's attack could just as easily have been the decisive one.

When you're in the midst of a race like that, everything happens ten times quicker than it does in a Grand Tour, which are more predictable – you know a lot more about your rivals as well because after five days you kind of suss them all out. I would say, though, the road captain's role is very similar in both types of racing. No matter what the race, you're still focused on keeping your troops where they need to be and staying with your leader. In more recent seasons at the Classics that's been Tom Pidcock, and the fundamental command would be 'Never, ever leave Tom'.

Doing that in a Grand Tour is a bit more chilled than it is in the Classics simply because you've got more time to make decisions and you're more certain of the unfolding scenario. Whereas in a Classic, everything can seem to be going smoothly, then suddenly something happens and you've missed a split, or you're out of position and attacks are firing on small roads, and sometimes you don't even know who's in the break. It's very hectic, often relentlessly so.

The tactic based around getting Brad through the Arenberg also worked well in 2015, although we missed the podium again. I was eighth and Brad eighteenth, the pair of us just seconds behind the winning group. By the next season, there'd been a big turnover on our roster, with Brad among those who moved on, which gave Ian Stannard and me the opportunity to lead. Yogi was a level above me. He'd won Het

Nieuwsblad two years on the trot and was knocking on the door of some of the big ones.

That said, the Classics were still a minor focus for the team in the middle of our Tour de France dominance. We were probably 95 per cent focused on stage races and 5 per cent on the Classics. We often had the same wheels as the year before, the same bike. Whereas, for a Grand Tour there was so much attention to detail on Froomey's bike. They'd do anything to get its weight down. If there was a lighter bolt and it cost a grand, they'd buy it. They were fixated on saving every gram.

Despite this, there was an opportunity for me, and I wanted to grab it. Prior to Het Nieuwsblad, I was told I was going to be the team leader, the first time I'd ever had that role. That race all comes down to the narrow, cobbled climb of the Taaienberg that comes with 50, 60K to go. In certain events, the smooth gutter on the climb is closed – Flanders and the E3 Saxo Classic for instance. In others, it's open, so you can use it. This means, though, that the peloton very quickly funnels down to a single file of riders. Obviously you don't want to be too far back when it does.

I did a recon with Andy Fenn a few weeks before the race and we were riding with Phil Deignan, who asked me what the plan was. I told him you have to be top ten minimum, top five ideally going on to the Taaienberg, and if you're first that's perfect. 'I'm either going to go in first or crash trying,' I said to him. That was honestly what I was thinking. I did not give a fuck. In my head, I was going in first or I was going to crash.

Come the day, Andy did a great job and I was third or fourth coming out of the right-hander at the foot of the Taaienberg. I accelerated and was shoulder to shoulder with Greg Van Avermaet. I slightly closed the door on him and got on to the climb first. Amazing! I big-ringed it up there. I was on fire. I ended up clear with Van Avermaet, Peter Sagan and Tiesj Benoot. It was surreal. They were all well-established, pedigree riders and I was a relative nobody. I was like a pig in shit. We then caught the breakaway, from which Alexis Gougeard was the only one able to stay with us. The five of us went all the way to the finish. Unfortunately, I got a bit overexcited, completely ballsed up the sprint and finished fourth as Van Avermaet won it. But it was still one of my breakthrough results in the Classics.

G and Yogi came in for Flanders a month or so later, and I finished fifth there, which turned out to be my best result in a Classic – I was third in Kuurne the following year, but fifth in Flanders was a bigger result. Then we went on to Roubaix, where I was in the mix again, finishing fourteenth, while Yogi was in the winning group, taking third behind Mat Hayman and Tom Boonen.

I kept knocking on the door for a couple of years after that before I accepted that I wasn't going to be able to compete for the big races and dropped back into more of a domestique's role again. The next wave of talent were too powerful and too punchy, so knowing the roads only got me so far against riders who have become the gods of the sport, the likes of Wout van Aert, Mathieu van der Poel and Pogi, of course. Although I'd sussed out the Classics and knew where the key locations were in each of them, that didn't mean anything when you were up against three or four guys who were simply unbeatable. If one of them went full gas on a climb like the Oude Kwaremont or Paterberg in the finale of Flanders, the other gods were the only ones able to stay with them.

So how do you combat that? The whole peloton basically

decided that the only way to do this was to be ahead of them, and the result of that was what we called front-foot racing. Every team thought, 'If the moment for their attack comes with 50K to go, we need to try to attack with 70K to go.' Everyone needed to be ahead of van Aert or van der Poel when they made their move, but when twenty teams were trying to do this that pre-emptive move began to happen further and further out – with 80K to go, 90 . . . Now it's like 'Why don't we try to stick a guy in the early break?' If you can manage this, that rider can get a result themselves or support a teammate in the final. As a consequence of this, though, the fight for the break goes on longer and longer because so many teams want to be in it.

At Roubaix, more often than not, the break hasn't formed by the time you hit the first cobbled section close to the 100K mark. It's been the same at Flanders for the last few years. Those two Monuments have become predictable in a way, because you know they're going to be full gas from start to finish. You don't see the traditional scenario of the break going in the first 50K and the peloton then cruising for the next 50K or so on the asphalt before the carnage starts when you hit the first section of cobbles in Roubaix or the first climb in Flanders. Now it's attack, attack, attack.

To illustrate what that means from a physiological perspective, I know that someone who was in the front group at the 2024 edition of Flanders averaged 4.2 watts per kilo for the five and a half hours or so that race lasted. When you consider that a lot of the time you're free-wheeling downhill, that you're going up, left, right constantly and having to take your foot off the gas incessantly to do this, this baseline average power output is staggering. The level is so high because that's the only way of trying to compete with these three freaks of racing. We've been seeing that their answer to these earlier attacks is to move even earlier than anyone expects. In order to prevent a group establishing that they will have to fight their way back up to, they defend their interests by attacking from further out, as we saw Pogi doing at the 2024 Worlds. It's like an arms race, with attacks going earlier and earlier.

Of course, the gods don't get it their own way all of the time. We saw that in the wet Roubaix of 2021, when Gianni Moscon flirted with success, and the following year, when Ineos finally emerged victorious from the Hell of the North thanks to Dylan van Baarle. That 2021 race was one of the very last events of that Covid-affected season, taking place on the first weekend of October rather than in early April. We did the recon in the days before it and the cobbles were an absolute mess. We had loads of crashes and were wondering how it was going to be possible to race on the pavé. The organizers 'cleaned' the course after that and it dried out a bit on the Saturday, but it was raining again as Lizzie Deignan won the women's race that afternoon. Overnight, it hammered down.

The next morning was probably one of the few times I was ever on the bus and could sense the nerves of everyone around me. I know I wasn't the only one who'd gone to bed the night before thinking they were on the fence about whether they were all in or not. On the bus, Dylan told us he wasn't up for it. He was at the back when the race entered the first section, just wanting to survive the hellish conditions. I was almost leaning the same way on the bus. Then I said, 'Fuck, you know what? I'm all in. If I go down, I go down.' Whatever happened, though, I was determined to be in the breakaway. I'd go with every move, burn some pennies, poke lots of holes in my bag of sand.

There was a bit of crosswind and the break kind of went partly due to a push at the front of the peloton and partly due to a split. It was huge, thirty-one guys, including Owain Doull, Gianni and me from Ineos. Doull punctured before the first section of cobbles, so we lost him. As we approached that section at Troisvilles, I told Gianni that I'd look after him. I did back myself in that group, but Gianni was better. I led him and the group into every section. Even without riding hard, that group was splitting, but I just felt so at home on the cobbles. I didn't have a difficult moment, didn't slide, nothing.

Going into every section, we were first and second. Then it split and I was in a group of four off the front with Max Walscheid, Florian Vermeersch and Niels Eekhoff. I said to them, 'This is the golden ticket. Let's just commit.' We knew it was going to be messy behind us, with riders everywhere, but Eekhoff wouldn't ride. To this day I still think, 'Dickhead!' He was pointing to his radio saying, 'I've been told.' The other three of us really got at him about it. We couldn't understand it. If you'd written a script of the perfect race, this would have been the scenario. But he didn't ride and didn't get a result in the end, which was good because he didn't deserve one.

I punctured out of that group, but I was so at home that I decided to drop back to the original group of thirty, which had been whittled down a lot. As we approached the Arenberg, I said to Gianni, 'Let's try to get this group down now.' We needed a good working group of six or eight guys. We knew that the big guns would be arriving soon. So I entered the Arenberg first, Gianni was second. The first bit is downhill and I was thinking that it didn't matter how fast I went, I just had to keep it upright because if I crashed there I was really going to fuck myself up. I managed that, and as it started to rise again slightly I began to squeeze. The group had been reduced right down, and then . . . front wheel puncture. It went flat, and it was another one of those moments when I went, 'FFFFUUUCCCCKKKK!'

Every team has zone hoppers who have spare wheels on most cobbled sections. They're usually stationed halfway through and at the end of them. In 2024, for instance, we had five teams of zone hoppers who covered forty-seven spots in total, so there were forty-seven opportunities to grab bottles and, more importantly, wheels. But when I punctured, I was past the halfway point. I had to get to the end, and it was still a long way to the end, the best part of a kilometre.

I stayed to one side, trying to ride on this front flat. I was doing all right, wobbling a bit, but if you get off and walk it's game over. Guys were shooting past me, and then a fan reached out and pushed me on the arse to try to propel me forward. I wasn't expecting it and, as he pushed me, my wheel turned to the left and I veered across the cobbles. A split-second later I collided with Mads Pedersen, who was doing 40kph. It was like being hit by a truck and left me winded and a bit dazed. Mads came off worse, though. He was a bit of a mess and his bike had snapped in two.

The crash was my fault because you've got to have control of your bike. It's on you to keep it straight. But if the fan hadn't pushed me out, I'd have been fine. I was 200, maybe 300 metres from the end of the section. When I got to the finish I wanted to apologize to Mads for taking him out. I got his number straight away and said how sorry I was. He was like, 'No worries, shit happens.' He could not have been nicer.

I then had a look on social media and I was getting absolutely battered. People were saying that I tried to take out the riders in the group of favourites that had van der Poel, Colbrelli and Pedersen in it because Gianni was up the road. That really pissed me off. I was depicted as a kamikaze-style rider. I was fuming and thinking, 'Do you realize how much that hurt me?' Almost all of it was from Danish fans who were mad at me. I had death threats. I did a video the next morning when I was hung over after a very big night out and went on a rampage, which I shouldn't have done.

That was an interesting Roubaix, that's for sure. Gianni looked like he was going to win it till quite late on. He had a lead of about a minute and a half with 25K to go. Then he started sliding, he had a puncture, and then a crash. He was caught about a kilometre before the last difficult section of cobbles at Carrefour de l'Arbre.

As it turned out, we didn't have to wait long for that elusive Roubaix success, little more than six months in fact as the calendar returned to normal. I played quite a significant role that day as the road captain, because we made our initial move in the crosswinds after about 50K, and that certainly wasn't the plan we'd had on the bus a couple of hours earlier. That was my call, it didn't come from the car. We all just found ourselves at the front, but not specifically by design. We knew that there was wind, but as we left the bus it wasn't blowing enough to split the race. However, the breeze was strong enough to make it hard if you were at the back, so we were staying in the front, holding position among the first fifty guys, remaining sheltered as attacks went and came back. It was a bit niggly at times and drew on our energy a bit, but it was purely about self-preservation. We weren't thinking the race would split.

Then, as we went over the brow of a hill, there were some attacks and it all went in one line. I felt the wind on my right, and was thinking, 'I'm top fifty, apparently sheltered, and I can feel this.' Things just happened so naturally after that. We all found our way to the front, and I spoke to Servais Knaven, our DS, and asked him, 'Where's van der Poel?'

'At the back.'

'Where's van Aert?'

'At the back.'

I remember saying to the team, 'Let's try one time. Guys, we're going to try. If it doesn't work, it doesn't work.'

You can't race individuals. There are 200 blokes and you have to race everyone. But there are some guys you do watch very closely, you do wonder where they are. Those two were at the back, and that made it even more worthwhile giving it a try.

We got together really well, QuickStep were also there with three or four guys, and we just started rotating and kept it going all the way to the first section of cobbles. All that time I was making the calls on how to play it in the echelon.

They can be half-road or full-road. If you're full-road, it means you use the full width of the road, fanned across in the direction the wind's coming from. Half-road is self-explanatory. The echelon only extends as far as the white line in the middle of the road, with the result that fewer riders can be in the rotation. If you think of a stereotypical road, you'd probably fit around twenty-five people in an echelon when it's full-road. If you go half-road, it'll be about twelve, so it halves the amount of people who can get protection and is likely, therefore, to split the group even more.

You tend to use this tactic in a situation where riders are

sitting in the wheels and not contributing to the rotation. If it's full-on crosswind, you've got to be rotating in the echelon because it's the only place you can get shelter. If it's slightly more tailwind, or it turns to cross/head, it becomes easier to sit in the wheels than rotate. In that situation, if you're full-road, some riders can sit inside and get protection from the riders at the front of the echelon without needing to rotate. To counter that, you go half-road, so you end up with twelve guys rotating and the rest in single file at the back. Then, when the group is slightly whittled down, you open it to full-road and you can use the strength of the whole group. If, though, some guys still don't want to contribute because they're protecting teammates behind, you'd go half-road again.

This was exactly how we played it, with me taking responsibility for dictating whether it was full-road or half-road. I'd do that by simply stopping in the middle of the road, on the white line, and not following the string moving into the wind any more. Then the next guy would come around me and, as he was coming through, I'd be saying to him, 'Half-road! Half-road!' so that he didn't go full-road. I was absolutely in the zone. It went perfectly with maybe forty to fifty guys in the group, including seven from Ineos. We achieved the dream scenario of going into the first cobbled section at the front as a team. It couldn't have turned out any better for us. We had about a minute and a half on the likes of van der Poel, van Aert and Kasper Asgreen at that point. It was textbook.

Cameron Wurf, who wasn't a cobbles specialist and struggles when riding in a bunch, was able to have a massive impact that day. Before we went on to the first section, I said to him, 'Cam, your job now is to ride as hard as you can for as long as you can. Just commit. Do a time trial until you die.'

While Cam was giving it full beans, I was thinking, 'What are we going to do next, and with who?'

My job that day was to look after people, and the way you do that on the cobbles is often to sit behind them, because in the chaos, with the crowds and the noise of the clattering bikes, you don't have any idea what's going on if they're behind you. As a result, you want to lead them on to a section and then slot in behind them. This meant that as we were riding as a unit through the second section of cobbles I was behind Pippo Ganna, and he got a slow puncture about 300 to 400 metres before the end of the section where the zone hoppers were waiting. I told him to stop next to them. My thinking was that he'd get a wheel change and by the time the back of the peloton came by he'd be able to hop on again with a small acceleration. I also decided I'd drop to the back of the group so that if he ended up off the back I could drop off and pace him back on. Alternatively, if he managed to get going without getting dropped, I could take him back up to the front of the group.

This isn't a big issue, and I don't know why he did it, but Pippo rode right past our zone hopper who was kitted out in bright fluorescent green kit. He completely missed him, then pulled over at the right and stopped. This meant that I had to stop to give him my wheel. He got going quickly and got back on pretty easily. I was absolutely gutted, though, because I had to wait for the zone hopper with the new wheel. Thankfully he'd noticed us stopping and ran up to assist me, but my race was effectively over. I'd felt so strong as well. My legs were good, I was guiding the team in that road captain role. I felt like I had control over the situation, that the team had really bought into the tactic and the group was fucking solid.

They all believed in me and I believed in each and every one of them.

Roubaix is the race where numbers count more than any other event, because you need teammates to bring you into position. Dylan van Baarle is one of the strongest blokes on the planet, but he isn't great at positioning himself, so he relies heavily on being positioned if he's looking for a result. The fact that we had numerical advantage in that group of fifty meant that he was always in position. Pippo Ganna is a little similar. He's not brilliant at riding in a bunch, but physically, needless to say, he's off the charts. He had a great race that day, leading it on to the Arenberg, with Dylan just where he needed to be.

One interesting tactical thing about Roubaix is that a lot of the winning moves don't start on the cobbles. They go on the asphalt. You put the pressure on when riding the cobbles, put people in the red, then moves come after them. When you come off the cobbles, you're already thinking about the next cobbled section. Riders effectively pause for breath when it gets easier, letting down their guard a little. Dylan is an expert at attacking at moments like this. When he moves, he looks as if he's going quite easy, but he's got this perfectly fluid pedalling rhythm, beauty and power combined. He's brilliant at these silent but deadly attacks, accelerating when in the saddle. Once he'd gone, they weren't going to catch him.

We were all on cloud nine when we got on the bus. We couldn't believe what had happened. Dylan gave me a massive hug when I got there. Once we were on the way back to the team hotel, Kwiato started organizing the evening. He's Mr Logistics – he can sort anything. We'd already arranged a bit of a party, but after Dylan had won we wanted to ramp it up a level. So Kwiato booked a DJ, we had wine and champagne. It was quite an evening.

Traditionally, we'd always finish with a big night after Roubaix. This has become trickier, though, because a lot of the guys now roll on to the Ardennes Classics. Historically, teams would have a Cobbled Classics squad who would all finish at Roubaix. There might perhaps be one guy who'd do the Amstel Gold Race or something else after, but essentially a whole new squad would do the Ardennes. Now there's quite a big crossover. In the last Classics team I was part of at Ineos, Tom, Kwiato, Big Ben Turner, Dylan and me would go on to Amstel and Liège–Bastogne–Liège, while some would do Flèche Wallonne too. So the big nights out are fizzling away. We couldn't miss that one though.

Hopefully this chapter's offered a good insight into the unpredictable nature of the Northern Classics and the skills required to race them, as the final thing I've got to say – and I know that most bike fans will disagree with this – is that I don't think cobbles have a place in the Tour de France, and gravel shouldn't have a place in the Grand Tours either.

Although there are exceptions, Pogi being the most obvious on the gravel stage at the 2024 Giro, most GC riders start stages like these with the mentality that they don't want to lose the race. They're often so scared of losing their chances of contending for the jersey in a Grand Tour that they start with a bit of a negative mindset, one where their focus is on being safe and staying in position. There's no real intent to go and grab the race by the balls and exploit the weakness of other rivals, because they're generally just shitting themselves.

The one thing we all want to see in a Grand Tour is the best riders in the world going head to head. Thinking back to the

2018 Tour won by G, one of his rivals for the title should have been Richie Porte, but he crashed out on the pavé. Fans got one day of great entertainment on that cobbled stage, but it had a significant knock-on effect on the rest of that race. If he'd got to the mountains, I believe Richie's presence would have added more entertainment value to the rest of the race, thanks to the way he used to light it up on the climbs.

There's simply too much at stake at a Tour de France to expect a 58kg GC rider to deal with a test like the cobbles or gravel. I know I'm coming over as a bit of a traditionalist, but I just don't think it's necessary. Bike racing is dangerous enough as it is. You've also got to bear in mind that the GC guys will have done six months' to a year's preparation, and all that can come to nothing in an instant. So why enhance that risk?

I realize we're in the entertainment business and that everyone wants to see a spectacle. I can understand too, as an armchair fan, that the cobbles are brilliant, but we've got plenty of one-day races taking place on them. We should push these as a spectacle rather than create what becomes a bit of a freak show on a Grand Tour because it's so dangerous for the GC guys. I remember Simon Yates, for instance, telling all his teammates to stay with him and ride a cobbled stage like a time trial. If they lost a minute, so be it. He just wanted to stay out of the jungle and as chilled out as he could. He knew that if there was a split he would have a lot of guys to time-trial back towards the main group. This was an understandable tactic, but it's one based on surviving rather than racing.

As for Pogi, he's just different. You can't base your assessment of what's suitable or not for GC guys on him because he's absolutely extraordinary. You just have to look at the way he tackled the cobbles into the Arenberg finish on the 2022 Tour, or at the way he thrived on the Giro's gravel stage in 2024. He's the ultimate all-round package. He's earmarked Roubaix as a race that he now wants to win. Can he do it? Of course he can. He can do anything. He can win anything. Although there is one race that has proved elusive for him . . .

15

The hardest Classic to win

Milan–San Remo is the first of the season's five Monuments and is, by general consensus, the most unpredictable of all five. It's such a complex race, so hard but so simple. It's a piece of piss to finish, but it's perhaps the toughest big race to win.

Although it extends to more than 300K in length, its principal difficulties are crammed into the final 50-odd kilometres on a course that's essentially remained the same since the early 1980s. It used to be dominated by the sprinters, but over the last two decades more and different types of rider have come into the mix. A sprinter still does come out on top occasionally, but they've got to be at the very top of their form to beat the more punchy riders in the Julian Alaphilippe or Mathieu van der Poel mould.

I raced La Primavera, as it's known – the 'Spring' Classic – nine times and never DNFed or even came close. It was the only one of the Monuments where I had a perfect record. Over that time, the team fared pretty well in San Remo too. Ben Swift was second in 2016, Filippo Ganna matched that achievement in 2023, and Michał Kwiatkowski was third in

2019. As was the case with the other Monuments, victory proved quite elusive for us, but we finally came out on top in 2017, when Kwiato edged a three-up sprint against Peter Sagan and Julian Alaphilippe at the end of a race that encapsulated what it takes to win La Primavera.

Unlike the other Monuments where there are numerous hurdles to clear, there are two key moments in San Remo: the entry into the Cipressa climb, which you reach with just under 30K to go, and the entry into the Poggio, the race's final climb, which is 10K from the finish. If you get either one of those wrong, it's quite hard to come back. You can perhaps recover from a mistake on the Cipressa, but you can't on the Poggio, because the speed that's set there lines out the peloton so much that if you go on to it in fortieth place, you're done. Nobody's good enough to pass forty riders at that point, not even the greats of the sport.

Kwiato had won a lot of big races before he joined Sky in 2016, including the world title. He's a Swiss army knife of a rider. He's got the tools to do almost anything. He can deliver someone on the flat all the way to a finish line in a sprint. He can climb well. He can do the medium mountains. He can do the crosswinds. He's strong in the team time trial. Thanks to this range of skills, he was one of the best teammates I've ever had and we spent plenty of time working as domestiques for the likes of Froomey and G. He also gives 110 per cent. He's the epitome of loyal.

He'd also stepped up to become a leader on plenty of occasions. When he's in that role, he's quite vocal and he expects 110 per cent from everyone else. If someone's not performing as he expects, he'll really get at them. On the bus before a race he'd be saying, 'Fuck, boys, I can win this.' Not many leaders have the balls to say that, to urge their whole team to support them. He'd tell us, 'Back me. I'm good.'

That's exactly how he was on the morning of that 2017 Milan–San Remo, fired up and getting us geed up too. While Kwiato was the leader, we also had our sprinter Elia Viviani there as a wild card. His role was to try to survive over the Poggio if he could, and if the race came down to a bunch finish. But it was all for Kwiato essentially. He'd just won Strade Bianche, and we were so confident in him that if we'd had to ride from the start in Milan, we'd have done it. As it turned out, Bora took control for their leader, Peter Sagan, and that took the pressure off us until we entered the last quarter of the race when the route on spectacular roads runs alongside the Mediterranean.

The first thing we needed to focus on once we were on the coast road was taking care of Kwiato over the *capi*, three imposing headlands that come one after another, the first arriving with 55K left. By that point the pace is very rapid indeed, and the constant sweeping curves on the road interspersed with narrow sections passing through the seaside towns make it difficult to move up if you're towards the back. But we kept together in our bubble and went on to the Cipressa right at the front as a team, totally nailing that, Danny van Poppel leading the way for us and then pulling aside, his job for the day done. It's the longer and slightly tougher of the two final ascents, but almost always too far out to be a launch pad for victory in San Remo. A break did go clear going up and over it, but Bora reeled it in well before we reached the Poggio.

The key to the Poggio is a roundabout that lies 1.2K before it. We wanted to be on the front there and hold that position into the bottom of the climb, and it was my job to make sure we were. Once again, we were right where we wanted to be. If you get a chance to watch the final few kilometres of the race, you'll see that I keep looking to my left as we're approaching the right turn on to the Poggio. I'm checking to make sure that no one is coming on that side of us, because if I'd let anyone come alongside us, the guys behind me would have got squashed out and forced back. You'll notice too how I'm tracking the TV motorbike as much as possible. At 50kph-plus you get quite a draught off the motorbike even when you're not that close to it.

We hit the climb as a unit of five, with me on the front – although not for very long once the climb started – then Łukasz Wiśniowski, Gianni Moscon, Kwiato and Elia. It couldn't have gone better. If you can do that, the whole team is on the front foot. From there, our guys had to keep the pace high until someone launched the inevitable attack about halfway up the Poggio. Given the work that Bora had done all day, it was no surprise that Sagan was that man. For a few seconds it looked like he might break the elastic and go away on his own. But Kwiato began to chase and Alaphilippe followed, the pair of them bridging up to Sagan.

The three of them had a few seconds at the top of the climb. They're all demon downhillers and they edged further away on the descent, where Sagan did most of the pace-setting. Once you're off that and into San Remo, there's a tad less than 2K to the finish.

At that time, Michał was known as 'Killer Kwiato' because he was so reliable when it came to winning big races, although I called him 'Kawasaki' because he was like a motorbike on a bike. He showed both of those qualities on the run-in. Both he and Alaphilippe let Sagan keep the tempo going at the front, doing the occasional small turn themselves but saving all they could for the sprint. On a flat finish like that, almost everyone would have backed Sagan, who'd won bunch finishes at the Tour de France and plenty of other races. He clearly fancied his chances too as he kept the tempo high. But a sprint after 300K isn't like any other. After seven hours plus of racing, they become very unpredictable. Sagan led it out, got a gap, then Kwiato started to come on his left, closer, closer, with Alaphilippe coming to the left of Michał. You could have thrown a blanket over them at the line, where Kwiato lived up to his Killer nickname.

The beauty of San Remo is that it suits so many riders, and if you're one of the favourites you get one shot at victory. You can fire it on the Cipressa, but that seldom works. Most save it for the Poggio, for the top part of the climb where Sagan attacked in 2017. Everyone knows attacks will come there and is ready for them. Only the strongest succeed. You can even fire your bullet on the descent off the Poggio, like Matej Mohorič did in extraordinary fashion in 2022. Or you can hold fire till the sprint, assuming there is one. Whatever the plan, though, what comes before the final attack is absolutely critical to success. Get one thing wrong, and San Remo punishes like no other race. Like I said, easy to finish, so hard to win.

Soon after Kwiato crossed the finish line in San Remo and we'd all arrived there to start celebrating his success, he told us, 'Nobody go home, we're going to Monaco and going out full gas. We've just won a Monument!' A couple of guys did go home, but most of the team stayed and we had a hell of a night out – a big, big one.

A day or two later, Kwiato WhatsApped all of us, asking for our addresses. As I mentioned, San Remo is known as La Primavera because it's in the spring and is the first major Classic of the season. Soon after, all the guys who were on the team that day received a red Vespa Primavera on their doorstep as a thank-you present. They're beautiful. Because I was living away from home I stored it away, but this summer I'll fit it with a new battery and get it running smoothly. I've got two matching red helmets, so I'll get the Aviators on and head around Cardiff on that bad boy.

Kwiato was always very good at showing his gratitude. Whenever he won a race, the whole team would get a nice present. After he claimed victory in the Amstel Gold Race in 2022, we all got a watch from him. What's more, when you're training with him, it's almost impossible to buy a coffee, to the point where it's awkward, because every time you go to pay the bill, it's already been settled. He's a very generous bloke.

He's long been one of the heartbeats of the team. When it came to Tour selection, I think he was probably one of the first on the list, certainly before me. Pretty much every year he was the all-round package. There were some years where he was climbing inside the last ten guys, but we also had to be careful in how we managed him, and, as road captain, I had to be aware of how much he was committing because he's always so loyal. At times he'd give too much and you'd be worrying how he'd back it up.

The problem always was that because he can do anything, the easiest thing to do was to ask him to do everything. You'd be looking at a flat sprint and think that Kwiato could help. Mountains? Yes, Kwiato. We would focus on strength in numbers and we never wanted to lose him because he was so consistent for us. Luckily, he had a big enough engine to absorb it.

There was definitely a sense, though, that we should protect him a bit, because no one can do everything through a race like the Tour and remain consistent all the way through. But we had to do this in the right way with Kwiato or he'd get pissed off. He likes to do things his way, which isn't a bad thing, because his way is usually the best way. So we were always treading a fine line with him. Although it almost always turned out that he had the engine to keep performing every day and do the job to 100 per cent, there were definitely times when we'd be thinking, 'Is he doing too much here?'

16

Switching seats

After thirteen seasons with Sky and Ineos, most of them spent as road captain, I'm on the verge of a major career change in 2025, swapping the saddle for the team car to become a directeur sportif. I suspect that many bike fans would have expected me to take up this role with the Ineos Grenadiers, and I can understand why as I'd probably have predicted this too a season or so back. I never thought I'd leave.

However, I've always performed best on the bike when I was out of my comfort zone. If you get too comfortable, you can end up going through the motions a bit, and I knew that if I stayed at Ineos this would happen. Consequently, I spoke to quite a few other teams and Decathlon-AG2R La Mondiale really stood out, and I agreed a two-year deal with them.

Dominique Serieys, their team manager, has a long-term plan for the team, one that really captured my imagination. They had this presentation that showed where they are now and where they want to get to. They were very realistic in terms of the time frame and the steps that need to be taken. Even though they won thirty races in 2024, they said that they were hitting above their weight, that they'd got lucky on occasions and had some opportunist wins. They told me that they needed to raise their standards right across the board, and that they felt I could help with that, particularly on the Classics side to start with.

I liked the fact that we had some very frank discussions, about the image the team has within the peloton, for instance. I said to Dominique that one of the issues Decathlon-AG2R La Mondiale faces is that riders don't want to join it because it's seen as being too French. All the French teams are like this. They focus on French riders and staff and do things the way they have always done them. Dominique and his management team have already set about changing this, sending all the French-speaking riders and staff to learn English as part of their prep for the new season. I've been having French lessons too. This is all part of a drive to get everyone pulling in the same direction, to boost confidence and put the team on the front foot so that it's challenging in the biggest races every season.

I'm looking forward to being part of this remaking of the Decathlon team and can't wait to get stuck into this new role. As I've already said, I think road captains make good DSs and I hope that I'm the latest in the line to demonstrate that. They tend to be clever and have unusually sharp insights into the tactical side of racing because they don't have the big engine so many guys rely on for success, whether that means taking victories or just being a pro who's reliable in terms of performance.

The road captain's role is one that requires a certain amount of homework and research, not only with race routes, but also when it comes to exposing the weaknesses of other riders and teams. Nico Portal was certainly that type of rider and then went on to become a sensational DS. Mat Hayman is another in that mould, comparatively limited physiologically, but very clever tactically. You just have to look at his Paris–Roubaix victory to see that. I thought Gabriel Rasch was a good DS at Ineos too. He achieved quite a lot in the sport with a limited engine. He was clever, he learned to fight, to navigate his way around the roads, and he used that to his advantage. All those qualities are fundamental to being a good DS.

Although I've got no idea whether I'll adapt to the role as well as these renowned DSs did, I do know that I've got plenty of the qualities required for it. While most guys get fixated on certain details within a race, as road captain I would always try to zoom out and look at the bigger picture, by studying the start sheet closely, looking at the parcours and checking the weather. A DS certainly has to do that, and even zoom out further from there and look at the whole of the Classics campaign, for instance, and then zoom out again to assess the entire season. You've always got to think about what might be down the line, partly by drawing on what you've experienced before.

When it came to racing, I always had a pretty good idea of how the action would unfold, unlike a lot of guys on the start line, who can't predict what's going to happen. I used to have an idea of who I thought would be in the break, which teams would control the race, which of those teams had a good lead-out the day before, which teams were organized and which weren't. By piecing all of that information together you can suss out how the day is likely to pan out.

I'm not naive, though. In saying all this, I realize that I've got loads to learn as well, that I'm pretty green in this role – a fact that was underlined by the experience of being a DS for

Ineos at the Czech Tour in 2024. I learned a huge amount in that one five-day stage race and could clearly see that I've still got so much more to pick up. Some of these gaps will, I think, be filled naturally, by drawing on the knowledge I gained while working with so many insightful coaches and DSs, the likes of Max Sciandri, when I was on the academy, and Rod Ellingworth, who was a big influence on me both there and during my pro racing career.

Rod worked out very quickly that I had the ability to see a race. He not only helped bring that out in me, but also pushed the team to push me. I've taken plenty from him too. He's old school, likes the bare bones of a bike race and to simplify things. He was always great at sweeping away the bullshit around racing, not only getting the riders to focus on the key aspects of the job we had to do, but also removing some of the pressure and reminding us that we were meant to be enjoying what we were doing, which can get lost in modern-day sport when athletes have to invest in so many different fields to be at their best.

I obviously learned a lot too from all the DSs I worked with at Sky and Ineos. Nico, of course, was the one who really stood out. He retired from racing to become a DS with Sky in 2011, the year before I joined the team, and I think we were both on the same trajectory, me as a rider and him as a DS. Each of us was stepping into a world where we had loads to learn and we ended up spending a lot of that journey together.

Nico was one of the kindest and most generous people I've ever met and I guarantee that everyone who came across him in cycling and beyond would say the same thing. While he was incredibly hard-working and devoted to the team, he was a family man first. When we reached Paris having been away at the Dauphiné, training camps and then the Tour de France, everyone would want to party pretty hard, but he'd be there with his family, dancing with his son and daughter, having a drink with his wife, Magalie.

Just before he passed away in March 2020, we did the Tour of the Algarve. Most of the time that race finishes early on the Sunday afternoon and you can get a flight out the same evening. But that year there was no flight on the Sunday night and the timings weren't good the next morning, which meant we flew out on the Monday afternoon. So Kwiato, G, Nico and I kept our bikes and went for a ride that morning. We did an hour or so, then stopped at a café, where Nico had a Nutella pastry – he had such a sweet tooth and his love of Nutella was an ongoing joke.

After that beautiful ride, we all got our flights, and I can remember where we were when I said goodbye to him. A little over a week after that, he was sat at his desk preparing for Paris–Nice and had a heart attack. Reflecting on the tragedy of his death, I realized we were so lucky to have those final few hours with him on the Algarve, with the pressure off, just enjoying each other's company.

Later that year there was a stage start in Pau, quite close to his home in Auch. Magalie and his kids were there with us, and it was a really emotional experience, quite hard for us and very obviously so for them. They were so brave. We lined up at the start and there was a minute's silence beneath a big picture of Nico and his family. As we stood there, I kept my glasses on because I was crying.

People talk about certain exceptional riders being generational talents, guys like Pogi and Mathieu van der Poel who dominate the sport, who are the very best. That same analysis can be applied to DSs, and in Nico we had a generational talent. I want to stress that Ineos have still got some great DSs, but have they got someone at Nico's level? Absolutely not. Are there many guys like him within the peloton as a whole? I don't know, but I don't think so. He was the GOAT, and very few achieve that standard.

Whenever you had him in your ear at a race, it felt like nothing could go wrong. If something did go wrong, he'd put it right. He was gentle, mild-mannered, and had this aura about him that meant he couldn't really piss anyone off. He didn't know how to. That said, he wasn't a pushover by any means. He would not take *any* shit, not from the riders, from his bosses, from anyone. He did things his way. He'd ridden for AG2R, Caisse d'Epargne and Sky, working with some exceptional DSs at all three teams. Then he carved his own path, which is what I hope to do as well. But I'll lean heavily on what I learned from him, and if I end up being 50 per cent of what he was, that would still make me a very decent DS.

Nico was always very good at instilling belief in his riders, essentially by making it clear that he believed in you. He knew when to say the right thing – a good example being that day I quit the 2013 Vuelta and he told me that he was sure that the Tour was the race for me. You can say anything to anyone if you phrase it in the right way, even something negative, and he was very skilled when it came to that. He might have picked up a mistake you'd made or sensed some kind of weakness, but when he brought it up you didn't feel like he was criticizing you, rather that he was helping you to improve as a rider.

I'd also admit that I've got to try to replicate his calmness during races because having someone yelling at you is one of

the worst things for a rider to deal with. You don't want someone in your ear, telling you, 'Come on! Come on! Get in the
front! Move up! Do it now!' You're in one of the most stressful of sporting environments, and if your DS comes across as
stressed it just pours fuel on that fire. Whereas, if your DS is
calm, you'll feel the same way.

Nico was great at staying calm whatever happened, whether
things were going right or wrong. I think being able to do
that is a quality that sets the very best road captains and DSs
apart. They don't panic under pressure. Nico remained totally
serene when Froomey was isolated in the yellow jersey on
the Cauterets stage of the 2013 Tour, with no teammates close
by and surrounded by Movistar riders. He talked Froomey
through the stage, telling him to think of himself as a Movistar rider and go wherever they did, while always making
sure that he didn't allow Nairo Quintana or Alejandro Valverde to attack and drop him. This might sound a bit mad,
but Nico knew Froomey inside out and he knew the Movistar
managers and strategy well having raced within that set-up.

He was totally calm too when on that key cobbled stage
at the 2015 Tour with Froomey. We were supposed to be top
ten in the peloton and we were sixtieth. It might seem easiest
in that situation to tell your riders, 'Keep pushing. You'll get
through. Chop some people up. Take some risks, go up the
side.' You can stick with the plan and do what you were told to
do at that point in the race. Stick your blinkers on like a race-
horse, basically. Nico didn't do that, though. 'It's OK. Chill
out. We'll get where we have to be, but let's stay rubber side
down,' he told us – just ride, chill out, we'll get there, and
Froomey won't end up on his back.

He'd have a big influence in other ways too. I remember

on the penultimate stage of the 2015 Paris–Nice, Richie and G both crashed in the wet on the descent of the Col de Peille into La Turbie before we headed into Nice. Back at the bus, we were all saying that the tyres we were using were fast and were great in dry conditions, but they were no good in the rain. Nico revealed that he'd been telling the team for a while that Continental were the best tyres, particularly in the rain. By the time we got to the Tour that year, the whole team were running Continental thanks to that call. It was a pretty big change to make, as there was a sponsor and money involved, but Nico had by then earned that kind of influence and respect.

He had an incredible work ethic, too. He'd be studying maps before and during races, trying to work out where the best places to attack were, where the pinch points were, where we needed to be ready to respond to attacks. I think all the teams have DSs who do that now, guys whose ethos is 'If you fail to prepare, you've got to be prepared to fail'. You've got to do your homework as a DS. During my very short stint in the role at the Czech Tour, I realized first-hand how much time goes into it. What's more, the more you do, the more you know.

With that in mind, as one of the guys looking after the Decathlon-AG2R boys in the Cobbled Classics, I'll be doing my research. Even though I think I know those roads like the back of my hand, I still intend to drive every single one of them well before we get to race day. If the guys are out there on their bikes and it's 2 degrees, raining, they're fighting for victory or for a top ten or twenty finish, I've got to be able to tell them where the key moments are. It's your responsibility, your primary job. You've got to nail it.

None of the DSs we had at Sky and Ineos were work shy. They were all hard-working blokes, but Nico was probably ahead of the curve in terms of doing recons of race routes. You'd see him and he'd have been away somewhere for a few days, checking out the Tour route probably, and he'd be telling us about the climbs we didn't know, the descents that were a bit shit. There were years when he drove almost the whole Tour de France prior to it starting, so he ended up covering it twice.

Nico also personified one of the critical factors required for any road captain or DS to excel – the ability to put your ego to one side and focus on the overall good of the team. In both of those roles, you're doing all you can to help somebody else win or succeed in some way. It's all about putting the group first. As road captain you may well be doing that because, if you were like me and Nico when he was racing, you very rarely have a realistic chance of victory or even contending for one.

I never had a big engine like Ian Stannard or Vasil Kiryienka; I couldn't train for the same number of hours as a lot of the other guys, or produce the power that they did. But I was always thinking, making calculations, trying to be smart with what I had, and I think I got more out of myself than some riders with bigger engines who weren't as clever or perhaps felt they didn't need to think, that brute force was all that was required. I was also able to apply that management of personal resources to other riders, and, like Rod had, I think Nico saw that and other qualities in me. I like to believe that he saw a bit of himself in me.

Thinking ahead, one of the things I'm most looking forward to about being a DS is helping the younger guys to find their place in the peloton and avoid making some of the mistakes I did over the years. As I've already laid bare, I got into all kinds of scrapes and situations that I later regretted, but I wouldn't have had such a long and successful career if I hadn't listened to the older riders on the team or learned from those errors.

There are all kinds of smaller things I can pass on too, especially when it comes to preserving that most vital resource, a rider's energy. I always tried to live by the adage that you shouldn't stand when you can sit, you shouldn't sit when you can lie down. Consequently, when you're in an airport, look for a seat. After a stage, it's always ideal if your room's on the ground floor, but if it isn't you need to be told exactly how to get to it. You don't want to be going the wrong way after racing and wasting a little bit of energy. Self-preservation of this kind is essential.

In the mornings, G and I always went down to breakfast late, and a few others caught on to this. If it started at eight and you were leaving at half nine, most riders would go to breakfast at eight then go back to their room for half an hour, then come down again to get on the bus. I'd always go down at quarter to nine and go to the bus from there just to save myself that trip back to the room. This all goes back to that bag of sand and trying to avoid popping unnecessary holes in it.

I used to calculate all of the time, thinking of ways that I could cut corners and save myself just a little bit. On a sprint day, when we reached the 3K-to-go banner, where you drop off your GC guys, as soon as I'd done that I would swing off, slow down to 15, 20kph and tickle the legs over. It made no difference to me or to the team where I finished, whether I was in the bunch or if I lost three, four, five minutes. But if you do stay in the bunch you're expected to do a cool-down on the rollers once you get back to the bus, with the result that you'd spend an extra five to ten minutes riding your bike. It made sense for me to sit up once my job was done, do that cool-down on the run-in and save myself the need to get on the rollers and the extra minutes that demanded.

Over the last few years, I've tried to give some of this advice to the young lads doing their first Grand Tour, such as Josh Tarling, Tom Pidcock and Kim Heiduk. In 2023, Kim got selected in the Vuelta ahead of me and, even though I was gutted when I got the news, I messaged him to say well done and that he deserved it, and he did, because the better man went. As with Josh and Tom, I also gave Kim a few pointers, minor things that might help him get through that race. For instance, when you're on the bus after a race, you can talk to the lads, read a book, you can sleep, which is the best thing really, but try to avoid staying glued to your phone, which I know everyone does. I was guilty of it too at times, but on a long transfer to the hotel I'd try to put the phone down after I'd spoken to my family, had a catch-up and told them I was OK. Staying on it saps your mental energy because a lot of the time you're looking at bullshit. I told them all that you absolutely don't need social media. Don't get sucked in if someone at home has seen something written about you on a news website. It doesn't mean anything and won't help you in any way. The most important thing is the next day and the job you can do to support your team.

On another occasion, I explained to Pippo Ganna how time cuts work. He'd ridden the Giro twice already, but when he first raced the Tour, he had no clue how to do this. I took

him through the Tour's roadbook and the rules, showed him
the percentages that are used to calculate the time limit on
different types of stages and how to do the calculations. Then
he would send his estimates through to me and ask if he'd
worked it out correctly. I said to the boys that they can always
speak to the DS about this, but that it's important to be able
to work out the time cut themselves.

I've always thought that you need to try to help young guys
in situations like this. What's more, I think that a road captain
has a certain responsibility to do this. I wasn't trying to be
arrogant, bigging myself up as the guy who knew it all. I just
wanted to pass on my experience, in the same way that senior
riders had when I took my first big steps as a professional. I
did feel that some of the younger guys weren't bothered, but
most did listen and appreciate it.

I know from my conversations with Dominique Serieys and
other members of the backroom staff at Decathlon-AG2R La
Mondiale that my experience of racing and particularly the
knowledge I've built up being a road captain was a significant
factor in them signing me as a DS. They believe that I can
help the team step up, in the Classics to begin with, and I look
at the riders on the roster and I'm sure that we can.

We've got a good few riders who've got a lot of experience
in the Classics, and in those races, more than any other, that
counts for a lot. If you don't know the roads, you've got pretty
much no hope of a result even if you're the strongest bloke in
the world. You've got to be in the right position at the right
time. Guys like Oliver Naesen and Dries De Bondt are right
at home in these races, and they can not only be contenders
but also help the younger one-day specialists, such as Pierre
Gautherat, who really impressed during the 2024 Northern

Classics campaign, and Stan Dewulf, who won the under-23 edition of Paris–Roubaix a few years back. The team have added Stefan Bissegger this season as well, a powerhouse in time trials but a rider who could thrive in races like Paris–Roubaix too.

Naesen is an interesting racer, one who's never quite delivered on his potential yet. When he joined the team in 2017, he looked set to be one of the outstanding Cobbled Classics riders of this generation. He had some great years initially, and I particularly remember him working for Romain Bardet on one Tour de France when he was the best domestique in the race. He was back at that level last year. At Flanders, he was in the group that came in behind solo winner Mathieu van der Poel, and he had an incredible Tour once again. I wasn't there, but everyone I spoke to said how strong he was working for Felix Gall, ferrying him up the outside of the peloton any number of times. In fact, I recall G saying on our *Watts Occurring* podcast that he was riding alongside Oliver at one point and congratulated him on the work he'd done. Hopefully he can relight the fire he had a few years ago. He does know the roads, he's hungry, and I fully believe that he can be at the pointy end of a big race. Whether he can win one or not, I don't know. That's a huge ask bearing in mind the generational talents we're up against, but I'm confident that he can be in the mix.

In fact, my sense is that the whole team has had a lift going into the 2025 season. Decathlon have committed for the long term, we've got a great new bike to race on, the team have made some great signings, and some of the kids they're bringing into the WorldTour look exceptional. I can't wait to get stuck in.

17

The future

My aim in writing this book has been to give fans a very particular insight into racing from the heart of the peloton, into the tactics of the sport but also into the nuances of those tactics. I hope that I've shed some light on the complexities of bike racing, which can be extremely difficult to pick out and understand. As a result of this, I hope, above all, that you'll get more from a sport that I've totally devoted myself to since I was a kid and still find completely compelling.

As I prepare to make the switch from racing to directing, I wanted to end by offering my take on the role of road captains as the sport becomes increasingly impacted by technology of all kinds, the next steps for the Ineos team which has been my home for the past thirteen seasons, and the future for the sport as a whole. However, before going down those various paths and delving into some of the critical issues that cycling is facing, I want to start by saying that the sport has never been in a better place than where it is now. The season's most important races are more captivating than ever, on the women's side of the sport as well as the men's, and the battles between the peloton's biggest stars are more enthralling. As someone who's still very much a fan, I'm relishing what the coming seasons will bring, while hoping that I can still have some influence and help to make my new team more competitive, consistently challenging the leading teams for major titles.

Like any DS, a key task in this new position will be to forge a bond with the road captains at Decathlon-AG2R La Mondiale, notably Oliver Naesen, who took on this position at the Classics and the Tour de France in 2024. In some ways, the role's become less important because technology has superseded some of the skills required by a road captain – judging the wind, the terrain, and trying to exploit other riders and teams by means of this knowledge. Nowadays, everyone has that information at their fingertips thanks to the technology that's available, like Veloviewer, which details every aspect of a race route – the turns and undulations, how exposed it is to the elements. What's more, every team has a recon car ahead of the race that can provide live updates – whether the wind is switching direction, for instance, or its intensity is changing.

Despite this, I believe the role of road captain has become more significant in an era of generational change, one in which the sport has a much greater focus on younger riders. No matter how talented these budding stars are, they don't come into the peloton fully formed as racers. They still need to learn the little details, and to be steered away from bad habits and mistakes on and off the bike, just as I was by Mike Barry, Mat Hayman and Bernie Eisel as a new pro. They need to learn about positioning, about how to move through a bunch at a key moment, the practical stuff that will make them even better racers, but also about how to get ready and be in the right frame of mind for the big events, as well as be mentally prepared to hurt themselves, to push right to their physiological limit.

Saying this, I think back to the 2023 Classics campaign. I'd missed a few of the races because my mum was ill, and I came back in for Flanders. Speaking to the other guys the night before the race, they were saying that they felt physically good enough to compete, but were struggling to get into the right position at the right time and missing out at the crunch points. Right before the race, we were talking specifically about positioning coming into the Oude Kwaremont for the second time and how we had to approach the foot of the climb at the front. As I've already said, you're on a three-lane highway that's descending pretty rapidly and you turn into a sharp right-hand corner. It's sketchy, there's no two ways about it, because you're coming in at 8okph.

I said words to the effect of 'Boys, I think there's got to be a certain level of acceptance here. It is as sketchy as fuck, but we can't get away from that. You're better off accepting this now, getting your head around it and starting to figure out how you're going to do it. Envisage which side of the road you need to be, when to accelerate, when we're going to try to move to the front.' There was no point sitting there dwelling on the fact that it's a very tricky point, dangerous even, because that wouldn't have helped in any way. The corner would still be there and we'd have to negotiate it. In order to make sure we did it right, I had to get the guys into the right mindset. As it turned out, we didn't nail it perfectly, but we did a pretty good job. While I can take some of the credit for that, more than anything this underlines why experience matters.

One question I need to answer having stepped away from

Ineos and my position there as road captain is who might succeed me in that role. I think Big Ben Turner is physically better than I was but hasn't quite got the vision yet. Kim Heiduk, meanwhile, has got the vision, but perhaps not the confidence, nor the experience quite yet. He's definitely in the pipeline for the role, though. However, I'd qualify this by saying that the ideal road captain is a guy who isn't racing for results himself, but is simply aiming to do what's best for the team. For a few years at the Classics I combined the positions of road captain and leader, and found it quite tricky. It's definitely easier getting guys to rally around you when you're not racing for and thinking of yourself.

You need a guy who thinks of himself purely as a domestique, someone who can take a step back, think what's best for the team, analyse the guys who are available to him, what level they're at, what the race is and who's the opposition, the state of the weather conditions – someone, essentially, who's got the time, desire and experience to answer all of these questions. It's more complicated to do if you're chasing results, which Ben and Kim still are. I certainly think Ben is on the cusp of a major success as a racer.

Listing all of these qualities, I do wonder whether Kwiato might be the best guy for the job. He's proved he can still contend with the best on his day, but he's obviously not the winner he was in 2017 or 2018. We all get older and a little weaker while other guys get stronger. But he's still at the level where if he decided to be a full-time domestique, I think that he'd be the best one in the world. He'd be a good fit as road captain as well. He's very vocal, doesn't mind putting his neck on the line and getting his teammates organized. He's a master tactician too, very smart. If, for example, he decides he wants to get in the breakaway that day, nine times out of ten he'll manage it. He's also very good at finding his way around the peloton, taking a leader into crucial sections, ducking and diving when the pressure's on, but going incognito when it isn't.

Thinking about the Ineos team as a whole, they've clearly had some difficult moments in recent months, but some of the stuff I've heard and read, writing them off as one of the peloton's leading teams, has been way off the mark. I think the infrastructure there is still up with the best – the staff, the approach to racing and training. They've also got the riders to support a leader at the Grand Tours. If you look at the 2023 and 2024 Giros, they controlled the race brilliantly for G on both occasions, but Primož Roglič edged him out in the first and Pogi was simply stronger in the second. But those performances underlined that it remains a great squad. Several of their domestiques are among the best in the world – Laurens De Plus, Thymen Arensman, Jonathan Castroviejo, Kwiato and Turner. They've got a team ready to go when a new GC leader comes along. If they went to the Tour and took the jersey, they'd be able to defend it if they had that one guy they're missing. The problem is that there's so few leaders of that standard out there and they're tied to very long and big contracts.

Over the last three or four seasons, Ineos have tried different strategies at the Tour in an attempt to rival Tadej Pogačar and Jonas Vingegaard, but it's very hard to beat guys who are substantially stronger than you over three weeks. I never want to use the word impossible, but I don't see how you can do it, unless there's an incident of some kind, a crash most likely. The gulf in class between those two GC hitters and everyone else is huge. They're generational talents, GOATs like LeBron James and Kobe Bryant or Lionel Messi and Cristiano Ronaldo. This means that the other teams are turning up to the Tour with the aim of fighting for the bottom step on the podium. There are maybe ten guys who could take that third spot on their day, although Remco Evenepoel is a level above all of them, in a class of his own now between the top two and the rest.

Looking at this with an Ineos hat on, I don't expect much change in 2025. Carlos Rodríguez is an extremely talented bike rider, a lovely bloke, but I don't think he can beat the dominant GC stars. He'd have to get 5 per cent better – and that's an immense ask when it comes to watts per kilo. Carlos is already crossing the t's and dotting the i's when it comes to preparation. He's doing everything right, he's at his absolute pinnacle. When you're already at that level, no one can find another 5 per cent. The answer lies elsewhere for Ineos.

The sport has always gone in cycles. There's never been a team that's dominated for twenty years, so you have to weather the storm sometimes. We were the top dogs for seven, eight years, but Ineos now have to build new characters and a new culture. They've got to put a strong focus on recruitment and look further down the line for their next Tour de France leader. If they can't win it now, when can they win it next? They need to be thinking about the guy who's going to win the race in 2028 or even 2030. Where is he now? Is he on their roster? Another team's? Do they have to buy someone in? One thing I'll add to this is that the sport is still essentially all about the Tour de France, and that every team is judged by their performance there. Ineos could win a lot of other races, but the Tour's the one event every fan knows and every rider wants to win. If a professional cyclist tells Joe Public what he does for a living, the standard response will be, 'Have you ridden the Tour de France?' If you say no, but you've done the Giro d'Italia, they probably won't know what you are talking about. The Tour is the pinnacle, the race that Ineos wants and needs to get back to winning.

There's been another very significant change since Ineos lost its crown as the top team. UAE have taken over and they're doing things completely differently, because they're the best all year round. Sure, they've got Pogi, who's already one of the all-time greats, but they've got such strength in depth. When we were top of the tree, we were focused on the Grand Tours, Paris–Nice, the Tour de Romandie, Tour de Suisse, and that was it. UAE won eighty-one races in 2024, including twelve stage race successes with seven different riders. We just won the big ones, but they've established a new standard. They don't set any limits. They want to win everywhere.

Tadej and his crew have played a massive role in spicing up the whole season, helping to make racing better than ever. There are, though, plenty of issues that need tackling in order to keep moving the sport forward. Rider safety is the primary one. There are all manner of aspects to this, with Tour de France director Christian Prudhomme suggesting that the solution lies in reducing the speed of races, which has risen significantly thanks to better training and nutrition, improvements in bike and equipment aerodynamics, and the wholesale switch to disc brakes. He's advocating for some of these advances to be reversed.

I definitely agree that the sport is getting more dangerous. In fact, I'd say cycling's become the most dangerous sport of all. There are a few reasons for this I think, starting with the fact that there's more money in it than ever before. The greater the rewards, the greater the risks riders are willing to take to reap them. They're thinking, 'If I win this race / get through that gap / enter this cobbled section first / get that result, I'll be on my way ...' You don't need that many results to be suddenly in demand and signing a contract for hundreds of thousands of euros. You have to be good to get that kind of salary, but you don't need to be a superstar. Given this, riders will think, 'If I just take that risk ... if I fly around this corner a little bit faster than them ...'

Another reason for the sport being more dangerous is that roads are getting cluttered with ever more road furniture. They talked to us about it in one of the Tour presentations once, telling us that the number of roundabouts in France had doubled within the previous decade or so. As well as these, you've got to take into account traffic-calming measures – the bollards in every village, the speed humps. The Netherlands used to have a reputation for the amount of road furniture, but now you find it everywhere. Ironically, the push towards having dedicated cycling paths and routes is making the situation more hazardous too. There are more kerbs, roads are narrower, and this makes it ever more difficult for race organizations to flag everything. You'll be whipping round a roundabout at 40kph and be confronted with a kerb separating a bike path from a road that you're not expecting to see.

The bikes and components are making the sport faster as well. Frames are getting more aerodynamic and they're all fitted with disc brakes, which allow you to brake later. However, I view better stopping power as a benefit, not a drawback. And when it comes to frame design, I don't see how the UCI could roll back and restrict the aero innovations that manufacturers are making. This would go against the whole ethos of a sport that has always been technology-driven, and would only work if every team was riding exactly the same bike, which will never happen because it would cut off a vital source of sponsorship money to teams and race organizers.

I think the best solution to this issue is to improve safety measures and procedures at races, which is something the riders' union, the CPA, has been very vocal in pushing for. We've seen better barriers introduced at stage finishes, and more and clearer warning signs about dangers on descents and corners, but often it's only the biggest races that can afford to implement these measures because of their cost. Resources need to be found to change this, which I realize is no easy matter given the financial structure of the sport as a whole.

As my career progressed, I did become increasingly aware of the dangers. When I was twenty-two, twenty-three, I didn't bat an eyelid and would always go into races all guns blazing. I never second-guessed myself. If it was raining, I'd be thinking, 'Mega, let's go slide.' As you get older and you've seen the crashes, the guys in a real mess, you do start to think about braking half a second earlier. I certainly did once I was married and had two kids. I'd be more inclined to give up a wheel when previously I'd have fought like hell for it. Yet, whenever I raced, I did tend to put all of this to the back of my mind. Pre-race, I'd think about it, and if things were quite relaxed when we got going I'd sometimes be telling myself to be careful – 'Don't fucking crash, Luke!' But a moment would always arrive when the race was on and those thoughts simply evaporated. I just rode like I always had. We are racers, after all.

It's also interesting to consider how technology is affecting the tactical side of racing. As a rider, this was where I gained my edge and was what made me so useful to my team as its road captain. If it were down to me, I'd ban Veloviewer and tools like it that serve up route and weather information that I had an instinctive insight into. I'm not serious, of course. Like aero frames, disc brakes and all kinds of other advances, you can't force the sport to go retro and ditch advances like this, although this innovation didn't help me.

Following this same logic, I'm also against the banning of race radios and power meters, which some people claim have turned riders into robots controlled by their DSs. Having read this far, you can no doubt understand my perspective on this. Racing is so fluid that riders still have to make their own decisions, hundreds of them in a day, thousands if you're a road captain. Your DS can't ride your bike for you. The indispensability of radios with regard to ensuring rider safety can't be underplayed either. They do change the racing, but you simply can't do without them. Nothing is more important than safety.

As for the argument for removing power meters, I'm definitely against this. They don't really change racing at all. I think that those people who say that they do have either never ridden at the top level in recent years or have simply got a dinosaur mentality. When I was riding on the front, I wouldn't be concerned with my power output. When I was riding on the front, my focus would be on the breakaway and remaining in a unit with my teammates.

The only time I would focus on my power was if I were trying to pace myself up an early climb. If we had a 10K ascent from kilometre zero, I'd have been thinking, 'OK, that's half

an hour. The best I can do for half an hour is, say, 400 watts.'
So I'd want to avoid starting the climb at 450, trying to hang
on and then fizzle out to 380 at the top. I would just ride
bottom to top as quickly as I could, which would mean sticking to a baseline 400. I might be one of the first twenty riders
dropped, but soon after that I'd start to pass and then keep on
passing riders who had tried to hang on – they'd set off too
fast and blown their doors. You'd get even more exposed in
these situations when you were racing at altitude.

In my experience, the GC guys don't focus on their power
meters too much either. In training, it's a different ball game.
Everyone is fixated on numbers. Everyone is training on
numbers, and in super specific ways. But that's just a generational change within the sport, one that's taken it to a whole
new level of professionalism. If you're coaching riders, you
can't base training programmes on a rider's feel or sensations.
You're dependent on that data. Every sport develops over
time and this is just another indication that cycling is doing
precisely the same.

I also believe the availability of these devices and the related
data massively benefits the commercial side of the sport. A
lot of riders stick their full file on Strava, which allows ama-
teurs and armchair fans to examine and evaluate what they're
doing, to see how impressive their numbers are. I think it's
brought in a whole new dynamic into what has always been
quite a geeky sport in a lot of ways.

One final thing I'll add to this is that everyone should
remember that the display on your head unit can be custom-
ized. I'd set the Garmin that we used at Ineos so that 90 per
cent of the screen was filled by the race map, and I'd have
power and distance displayed too. If you saw me on TV

looking at my computer, I guarantee that I was looking at the map. If it was a really hot day, I might even replace the power reading with the temperature. On other days, I might display the total altitude gain so that I knew how much climbing I'd done during a stage. I liked to see it clicking down. It was a mental thing that gave me a boost. A lot of guys are more fixated on heart rate than on power because this gives you an indication of your level of fatigue during a Grand Tour.

Although this isn't relevant to this debate, my pet hate and something that really cracks me up is seeing guys crossing the finish line and pressing pause on their head unit, sometimes doing it even before they've reached the line. I've seen people lose a position in a sprint because they're that fixated on pressing 'pause'. I've seen guys who are riding in for a win do this and then put their arms in the air. Why don't they just enjoy the moment? It makes no difference whether you do this after five hours, five hours and ten seconds, or five hours and one minute, because your coach can crop the file exactly where they need to.

While this short diversion might make me sound like a bit of a dinosaur myself, I actually don't feel that way as I step out of the peloton and into one of the team cars behind it. Having been on the sidelines due to my concussion since the Spring Classics campaign in early 2024, I've not missed racing a bike as much as I might have expected. I've enjoyed watching races and being in regular contact with my teammates and other mates in the bunch, but I've been thinking more about this next step.

Having done some early camps with Decathlon-AG2R La Mondiale, I'm feeling that same excitement I had when I joined Team Sky back in 2012. The sport has changed immensely since then, and I have too. What remains unchanged, though, is my desire to succeed. Whether road captain or directeur sportif, I'm determined to pitch in and help my team win, get good results, beat our rivals.

Let's fucking do it, boys!

ACKNOWLEDGEMENTS

First and foremost, I would like to thank my beautiful wife, Cath, and the boys, Ollie and Alfie. When I turned pro in 2012 my wife soon realized what she had signed up for and she never batted an eyelid. Always by my side with a beaming smile and supportive until the bitter end. My two children keep me on my toes, but are the life of the party – two weapons.

To Mum and Dad, you carved me into the man I am today. From letting me ride on the back of the tandem down the lanes of South Wales to driving me the length and breadth of the country to compete, you've always been there. To my best mate, who also happens to be my brother. We've shed blood, sweat and tears together, and he's had my back through any situation. My thanks too to my extended family, who were always there to look after my wife and children when I was on the road.

When it comes to my cycling career, the names at the top of my list for gratitude are Fran Millar, Rod Ellingworth, Dave Brailsford and Richard Usher. They saved my career in 2017 after my leg break. Fran and Rod are some of the most ferocious businesspeople you'll meet but are big softies with big hearts deep down. Richard 'Doc' Usher has sadly passed away, but he's certainly not forgotten, and he and his family have a special place in my heart. Dave took me under his wing as a young boy and helped me to progress through the ranks, always under his watchful eye. If I had to go into battle, Dave would be the first person I'd take with me.

To all the teammates I've had over the years, I always tried to get the balance right between work and pleasure and hope that you look back at our time together and think that we had success while having a laugh.

Thanks to G, my compatriot and *Watts Occurring* butt. To Pidcock, good luck on your new chapter, champ, go light it up. To Kwiato, my IT manager and the best wingman while manoeuvring through a hectic peloton. To Cav, for showing me the ropes as a first-year pro and a top camper. To Froomey, one of the craziest blokes I know – riding through France with you in yellow was a pleasure.

Thanks for the memories 'the awesome foursome' – yes, you read that right. Caleb Ewan, Ryan Ewan, Cath Rowe. Our families have grown close and we've got a gang of loving children. We look forward to spending even more time together after Caleb's hung up his wheels. To Caleb, my training partner – we were never conventional, but we always got it done with smiles on our faces.

To my best mates Tank, Akon and the Foxy Bros. You boys have always appreciated the intensity of my job and supported me through thick and thin. To all my friends that I keep in touch with from my school days. We don't talk too often, but when we get back to 'The Griffin' it's like nothing has ever changed.

I'd also like to thank everyone who made this book

possible, including all of the team at Transworld, my agent Jay at Rocket and my literary agent David Luxton. Thanks also to Peter Cossins for his job as road captain on the words.

To all of you reading this book and the people on the roadside over the years, thank you. As a rider in the peloton, a lot of the time racing is a blur, but somehow you always hear when your name is shouted out. This always gave me a little buzz. Don't be strangers, come say hello if you see me at the races.

PICTURE ACKNOWLEDGEMENTS

Page 1: All author's own.

Page 2: Author at Team Sky's 2012 season launch © Dean Mouhtaropoulos/Getty Images; winning opening stage of the 2012 Tour of Britain © Jamie McDonald/Getty Images.

Page 3: Topping the Paterberg during the 2013 Tour of Flanders © Bryn Lennon/Getty Images; author with Bradley Wiggins after the 2015 Paris–Roubaix © Bryn Lennon/Getty Images; being checked over by race doctors during the 2018 Paris–Roubaix © Luc Claessen/Stringer.

Page 4: Team Sky during the 2013 Tour of Qatar © Bryn Lennon/Getty Images; author with Geraint Thomas and David Millar on the presentation podium before the 2014

Championships in Ponferrada © Bryn Lennon/Getty Images; with Geraint Thomas and Ben Swift during the 2015 Milan–San Remo © Tim de Waele/Getty Images.

Page 5: Retaining the white jersey for best young rider at the 2015 Tour of Qatar © Bryn Lennon/Getty Images; with Chris Froome at his victory in the 2015 Tour de France © Lional Bonaventure/Getty Images; with Ian Stannard and Chris Froome at the 2016 Tour de France © Christophe Ena/Stringer.

Page 6: Author with Niki Terpstra during the 2016 Paris–Nice © Tim de Waele/Getty Images; riding with Geraint Thomas at the 2016 Tour of Flanders © Bryn Lennon/Getty Images; with Geraint Thomas winning the 2018 Tour de France © Tim de Waele/Getty Images.

Page 7: Author with Geraint Thomas during the 2022 Tour de France © Tim de Waele/Getty Images; with race commissaires during the 2022 E3 Saxo Classic © Tim de Waele/Getty Images.

Page 8: With Dylan van Baarle and Wout Poels during the stage 12 finish at the 2019 Tour de France © Justin Setterfield/Getty Images; crashing at the 2024 E3 Saxo Classic © Tim de Waele/Getty Images; with sons Alfie and Ollie after the 2023 Milan–San Remo © Jasper Jacobs/Getty Images.

ABOUT THE AUTHOR

Hailing from a cycling-mad family from Cardiff, Luke Rowe represented Great Britain at junior and under-23 level. He turned professional with Team Sky in 2012 and won a stage of the Tour of Britain that season. He quickly established himself as one of the British team's key riders in both the one-day Classics and the Grand Tours, including the Tour de France.

Luke rode the Tour in every season between 2015 and 2022, playing a key role as the road captain as Sky won the yellow jersey in 2015, 2016, 2017 and 2018, and when Ineos retained the title in 2019. After retiring in 2024, Luke co-presents the *Watts Occurring* podcast along with his teammate and long-time friend Geraint Thomas.